ENOUGH
IS
ENOUGH!

DISCLAIMER NOTICE

The book to read is not the one, which thinks for you, but the one that makes you think. No book in the world equals the Bible for that.

— *HARPER LEE*

ENOUGH IS ENOUGH! *Trojan Horses and A Dangerous Hubris Exposed.*

All matters discussed in this publication are the author's research or creation, reflecting what is deemed good for America, Americans, and the World at large. The author has no party affiliation. The materials do not represent the views of the author's family, political party, or any organization, are not binding, and are without obligation. The author reserves the right not to be responsible for the accuracy and completeness of this publication. Liability claims regarding damage caused using any information provided in this publication, including information that is incomplete or incorrect will, therefore, be rejected. Readers that are younger than ten years old will need parental guidance.

Thank you and God bless you and God bless the USA.

Yakob Kidane Adhanom

ENOUGH
IS
ENOUGH!

Trojan Horses and A Dangerous Hubris Exposed

YAKOB KIDANE ADHANOM

AUTHOR'S NOTE

"Precious in the sight of the LORD is the death of his faithful servants."

— *THE BIBLE*

June 8, 2020, The Capitol Hill Autonomous Zone (CHAZ), also known as the Capitol Hill Occupied Protest (CHOP), occupied some blocks. It was an alarming moment remembering the kind of situation that made him and million across the globe to be refugees and migrate countries where the governance is functional and stable. He wanted to fight back. When such a junta takes control of a State, the immigrants and people of color are their first targets for inhumane treatment. Socialist, Communist, and dictatorial ideologies are evil. No one wants to immigrate to such countries. Whoever got involved in such activity should have no inheritance or portion of property in the American society. That is when the author said, *'Enough is Enough'* and decided to write this project.

Thank God, with Him all things are possible.

All biblical quotations come from Kenneth Baker (ed.), *The New International Version Study Bible*, Grand Rapids, MI: Zondervan Publishing House, 1995.

TO:

The United States of America- "For I was hungry, and you gave me something to eat. I was thirsty and you gave me a drink. I was a stranger and you invited me in. I needed clothes, and you clothed me, I was sick, and you looked after me." Thank you, the United States of America.

Also, to you, refugee, and immigrant welcoming nations: "Do not oppress a foreigner; you yourselves know how it feels to be foreigners, because you were foreigners in Egypt" (Exodus 23:9).

ACKNOWLEDGMENTS

We may have all come on different ships, but we are in the same boat now.

— *REV. DR. MARTIN LUTHER KING JR.*

Thank you, Jesus, for making this project possible.

I would like to acknowledge my wife, Elsa's great support, and critic of my project. Thank you Sarah Baraki's for your help in making this project successful. There are few silent warriors that I would like to acknowledge for taking their time to help. Thank you!

Finally, I would like also to acknowledge my sister-in-law Roman Tesfamariam (Emory Hospital and Northside Hospital) who died on December 2, 2019. She tirelessly worked hard to make sure that we get adjusted and be successful in the USA. Thank you Roman for your service, gone too soon. I will always remember your loving tears. As we prepare to commemorate the first anniversary of your departure, I would like to say, Love you Roman.

Yakob K. Adhanom

SINCERE PRAYERS FOR FIRST LADY MELANIA AND PRESIDENT TRUMP'S QUICK RECOVERY FROM COVID-19.

I PRAY THAT YOU COME OUT BETTER AND STRONGER, ROARING LIKE A LION TO FINISH THE JOB THAT YOU STARTED.
"NO WEAPON FORGED AGAINST YOU SHALL PROSPER" (ISAIAH 54:17); AND "YOU WILL NOT DIE BUT LIVE AND WILL PROCLAIM WHAT THE LORD HAS DONE" (PSALMS, 118:17). ALSO, "THE LORD YOUR GOD WOULD NOT LISTEN TO BALAAM BUT TURNED THE CURSE INTO A BLESSING FOR YOU, BECAUSE THE LORD YOUR GOD LOVES YOU" (DEUTERONOMY 23:5).

The Bible

DECLARATION

Hayet is an African immigrant. He loves his African heritage; whether readers like it or not. His allegiance is to no race, no person but to the kingdom of God and His righteousness; the people and the governance that are in favor of it. As recognition and appreciation to the services African ancestor slaves endured in the USA, he put the following front cover on one of his books:

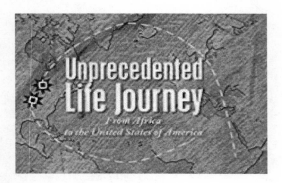

He believes that the people of color got their freedom because former slaves such as Fredrick Douglas and white abolitionists struggled side by side. In recognition of a man who fought for anti-slavery, he named his good character in the story in the book as Mr. Garrison.[1] Therefore, people should carry on their legacy by doing what is right for themselves and for their community.

Black people: people of color in general are conservatives in nature. They love, serve, and died for the USA. They are free whoever they want to be and should not be considered as victims. As a person of color, for the author, the Black Lives Matter organization which treats our white neighbors who love, adopt, feed, and care for our children should not be labeled as bad just for being white people. Everybody is a child of God. Any race that says one race matter over other races is wrong. Black Lives Matter which is engaged in Burning, Looting, and Destroying the USA. BLM's foreign or domestic accomplices who are making the Black People's life miserable do not represent for the author.

MAKING A WISH

HOW DOW WE STOP RACISM? Stop talking about it. I'm going to stop calling you a white man and I'm going to ask you to stop calling me a black man."

— *MORGAN FREEMAN*

On the 2020 Election and Beyond, Hayet has a wish to make and may the wish be fulfilled: "What the wicked dread will overtake them; what the righteous desire will be granted" (Proverbs 10:24).

❖ I am calling upon The House of Representatives and the Senators to please introduce a bill for amendment to impeachment. The voters should have a say. What happened to President Donald Trump should never happen to any future President. It is not fair for an elected President to be impeached along party lines. Such impeachment will put the USA into a civil war that cannot be healed. If one party has the majority in the House of Representatives and in the Senate, they can decide the fate of a President: impeachment or not. That is not fair. Members of Congress and Senators who did not vote President should not decide their fate, voters should have a say. This amendment will be fair for both parties, and for the voters.

CONTENTS

Chapter One

"How long, Lord, must I call for help, but you do not listen? Or cry out to you, "Violence!" but you do not save? Why do you make me look at injustice? Why do you tolerate wrongdoing? Destruction and violence are before me; there is strife, and conflict abounds. Therefore, the law is paralyzed, and justice never prevails. The wicked hem in the righteous, so that justice is perverted."

— *THE BIBLE*

ENOUGH IS ENOUGH EXPLAINED

Evangelist Billy Graham said, "My heart aches for America." While reading the draft of her husband's book, Mrs. Ruth Graham describing the terrible descending spiral of our nation's

moral standards and the idolatry of worshiping false gods such as technology and sex, she stunned him by crying, "If God doesn't punish America, He'll have to apologize to Sodom and Gomorrah."[2]

He wondered what Ruth would think of America if she were alive today, where sin is widespread, millions of babies have been aborted and our nation does not seem concerned. Self-centered indulgence, pride, and a lack of shame over sin are now badges of the American lifestyle.[3] If you do not support their way of life, they treat you as racist and many other name callings.

America is in big trouble. These are bad days for America in the eyes of God. People indulge in all sorts of wrongdoing and consider them as their glory. No shame or remorse for wrongdoing. The clergies are either afraid of getting admonishment by government officials; or being complacent, they want to be known as good people. How long will America go the way people are going? If we do not repent and return, soon a time will come when we may not be able to do so when God will say *Enough is Enough!* God forbid!

Prophet Habakkuk has had enough of violence, injustice, intolerance, destruction, wrongdoing, strife, conflict abounded him, the law was pearlized, justice was perverted, and it never prevailed and he prayed to God, "How long, Lord must I call for help." He felt God was far off and did not listen. Even in a time such as this, the prophet had a strong faith in God and declared, "I will stand at my watch and station myself on the ramparts; I will look to see what he will say to me, and what answer I am to give to this complaint."[4]

Eventually, God showed up in due time. However, not in a way the prophet expected. God said to the prophet, "Look at the nations and watch— and be utterly amazed. For I am going to do something in your days that you would not believe, even if you were told. I am raising up the Babylonians, that ruthless and impetuous people, who sweep across the whole earth to seize dwellings not their own. They are a feared and dreaded people; they are a law to themselves and promote their own honor."[5] Does Habakkuk's concern sound familiar to what is going on in some of the American cities?

The author believes that America is a Godfearing nation. That is why God is giving us a time to return. The country's reverence of God and His principles have been eclipsed by the gutless politicians who in the name of human freedom put us in to where we are at. Unless America wakes up and return to God, saying *Enough is Enough*, it will be worse for us than other nations who do not know God.

In the same manner, Jesus warned two cities, "Woe to you, Chorazin! Woe to you, Bethsaida! For if the miracles that were performed in you had been performed in Tyre and Sidon, they would have repented long ago in sackcloth and ashes."[6]

My heart is in a deep pain for America. The enemy of America, the devil is so prevalent in American homes and cities, proclaiming to destroy what America made America, faith, family, and country. The enemy is saying unheard of cursed on the nation and doing abominable acts. Wake up America!

Saying Enough is Enough is also another beginning. Enough is enough means no more will it be tolerated. Tolerance has a beginning; it has also ending. When do people say, *'Enough is enough?'* To say *enough is enough*, when you reach the maximum unfairness, injustice, and so on you can tolerate, and you take another action to counteract.

There are several instances whereby God said *Enough is enough*. Example, The Lord said, "I have indeed seen the misery of my people in Egypt. I have heard them crying out because of their slave drivers, and I am concerned about their suffering. So, I have come down to rescue them from the hand of the Egyptians and to bring them up out of that land into a good and spacious land, a land flowing with milk and honey."[7] When God says *enough is enough*, that is when a meaningful solution comes. Sometimes God uses the least expected person.

For Rosa Parks *Enough is enough* was to refuse to give up her seat to a white passenger on board on a bus in Montgomery, Alabama. This happened during legal systemic racism, and oppression era in the USA.

For years, Ms. Parks was obedient to the segregation law. A time came when she challenged the white supremacy saying *enough is enough*. One thing to note here is that, if the *enough is enough* is from you, you keep on pushing and pushing hard. If the *enough is enough* is from God, it flows smoothly and achieves the goal. It is good to take self-inventory whether that *enough is enough* is from you or from God.

To be able to impact yourself and other lives, one should be able willing to do what others are not willing to do and say what others are not willing to say. That is when a meaningful change comes into effect.

THE TOWER OF BABEL

Before God said *Enough is Enough* for the tower of Babel, in the beginning, the people of the whole World had one Adamic language and a common speech. No matter what language it may have been, God spoke to Adam and Eve; they clearly understood. The language that began as the only and one has now resulted into thousands. Currently there are about 7,117 languages in the World of which most of the languages exist in Papua New Guinea where there are 840 living languages. Indonesia comes in second, with 710 living languages. Third place goes to Nigeria, having 515 living languages.[8]

While most of the languages have written scripts, a few still do not. It should be noted though that one language is not better or less than the other if it serves what it is intended for, to communicate. Also, one race is not better or less than the other. As people moved Eastward, they found a plain in Shinar and settled there.

They said to each other, "Come, let's make bricks and bake them thoroughly."

They used brick instead of stone, and tar for mortar. Then they agreed to build a city, with a tower that reaches to the heavens, so they may make a name for themselves, otherwise they would be scattered over the face of the whole earth.

Scripture says, "What the wicked dread will come up on them; what the righteous desire will be granted. The people dreaded of being scattered and what they dreaded overtook them."[9]

Thus, the Lord came down to see the city and the tower the people were building. The Lord said, "If as one people speaking the same language, they have begun to do this, then nothing they plan to do will be impossible for them. Come, let us go down and confuse their language so they will not understand each other."

So, the Lord scattered them from there over all the earth, and they stopped building the city. That is why it was called Babel—because there the Lord confused the language of the whole world. From there the Lord scattered them over the face of the whole earth.[10] Thus, the language became a curse instead of a blessing. That became the beginning or racism. One language speaker treats people of other languages with disrespect. People have been discriminated against, properties looted, destroyed, burned, kicked out of regions they were born, and much worse killed for speaking (undesired) languages. Hayet has witnessed tribal clash in Kenya, in Ethiopia, Rwanda and Burundi that affected millions of innocent citizens.

The language curse has devastated third World countries and affected in some way the first World as well. For example, in Canada, the French speaking Quebecers wanted an independent sovereign nation. After two referendums failed to separate Quebec from Canada, still more attempts will come. Let the people that perished, property destroyed due to language racism be enough. The language and the race that each one has is temporary.

To the people that live as earthly bound fighting one another, the Bible informs how aiming for heavenly citizenship is beneficial. Paul says: "Join together in following my example, brothers and sisters, and just as you have us as a model, keep your eyes on those who live as we do. For, as I have often told you before and now tell you again even with tears, many live as enemies of the cross of Christ. Their destiny is destruction, their god is their stomach, and their glory is in their shame. Their mind is set on earthly things. But our citizenship is in heaven. And we eagerly await a Savior from there, the Lord Jesus Christ, who, by the power that enables Him to bring everything under His control, will transform our lowly bodies so that they will be like His glorious body".[11]

Chapter Two

"You cannot go back and change the beginning, but you can start where you are and change the ending."

— *C.S. LEWIS*

IN THE BEGINNING

The earth was with no light, formless, shapeless, and empty. Darkness was over the surface of the deep, and the Spirit of God was floating over the water. That was the beginning.

The beginning is the source, the origin, the starting point. The Bible begins with the phrase, "'In the Beginning,' God created the heavens and the earth."

When God created in the beginning, he created all what was, what is, and what is yet to come in mind. That includes you and me. Before we were created, He set a time, a season, and a plan for each. King David testifies that how God made all the delicate, inner parts of his body and knit him together in his mother's womb. He thanks, God, for making him so wonderfully complex! David praises how God's workmanship is marvelous—how well he knows it and how God watched him as he was being formed in utter seclusion, as he was woven together in the dark of the womb.

God saw him before he was born. Every day of his life was recorded in God's book. Every moment was laid out before a single day had passed. Precious are God's thoughts about him. They cannot be numbered! He can't even count them; they outnumber the grains of sand! And when he wakes up, God is still with him.[12] What is true of David's and God's relationship is true of each one of us. Hallelujah Amen!

David acknowledges how great are God's works, how profound His thoughts. The senseless man does not know, fools do not understand that though the wicked spring up like grass and all evildoers flourish, they will be forever destroyed.

Human beings start forming just four weeks after conception. By 24 weeks (about 5 and a half months) the baby's organs are fully formed. Hearing is also well developed by this stage; the baby will respond to external noises.[13]

Before human beings came to be, God filled each one to the measure of all his fullness; all that one needs and is meant to be. He is the one and only who can do immeasurably more than all we could ask for or imagine, according to His magnificent power and limitless knowledge that is at work within us.

God foreknew us. That means all our successes and failures, all our strengths and weaknesses are not a surprise to Him. He also predestined us to be conformed to the image of Christ. He predetermined a person's days: He decreed the number of everyone's months and has set limits that none can exceed.

After the creation, all things considered, the highest heavens belong to the Lord, He has given the earth to humankind until the time He gathers them up to Himself through death or at the second coming of Christ and end time.

Before the creation of the world, and to be specific, before one got conceived in the natural way, God finished all the plans and assignment He has for each one of us. He knows the assignments and plan He has and that is to prosper us and not to harm us, plans to give us hope and a future no matter how twisted, senseless, meaningless, joyless, purposeless it may appear at times. You have been created for a reason. You ought to figure it out.

CREATOR'S MANUAL

All one should do is to begin the beginning with the right mindset at the right time. Although God has set what is good for you, He will never force you to do it. One must take a responsibility and make a choice either to pursue God's plan or man's plan. God's plan is written on His Word, the Bible. By reading His Word, the Manual, the plan, the GPS (God's Positioning System), one gets to the destiny within a brief time. The sooner one aligns to that plan, the easier and faster one finishes the purpose.

The very thing that one needs to use in any invention is the manual. The manual for human life and for the World is written in the Bible, which is the Manual written in detail. In case of any deviation, perversion, modification, or alteration to that Manual, there is no guarantee that the product of God's creation could function as intended. The Lord has assigned and equipped each their task should they be willing to work it out.

For Timothy of the Bible, from infancy he knew the Holy Scriptures, which were able to make him wise. By reading the Holy Scriptures people of the current generation could also be wise. On the other hand, by ignoring the words of the Manual a person becomes a fool.

In reference to the value of the Maker's Manual, Jeremiah the Prophet spoke of how when he discovered God's words, he devoured them. They became his joy and his heart's delight.[14]

Every invented or created product has a manual in the box. The manual entails directions on how consumers should use the quality-tested product. The manual informs what it can or cannot do for guaranteed services and functions. One has the right to ignore the manual and use it their own way. However, one should be responsible to accept the consequences that come from not following the manual. An iron box is designed to iron clothes, should one choose to iron oneself, it will burn them.

The same applies to a person or everything that exists. Because Jesus created all things in heaven and on earth, visible and invisible, whether thrones or powers or rulers or authorities; all things have been created through Him and for Him.[15]

For example, in the beginning, God created Adam and Eve as a male and female. That was in the initial creation. In procreation gender is assigned at the time of conception. Your location, inside or outside the womb does not determine your humanity and gender.

When the politician Joe Biden was asked as to how many genders exist during one of his Iowa campaign stops, "There are at least three,"[16] he replied. This answer is from a man who Democrats say is a man of faith. Which faith Book does he read that guide his life? Of course, not the Bible which says, "He created them male and female."[17] Biden is not the only one. The Democratic plantation and Healthline list 13 to 64 terms that describe gender identities and expressions.[18] Trump's administration's legal definition of gender and as to 'how many genders exist,' the answer straightforward is 'Two.' So, the election of the year 2020 is between those who say there are two genders and those who say there are as many as 64 genders. We have been tricked by the devil for generations, *Enough is ENOUGH*, let us return to the maker's manual plan.

The Maker designed the male to function as a husband, the female to function as a wife. God's creation, be it a male or a female are equal. One gender is not better or less than the other. However, wanting to be one or the other gender and forcing people to acknowledge your gender preference is wrong. Because God saw all He had made, and it was incredibly good. God blessed them to be fruitful and increase in number; fill the earth and subdue it. Rule over the fish in the sea and the birds in the sky and over every living creature that moves on the ground.[19]

JESUS' BEGINNING ON EARTH

God said *enough is enough* and sent Jesus to save his people. Beginnings may not be for only one thing or only one time. There could be several beginnings for distinct sets of things. Christianity teaches that Jesus pre-existed father Abraham. Yet when He came to earth, He had a beginning. Jesus' earthly beginning was when the Angel Gabriel brought the good news to Mary. Mary was betrothed to be married yet she had not experienced premarital sexual relationship with her fiancé or with anyone else. May it be so for the current and future generations.

"Greetings, you who are highly favored! The Lord is with you," salutes the Angel.

Mary was troubled at his words and wondered what kind of greeting this might be. But the angel said to her, "Do not be afraid, Mary; you have found favour with God. You will conceive and give birth to a son, and you are to call Him Jesus. He will be great and will be called the Son of the Most High. The Lord God will give him the throne of His father David, and he will reign over Jacob's descendants forever; his kingdom will never end."

"How will this be," Mary asked the Angel, "since I am a virgin?"

The Angel answered, "The Holy Spirit will come on you, and the power of the Most High will overshadow you. So, the holy one to be born will be called the Son of God."

"I am the Lord's servant," Mary answered, "Let it be to me according to your word." Then the angel left her.[20]

The moment Mary said, "let it be to me according to your word," immediately, the seed of Jesus entered her womb.

Children are a heritage from the Lord, the fruit of the womb a reward from God. The seed inside a womb of a woman is holy and known by God. Thus, earthly life begins at conception regardless of what the abortionists who claim that 'life starts after birth' say.

Shortly after the Angel left Mary, she hurried to visit Elizabeth, John the Baptist's mother who was in her sixth month of pregnancy and greeted Zacharias' household. "The phrase Mary Shortly after the Angel left Mary, she hurried to visit Elizabeth," shows it happened immediately or right after Mary's encounter with the Angel.

"When Elizabeth heard Mary's greeting, the baby leaped in her womb, and Elizabeth was filled with the Holy Spirit."

In a loud voice she exclaimed: "Blessed are you among women and blessed is the child you will bear,"[21], responding to a just conceived baby.

The freshly conceived Jesus at the time of the visit was about twenty-four hours or a couple of days old. Elizabeth is addressing the pregnancy as a viable person, Lord, and the savior of the world. She is not addressing as a blip or a tissue that can be discarded at any time and for any reason. That is how the abortionists and the Democratic plantation leaders want to dehumanize a pregnancy. This election is between those who dehumanize a pregnancy and those who defend the right to live for every unborn child in the womb.

That is not all. As soon as the sound of Mary's greeting reached Elizabeth's ears, the baby in her womb leaped for joy over the visit of hours or days old baby. The leaping for joy in Elizabeth's womb shows an emotion of a baby who is at the end of the second trimester.

It is the same emotion though in a negative way that became a turning point for Abby Johnson, who was the former abortion clinic director. Johnson tells of how she went to assist in a live abortion.

Prior to that experience, she believed a pregnancy is not a person. After all, we are helping women to make choices with their body. During the abortion procedure, she saw on the ultrasound the baby flailing and screaming with inaudible voice, nowhere to go to, to escape while being drained through the abortion suction tube. That was the beginning of a new true perspective of life. She learned that she cannot go back and change the beginning, but she promised to start where she was and change the ending.

As Johnson exits from the gripe of abortion, Pastor Raphael Warnock enters it. He is a megachurch pastor of the congregation that Rev. Dr. King pastored, who is running for a Democratic State Senate. When you run as a democrat you will be required to believe what the party, believes. The same applies when you run as a Republican.

He believes that abortion is healthcare and reproductive justice, and God is cool with it, he would legalized abortion because it is consistent with Christianity and he would fight to ensure it remains lawful.[22] As a reward for his advocacy for abortion he earned the endorsement of Planned Parenthood What an embarrassment to the Church that was known for a good fight! The pastor chose to be an ally of Planned Parenthood.

Apostle Paul warns believers who to listen to. No matter who says biblically unsound doctrine, stop being bamboozled, your vote (if you claim to be religious) should be determined by the scripture. To the church of Ephesus John, the revelator wrote, "I know your deeds, your hard work and your perseverance. I know that you cannot tolerate wicked people, that you have tested those who claim to be apostles but are not and have found them false."[23]

To the easily swayed believers Paul says, "I am astonished that you are so quickly deserting the one who called you to live in the grace of Christ and are turning to a different gospel— which is really no gospel at all. Evidently some people are throwing you into confusion and are trying to pervert the gospel of Christ. But even if we or an angel from heaven should preach a gospel other than the one we preached to you, let them be under God's curse! As we have already said, so now I say again: If anybody is preaching to you a gospel other than what you accepted, let them be under God's curse![24]

There are those who have a form of godliness but denied its power. Believers should have nothing to do with such people. These are the individuals, whose condemnation was written about long ago have secretly slipped in among believers. They are ungodly people, who pervert the grace of our God into a license for immorality and deny Jesus Christ our only Sovereign and Lord.[25]

Television commentator and NFL analyst Tony Dungy, admonishes Pro-Choice Pastors they couldn't be reading the real Bible as a guide for their life and their decision.[26]

When a person chooses to honor God, God honors them in return. On the other side, when a person chooses to dishonor God, He dishonors them no matter who and where they are. These are golden rules, and they apply to everybody without exception.

While announcing the death penalty of the dishonorable priests, Eli's sons, God told the boy Samuel the following message: "Therefore the LORD, the God of Israel, declares: 'I promised that members of your family would minister before me forever.' But now the LORD declares: 'Far be it from me! Those who honor me I will honor, but those who despise me will be disdained".[27]

The Torch Bearers for Christ about honoring God say: God is saying to us that if any person, anywhere, will honor Him he or she will, in turn, be honored by Him. To make it personal God says to each one of us, "If you will honor Me, I will honor you." We often hear about the honor of representing one's country in sport, or the honor bestowed by a country on some person in recognition of a worthy act. But very few of us will ever qualify for that sort of honor. But it is within our power to honor God and to have Him honor us in return.[28]

Of course, life after birth is another beginning, but not 'the' beginning of life. In due time, Jesus was born, ushering into a new beginning. When Jesus finished his time on earth that was also another beginning. The second coming is also going to be another beginning.

According to C.S Lewis, there are so many good or bad beginnings people make in life. These beginnings could be intentional, unintentional, with good intention yet it ends bad, voluntary, or forced by others.

No matter the motive, or the intention, a wrong beginning cannot be undone. A wrong beginning is as good as dead. Of course, from a Christian perspective, there is a resurrection of the dead to face a judgment. However, in general terms a dead person is gone, and cannot come back to life.

There was a time when Jesus' disciples were so scared for their lives, locked down in a room. Three brave women went to anoint the body of Jesus, risking punishment, and they were too late, did not find the body in the tomb.

There was a beginning for the death of Jesus in crucifixion and it was an end for in the resurrection. Yet when Jesus was alive, one woman who was a sinner managed to begin and end anointing preparation for his burial. Should one feel doing what is right to a loving person, it ought to be now. Crying, wailing, lamenting, and pretending to be hurt after someone's death is useless to the dead person.

Regarding being unable to undo past wrongs there is an Eritrean proverb that says, "*zfesese ney hfes, etezerbe qal ney mles.*" The literal meaning of the proverb is, "that one is unable to fix the past mistakes."

In the computer World, there are few cases one can undo mistakes, edit, or rearrange while still on hand once saved, chances are the beginnings cannot be undone. In the texting world once a text is sent, it cannot be undone. That is why wise people say, 'Think twice before you do it."

There are some beginnings that can be corrected without many consequences; there are some that one must pay for the wrong beginnings.

Here is one example: Nike's slogan for years has been "Just Do It." Without exaggeration the author could say every American has multiple brands of "Just Do It" in the house or even now wearing appear. The slogan was inspired by the final words of a notorious killer and a marketing agent in Utah, Dan Wieden.[29] After being a major slogan for about three decades, in 2020 it has been modified to "For once, Don't Do It," Which is a new beginning, saying enough is enough.

CURTIS CARROLL'S BAD BEGINNING

Curtis Carroll had a bad beginning. In 1996 at age of 17, he was convicted of robbery and first-degree murder and was sentence to 54 years in prison. Between ages 9 and 17, his mother and grandmother were addicts to drug and cocaine. His entire family members were of the same sort one or the other, they had no job. All that he knew was poverty and the people that he knew were poor and not good role models. He never saw successful lawyers, doctors, and other role models.

One should take a note that success is measured by comparing the potential God gave you to what you have done compared to what you could and should do before you die. All that he saw was police force coming either to pick up dead bodies who are victims of shootings or arrest someone.

As a teenager, he says he could not read or write, nobody taught him how to take care of himself. He knew that crime was bad but justified in his household. In his mind he always knew that the police and the white people were the enemies, they got it all. He was told that white people were the reason the black people were living the way did. With no accountability, his real-life experiences of 'them, them, and them' thinking shaped his identity.

Carroll tells, the black people's problem is perpetrated by the white people for what happened about 500 years ago. This should not be a normal way of life for a healthy community to be bound by the irredeemable past.

Joseph and Paul of the Bible refused to be bound by the past. They know all things happen for a reason. The people who are bound by the past cannot improve themselves. In regard how important it is to focus for the yet to come, Paul says, "Not that I have already obtained all this, or have already arrived at my goal, but I press on to take hold of that for which Christ Jesus took hold of me. I do not consider myself yet to have taken hold of it. But one thing I do: Forgetting what is behind and straining toward what is ahead, I press on toward the goal to win the prize for which God has called me heavenward in Christ Jesus."[30]

Carroll always expected someone to provide for him, be it knowledge or other needs. He calls himself a victim of circumstances. In prison he learned how to take responsibility for his actions, caring for his community, that he could be a great person (self-worth), trading stocks, how to read, write, and became involved in investments in prison. While a prisoner, he has money now, known as "Wall Street" Carroll: A Finance Prophet Currently Serving Life.[31]

To change one's life one's beginnings should not be ones ending. There is a choice to make. By beginning a right direction, the second time, he created a name and wealth for himself while still in prison.

Just as Carroll did, the white people have been the center of all blame that goes wrong in America. That is unjust. It can take only so much to say enough is enough. To pay you back in kind, God forbid. What is the 13% black 17% other people to the 70% white people?

As a parent, a friend, or a relative what kind of negative beginning have you been told or are you telling others regardless of your race? Saying enough for wrongdoing and doing right too late is better than never.

ELIJAH'S BAD BEGINNING

Who do you blame for bad beginning or for where you are today? Prophet Elijah blamed Jezebel for where he was when God asked him at his hiding place, "What are you doing here?"

The background of the story is that people were wavering between two opinions. That is, worshipping Baal and God at the same time, enough is enough. Elijah challenges King Ahab to bring the four hundred and fifty prophets of Baal and the four hundred prophets of Asherah, who ate at his wife, Jezebel's table for a showoff or betting.

Elijah and his opponents were to set two separate stages for offerings, firewood, and sacrifice on it. The one who answers by fire — he is true God.

Jezebel's prophets were to lead in calling on Baal to answer by fire. They shouted louder, slashed themselves with swords and spears until blood flowed. Midday passed, and evening came. Yet there was no answer.

Elijah took his turn. The moment he called upon God, the fire of the LORD fell and burned up the sacrifice, the wood, the stones, and the soil, and licked up the water in the trench that was on the stage. After the true God proved Himself by answering with fire, Elijah managed to seize all the prophets and had them killed. When, Jezebel heard that Elijah killed her prophets, she threatened to kill him, and he had to flee to save his life.

At his hiding place, he prayed that he may die. He claimed he had had enough. He pleaded "Take my life; I am no better than my ancestors." Then he lay down depressed under the bush and fell asleep. Perhaps, one may be feeling hopeless. God is saying, this is not the end, the best is yet to come.

While he was asleep, twice an angel brought bread baked over hot coals and a jar of water to set him up for another beginning. "Get up and eat for the journey is too much for you." After he ate and drank, he lay down again. God was feeding him, to begin a journey, not to sleep. After the second provision, strengthened by that food, he traveled forty days and forty nights until he reached Horeb, the Mountain of God. There he went into a cave and spent the night. That is when God asked him "What are you doing here, Elijah?" God asked him the same question twice.

Elijah replied the same answer twice, "I have been very zealous for the Lord God Almighty. The Israelites have rejected your covenant, torn down your altars, and put your prophets to death with the sword. I am the only one left, and now they are trying to kill me too."

He was not aware that God "reserved seven thousand in Israel—all whose knees have not bowed down to Baal and whose mouths have not kissed him."

Elijah had to go back and begin another beginning.[32] The same message applies to each one of us. What are you doing here? Where are you and where am I? Do we blame others for where we are? Let people say the old way is enough and choose to have a new beginning by aligning with God's plan for their life.

HAYET'S SMALL BEGINNING

The author's pen name shall be Hayet Africa, the son of Sheden Africa. Hayet pronounced as Hayet as "hyat," or as "ha-yet," and Sheden is pronounced "she-den." Hayet means a lion cub. Sheden pronounced 'She' as in she and 'den' as in den means a lion, the leader of a lion pride.

Just as many other people, Hayet had a bad beginning. But that bad beginning does not have to be his ending depending on the choices he makes. All changed, by accepting Jesus as his savior and Lord of his life.

As an eight-year-old boy, at the beginning of life, Hayet remembers is agony of discrimination against his father at the place of work and against him by his peers. The very issues that were meant to kill him, made him stronger. Here is the glimpse of discrimination that he experienced. His father, Sheden, was an orthodox priest. He had an encounter with American Orthodox Presbyterian Missionaries in the 1950's. He accepted Jesus and his life was transformed. Due to the conversion, the community would not let him live peacefully. He had to move from the Southern Province to the Central Province where people were more diverse.

Hayet was the only Southerner among Northern and Central Province kids. Friends in the Central Province friends lived surrounded by uncles, aunties, grandparents, and relatives who boasted of their Central Province heritage as high class out of pride. They are viciously racists, undermining people from the Southern region. Nevertheless, depending on he chooses to handle life's unfair dealings and beginnings, the very peer pressure that set him apart could take him precisely to where God wanted him to be. Thus, he came to believe that in God's eyes favoritism and discrimination have no room, no matter where one comes from. "The earth is the Lord's and all in it, the World, and all who live in it."[33]

Hayet did not see his father much while growing up, on Sundays and holidays; he went where he was needed most, for work, out of town. The Holidays, more than any other days without a father feel so heavy. Sheden usually came home only after weekends and holidays, once per month, then he went back before the weekend.

During his days of isolation, Hayet pledged, *When I grow up, I shall always be present for my family.* He did not understand his father's endeavors, wishes, desires, and the sacrifice he was making to be with his family as much as possible. Nevertheless, the few evenings that Sheden came home were so tormenting for Hayet. Nobody comprehended his sufferings.

On Sundays, Hayet went to church. His friends earned hugs, kisses, and visits from their relatives. However, for Hayet, nobody knew who he is, and nobody visited, be it the church community or his own relatives, who had excommunicated the family due to their conversion experience.

It was commonly perceived, if Orthodox Christians eat any food from Evangelical Christians' homes, they would be converted as well. For fear of conversion, his relatives rarely visited the family. If or when they did visit, they would not eat or drink. That was also another emotionally damaging experience.

To defend himself against bullying peers, Hayet gave it an all-out effort, doing detective work, developing a spy mentality, and finding crafty ways to work. He embarked on personal physical training. He wants to fight potential enemies. He pledges, *People will take advantage of you, so make sure not to trust anybody—especially the rich and the powerful.* Consequently, he trains himself to fight physically, having a distrusting mentality toward whoever approached him.

Concurrently, he desires to bring up an unconquerable army of World changers who would be useful to themselves and to others, fighting for the right of the weak and serving the underserved fairly and justly. He offers his sincere prayer, *O God, please give me strength to defend and help the weak.* God granted his request.

As a kid, Hayet needed physical strength to fight. However, when he grew up, he needed a brain to fight and win legal fights. He served and helped several people, who in turn would bless him saying 'Brook kun,' meaning be blessed. As per the people's blessings, he always anticipated what kind of result the blessings may bring to him.

Right after the completion of high school, he began wholesale and retail business. He became successful in increasing profits. However, before long, he left his birth country and became a refugee, where he had an encounter with Jesus, the best decision of his life! Praise be to God! A few months later he received the baptism of the Holy Spirit.

Still in the country of his refuge he got married. His wife got pregnant and he was experiencing a great deal of life-threatening persecution. At a time when there seemed to be no sympathy from a person God remembered him. Sending a prophetess, God said, "Though your beginning was small, yet your latter end will increase abundantly." He has had several bad beginnings, discriminations, favoritisms, but it depends on him either to stay focused on the wrongs done to him, or to work to improve his future trusting in God in all things who for his good.

JESUS TRANSFORMS A BAD BEGINNING

Hayet has had enough, observing the church leadership filled with favoritism, and racism were harassing and discriminating his father for being from a different region and choosing to be a slave to nobody else, but Jesus.

Because of the bad leadership, the teenage Hayet hated anything that has to do with the Bible, Christianity, and the church. In fact, he concluded, *God does not exist. If he does, He would have intervened in my father's case.*

While living life without God, Hayet became a refugee. He had just a Bible on his hand which he forfeited a few years back. His older brother gave him the day he left the country. Hayet accepted the meaningless book, the Bible. He did so, just to obey his brother. In Africa, it is expected for the younger to obey the older. He was not aware all that he needs in his life is the Bible, and the script in the Bible would transform his life.

To make it short, up on arrival in the country of refuge, where there is no cage/enclosure, no shelter- rain or shine on the open field, no lavatory, no running water and many other basic provisions (at least for the few months). He had no choice but to begin reading the New Testament Bible. At the time, he had a chronic worry, *what is going to happen tomorrow?* And all the details that goes with it.

While reading, he reached Matthew chapter 6, a turning point of his life:

"Therefore, I tell you, do not worry about your life, what you will eat or drink; or about your body, what you will wear. Is not life more than food, and the body more than clothes? Look at the birds of the air; they do not sow or reap or store away in barns, and yet your heavenly Father feeds them. Are you not much more valuable than they? Can any one of you by worrying add a single hour to your life? "And why do you worry about clothes? See how the flowers of the field grow. They do not labor or spin. Yet I tell you that not even Solomon in all his splendor was dressed like one of these. If that is how God clothes the grass of the field, which is here today and tomorrow is thrown into the fire, will he not much more clothe you—you of little faith? So do not worry, saying, 'What shall we eat?' or 'What shall we drink?' or 'What shall we wear?' For the pagans run after all these things, and your heavenly Father knows that you need them. But seek first his kingdom and his righteousness, and all these things will be given to you as well. Therefore, do not worry about tomorrow, for tomorrow will worry about itself. Each day has enough trouble of its own.[34]

At the time of the reading, Hayet was away from God, because God did not intervene when he needed one. He was so mesmerized, shocked and could not believe that the Bible has a message that resonated with his current situation.

The main thing he needs to understand before all other things, "But seek first his kingdom and his righteousness, and all these things will be given to you as well."

Therefore, to get a solution to all that were worrying him, he must seek first the kingdom of God and his righteousness.

A kingdom is a state, or a country ruled by a king or a queen. Thus, God, Jesus, and the Bible are concerned about building the kingdom of God on earth, where God is the King.

In search of 'the kingdom of God and his righteousness,' he started going a place where the Ethiopian refugees were worshiping, at the house of Linda and Bill their daughter Becky, American missionaries. At the end of the first preaching, the preacher asked, "If you are willing to accept Jesus and change your life, this is the time."

Hayet did.

Right after the end of the meeting, he saw an immediate change in his life. He was set to learn about the kingdom of God and his righteousness. One challenge though is that the fellowship where he attended and the volunteer leaders were Ethiopians, who are Eritreans political enemies. Although, the Ethiopian Christians were friendly, some of the Eritrean refugees repeatedly question him, "Why do you go with Ethiopians?"

"I am going for church not for politics," were Hayet's common reply.

During some holidays, the Missionaries do provide lunch for the attendees. Hayet's Eritrean friends would tell him, "If there is lunch please tell us," which he did. The lunch usually comes after the preaching they had to accept both the food and the message.

Transformed by the power of Jesus, Hayet does not know what the future holds for him. But he knows who holds the future, by learning and accepting the principles of the kingdom of God and his righteousness he will have all the things that he needs.

DAVID'S SMALL BEGINNINGS

During the days of David and Goliath, the Israelites blamed the Philistines for the conditions they were in. Currently, it is vice versa. Not a blacksmith could be found in the whole land of Israel, because the Philistines had said, "Otherwise the Hebrews will make swords or spears! So, all Israel went down to the Philistines to have their plow points, mattocks, axes, and sickles sharpened".[35] Thus, on the day of the battle not a soldier with King Saul and his son Jonathan had a sword or spear in his hand; only Saul and his son Jonathan had them.

This was a heavy burden that the Israelites had to deal with, without adequate weapons they could not defend themselves effectively. No wonder they could not defeat Goliath and his army. As a result, the king promised a reward for whoever would kill the giant. The king would give great wealth to the man who kills Goliath. He would also give that person his daughter in marriage and will exempt his family from taxes in Israel.

David's brothers as a symbol of entitled establishments were there for years. They could not handle and deal with the single threat of their country. They could have and should have dealt with the giant and earned the reward. However, they could not and would not.

As a principle, it is better to try something and fail than not to try at all. When Hayet told that he wanted to write an English book, he was told by Eritrean academics please do not. Because of the admonishment, he doubted himself. At the same time, he wanted to prove the academics that he can. He strongly felt that he should. Who should he listen, to his inner conviction or to people who never walked on his shoes?

If you cannot and will not bring a solution to the existing problem, move away, and let someone else willing and capable do the job do it. The problem is that people feel intimidated or get comfortable where they are and do not see the need to change. People would neither bring solution nor would they want or cooperate with one who promises to bring a change.

When Eliab, his oldest brother, heard David speaking with the other men, he burned with anger at him and asked, "Why have you come down here? And with whom did you leave those few sheep in the wilderness? I know how conceited you are and how wicked your heart is; you came down only to watch the battle."

The loud majority tried to silence and strip away David's right to speech for which he replied, "Now what have I done?" said David. "Can't I even speak?"

Your worst fear could be your greatest victory. Do not be afraid, God has equipped you with what you need to be successful.

Regardless of the establishment's threats and intimidations, David used his past experiences and confidence, The Lord who rescued him from the paw of the lion and the paw of the bear would rescue him from the hand of this Philistine.

David eventually, decided to walk his conviction and wanted to get rid of the scolding from Israel. He triumphed over the Philistine with a sling and a stone; without a sword in his hand, he struck down the Philistine and killed him. He destroyed the reproach of his country with just one hit on the big target, and he got his reward.

David's success in killing Goliath put him in trouble. When the men were returning home after David had killed the Philistine, the women came out from all the towns of Israel to meet King Saul with singing and dancing, with joyful songs and with tumbrels and lyres. As they danced, they sang: "Saul has slain his thousands, and David his tens of thousands." Saul was terribly angry; this refrain displeased him. *They have credited David with tens of thousands,* he thought, *but me with only thousands. What more can he get but the kingdom?* And from that time on Saul kept a close eye on David and wanted to kill him.

When one harbors ill intentions, evil spirit possesses them and will do anything to bring the successful down. It is such evil spirit owned, jealous, troublemakers that plant seeds of strife and in sighting hatred in the USA.

The king made several close proximities tries to kill David did not get Him because, David's God is a God who saves; from Him comes escape from death. David's God is yours should you choose to make Him part of your life. If the Lord had not been on David's side when Saul attacked him, Saul would have swallowed him alive when his anger flared against him. The flood of persecution would have engulfed him, the torrent would have swept over him, the raging waters of the King would have swept him away. Praise be to the Lord, who did not let him be torn by Saul's spear or sword. He escaped like a bird from the fowler's snare; the snare was broken, and David escaped multiple times.

David cannot change the beginning of how King Saul treated him. When Saul went to chase David in the wilderness, David had at least two opportunities to kill Saul. Instead each time he chose a new beginning of forgiveness.

Chapter Three

"If my people, who are called by my name, will humble themselves and pray and seek my face and turn from their wicked ways, then I will hear from heaven, and I will forgive their sin and will heal their land."

— THE BIBLE

WHERE 'WE THE PEOPLE' AND 'WE THE WORLD' ARE?

The word 'where,' in this context refers to a place and a condition one is in, made either by a perpetrator or by a personal choice. The beginning of where is the point at which one may be perpetrated or makes a choice. But the ending to a destiny is a choice to make. So, a person ought to focus not on the beginning, but to the destiny where they are heading. What God would like us to focus is to his kingdom, which is everlasting. Whatever exists today will last, but God and his kingdom live forever.

Knowing where a person is and realizing how they got there would help them to comeback expeditiously.

The year 2020 is so unique than any other past years. What makes it unique is that it has revealed two invisible pandemic viruses that have been ravaging the world. These are Covid-19 and Livid-20. The author will discuss both.

COVID-19 PANDEMIC

The term Covid-19 refers to Corona Virus Disease 2019. It originated in the Wuhan Province of China. In a stunning revelation, a Chinese virologist, Dr Li-Meng Yan has claimed that the coronavirus was created in a government-controlled laboratory in Wuhan, the original epicenter of the outbreak.[36] That may be the reason why the virus targets certain people that the health insurance covering government does not want to pay for. With Communist and Socialist leadership, everything is a secret. The World will never know the real cause of Coronavirus or other such problems. However, the Chinese government denies it and blamed a fish market and at another time, a bat. Bats and fish have existed on the same market for generations. What makes 2019's market deadly? Anyway, regardless of where it originated, there are several facts that one should consider.

Covid-19 is the first disease of any kind that has affected the whole World simultaneously. There are no places or people directly not affected by it. All previous diseases or disasters no matter how huge the magnitude, were indigenous to specific geographic location, but not Covid-19.

Covid-19 has killed all indiscriminately. It has affected and crippled the whole World's daily business into lockdown, killing people of first, second, and third World countries in the thousands per day. As per WHO data of September 19, 2020, there have been 30,369,778 confirmed cases of COVID-19, including 948,795 deaths globally.[37] People cannot mourn and bury their loved ones as it had been customary. It is the same disaster as it has been written in the scripture, "A cry is heard in Ramah, weeping and great mourning, Rachel weeping for her children and refusing to be comforted, because they are no more."[38]

This pandemic is more than a disease. It is a sign from God "He who has eyes to see, let him see, and he who has ears to hear, let him hear".[39] Rarely is there one who would pay attention to what is going on seriously. If there is, God would heal.

Covid-19 is more than a sign, it is an apocalyptic symbol which has affected each continent. While the whole World was asleep and off guard, the enemy sowed weeds among the wheat and went away. It is true the Scriptures tell us that God does nothing without revealing His plan to His servants the prophets. Where were people such as millionaire Michael Moore and Christian prophets who predicted about Donald Trump's election as well as his reelection? They could not see or prophesy the coming of Covid-19 that is devastating our World and its inhabitants.

Covid-19 is an epidemic that stalks in the darkness, a plague that destroys at midday. One that terrorizes by night and an arrow that flies by day. The weak as well as the powerful governments do not know how to contain it and are brought to their knees. For just as the lightning comes from the east and flashes even to the west, so is the effect of the pandemic. Behold, he is coming with the clouds, and every eye will see him, even those who pierced him; and all peoples on earth will mourn because of him.[40]

This is the time when the World needs to reconsider how far people have fallen abandoning the Lord God! It is time to repent and do what is right in the eyes of God, put God first, families together, fewer divorce, reduction in crimes, less injustice, less unfairness, decline in abominations, fleeing laziness, and turning away of Sodom and Gomorrah practices.

It is not time to blame one race over the other, one religion blaming the other, as Marxists do blame one class over the other and wanting to eradicate social stratification. Fighting one another, in the end there is no winner, and all get destroyed. Saint Paul related to this habit (American, fighting and destroying another American, destroying American property) said, "If you bite and devour each other, watch out or you will be destroyed by each other".[41]

Hayet's father, Sheden once told him, 'Divided we fall, united we win.' To prove his point, he told him the following story, which is good to the current situation, what "We the People" and "We the World" are facing.

There were three oxen, red, black, and white. Divided they fall, united they stand. Since the enemy knows cannot win against united people, the enemy creates dissention, separation, discord to win. It could be by race, gender, economic status, religion and so on.

The oxen were sticking together as one and the hyena realized that it cannot break their unity to defend. Then the hyena came up with a scheme and said, "I came to eat you because of the white ox."

The black and red oxen told the white ox, "we don't want to get eaten because of you." So, they isolated themselves from the white ox. Then, in isolation, the hyena killed the white ox.

The enemies are not satisfied when you give them one. They need all that you have. The hyena tried and could not break the unity. Later, the hyena came back to the remaining oxen, "I came to eat you because of the red ox."

Eventually one said to the other, "I don't want to get eaten because of you," and went separate ways. Divided we fall, united we stand. The oxen, one blaming the other went separate ways. Eventually, the hyena killed three of them with in one night. Therefore, America, to win against the common enemy, the devil, let us unite.

Fighting, devouring, and destroying each other harms both sides. That is what made countries where immigrants to the USA come from become poor, unable to solve their differences peacefully. That is where Americans appears to be heading betrayed by both major political parties. Thus, one needs to "Be very careful, then, how you live—not as unwise but as wise, making the most of every opportunity, because the days are evil".[42]

All have made wrongs regardless of who they are. There is no difference between Jew and Gentile, Black and White, Muslim, Christian, Hindu, Buddhist, African Traditionalist. For all have sinned and fall short of the glory of God, and all are justified freely by God's grace through the redemption that came by Christ Jesus.

It is time NOW to repent in droves at God's rebuke and He will pour out His thoughts to us, He will make known to us His teaching. We must return to where we have fallen from as individuals and as a nation, not to riots that divide us even more.

The departure from Judeo-Christian values and has far reaching consequence and worshipping government and those who encourage people away from the teaching of the Word of God. God is calling, "Seek the Lord while he may be found; call on him while he is near. Let the wicked forsake their ways and the unrighteous their thoughts.[43] Yet people prefer not to return. This is the fulfillment Paul instructed Timothy to beware of when he wrote: "The Spirit clearly says that in later times some will abandon the faith and follow deceiving spirits and things taught by demons. Such teachings come through hypocritical liars, whose consciences have been seared as with a hot iron".[44]

For refusing to heed Truth there are consequences. However, since you refuse to listen when I call and no one pays attention when I stretch out my hand, since you disregard all my advice and do not accept my rebuke, I in turn will laugh when disaster strikes you; I will mock when calamity overtakes you— like a storm, when disaster sweeps over you like a whirlwind, when distress and trouble overwhelm you.[45] There is a time when God will listen, there is a time when He will not. That is the time when people will call to God, but He will not answer.

There was a time when America, Canada, and other Western nations were called God-fearing nations, reaching out the unreached! May it be said of us again that we are God fearing nations. Amen!

The fear of God, the beginning of all knowledge was the center of our governance and working curriculum in our school systems. It is no more. In those days there were very few crimes and community affecting problems because people were obeying spiritual law, moral law, civil law which is included in government law. Good old days passed when parents were involved in their children's education and when, chewing gum and wearing a hat were the worst crimes in our schools. No more God and no more prayers.

Nowadays, our learning institutions, teacher's union are holding students hostage demand on issues that have nothing to do with the teaching and learning met to do their job. Learning institutions changed into battlegrounds of politicians to own and possess the students. There should be checks and balances on the curriculum that involves love for the USA. These are not one or two incidents, there have been far too many reports of "rogue teachers" attacking Trump in the classroom. It's time to root out educators who have turned their classrooms into indoctrination centers."[46] *Enough is enough!*

Universities and colleges create an office of diversity and inclusiveness. However, they would not let conservative students or speakers on the very campus. The liberals can bring whatever they want to the schools, while conservatives are censored and cannot.

It appears there are external forces that influence and change the USA's history to be like any other nation. America's uniqueness is based on the USA's distinctiveness. God made America and the first World countries prosperous because of adopting Christian principles as a manual. When they abandon what made them prosperous in the name of human freedom purported by people who do not love God, they become like the ungodly nations. Thus, Christianity as it did for 2,000 years will survive without the first World nations. However, the first World nations cannot survive without Christianity that made them prosperous.

America does not have to be part of a union or be it NATO or WHO to be accepted if our distinctiveness of indivisible with liberty and justice for all is not welcomed and appreciated. The USA should be the leader not a follower. There are some leaders that want us to be followers and others who want us to be leaders.

The Lord is with us when we are with Him. If we seek him, He will be found, but if we forsake Him, He will forsake us to do things that ought not be done. The more a nation pushes God out of its governance, and society, the society grows worse and turns into chaos.

In the USA, the idea of pushing God out of governance worsened and was visible during the Obama administration more than any other American President. A government without God put us to where we are today. There is nothing worse than unjustified merciless genocide and daily killings of each other on our great cities. One injustice does not neutralize another injustice. Acquitting the guilty and condemning the innocent-- the Lord detests them both.[47]

For generations as it did during the days of prophet Jonah, the message has been preached against the great cities because people's detestable, abominable sin has come up before God. Yet people did not pay attention to the signs, warnings and did not care to return.

In the American context, one race blames the other, one party blames the other for the mess both parties 'We the People' put in. Everybody is to blame for the mistakes and generational curses that have been piling on for years. These are the days, "Parents are not to be put to death for their children, nor children put to death for their parents; each will die for their own sin".[48] At last, Covid-19 has come to warn, set a break, slow, or prevent our craziness and our worldly or perverse way of life.

These are like the days before the great flood, people were eating and drinking, marrying, and giving in marriage, setting up dynasty businesses, creating great inventions up to the day Noah entered the ark; and they knew nothing about what would happen until the flood came and swept them all away. It is time to wake up and return from the ways that caused Noah's generation to be wiped out.[49]

The people of Nineveh were smarter than the current generations of hubris who have excessive pride and self-confidence. When they saw and heard a sign that after forty days that the city would be overthrown, it was not time to fool around and do business as usual.

The Ninevites heed to the warning. A fast was proclaimed for everyone from the greatest to the least, everyone, put on sackcloth. Upon hearing the impending calamity, the king of Nineveh, rose from his throne, took off his royal robes, covered himself with sackcloth and sat down in the dust. He issued a statewide proclamation in Nineveh: "By the decree of the king and his nobles: Do not let people or animals, herds or flocks, taste anything; do not let them eat or drink. But let people and animals be covered with sackcloth. Let everyone urgently call on God. Let them give up their evil ways and their violence. Who knows? God may yet relent and with compassion and turn from His fierce anger so that we will not perish."

When God saw what they did and how they turned from their evil ways, He relented and did not bring on them the destruction He had warned he would.[50] This is what is needed of 'We the People' and 'We the World,' to avert the Covid-19 pandemic. Everyone should blame themselves not others.

In a Town Hall Biden with Anderson Cooper of CNN said, "If the President had done his job from the beginning, all the people would still be alive.[51] He blames Trump, not China. To speak the truth, the USA was better prepared to deal with such pandemic under the sleepless and hardworking Trump who was fighting multiple warfronts. Americans also were in a better position economically.

LIVID-20 PANDEMIC

LIVID-20 (Livid-20 also Livid) pandemic is global issue, generations older, slicky, and vicious than Covid-19. It has affected, afflicted, and killed more people than Covid-19 for generations. The people of the world do not notice its severity, CDC, and the WHO will never declare it a pandemic. Because they are cool with it. Perhaps the author chose to name it Livid-20 since it is discovered at the time of this writing.

Livid-20 does not heal you and does not kill you. It is not a bone-eating virus or one that contaminates the blood with abnormal cells. This pandemic is not something that slows or increases the heartbeat. Livid-20 is not a respiratory related virus that afflicts human respiratory anatomy. Physical medicine cannot treat or cure it. It is not one that afflict people with painful sores from the soles of the feet to the crown of the head. If people were to have a feeling like irritants in the eyes, thorns in the sides, they would have sought medical help. However, this pandemic is not anything like that.

Van Jones of CNN in the year 2020, and Malcom X about sixty years ago had a glimpse of the dangerousness of it. This pandemic is the Liberal virus disease of 2020 (Livid-20). Livid-20 is a spiritual problem. A spiritual problem needs a spiritual solution. Thus, only God can heal and deliver one from Livid-20. It is an enemy to whatever is true, whatever is noble, whatever is right, whatever is pure, whatever is lovely, whatever is admirable, whatever is excellent or praiseworthy.

Livid-20 is a communicable disease. The best way to keep oneself from Livid-20 infection according to King David is, by staying on the path of purity and by living according to your word.[52] One must return to where one left, to God to reclaim what one left.

COMMON SYMPTOMS OF LIVID-20 INFECTION

These symptoms are not all and may not be so for everyone infected by Livid-20:

❖　　Biblical symptoms to Livid-20. People are going to be self-absorbed, money-hungry, self-promoting, stuck-up, profane, disobedient to authority and parents, crude, coarse, dog-eat-dog, unbending, slanderers, impulsively wild, savage, cynical, treacherous, ruthless, bloated windbags, addicted to lust, and allergic to God. They will make a show of religion, but behind the scenes they are animals. Stay clear of these people or else you will be infected.[53]

❖   Unfulfilled promises. You promise one and you do another.

❖   Blame others. For whatever wrong goes in (the country) you blame others even if you have been part of the problem for generations.

❖   Hold others to a higher standard which you cannot do for yourself. In a related reference Jesus said to the crowds and to his disciples: "The teachers of the law and the Pharisees sit in Moses' seat. So, you must be careful to do everything they tell you. But do not do what they do, for they do not practice what they preach. They tie up heavy, cumbersome loads and put them on other people's shoulders, but they themselves are not willing to lift a finger to move them.[54]

❖   You say schools, jobs should not open, people should socially distance, wear mask to avoid spreading or contracting Covid-19. But you do not do what you say it should be done. The rule applies to them not to you.

❖   Hypocrisy. You blame Trump's organized parades or less than 2,000 RNC acceptance attendees as super Covid-19 spreader while you do 50,000 plus march in Washington and daily thousands protest not talking about your own following CDC guidelines.

❖   Bring or tell distorted information. You burn buildings, loot, and destroy businesses of hard-working citizens and you call it fiery but mostly peaceful protest.

❖   You demand from others. You demand from others what you would not give to others. Example, you speak about tolerance while yourself being intolerant.

❖   Chant death to America and burn American flag. For the country you claim to love you wish death. For the flag, many people paid their life to protect, you burn it and you feel no remorse.

❖   You say what is that to you. When someone, 'a brother keeper,' tells you God created male and female, 'you say what is that to you'.

❖ You portray to care for life. You claim to care for human dignity and life. Yet you legalize late term abortion and partial birth killings.

❖ No fear of God. A Livid-20 infected person is a barbaric person, no mercy to humanity or to their property.

❖ Blaming fascism and racism. While doing fascist and racist acts, you blame others for being fascists and racists.

Let this list be enough for now.

TROJAN HORSES

The Trojan Horse is a story from the ancient Trojan War. The tale is about the deception that the Greeks used to enter the independent city of Troy and win the war. In the canonical version, after an unsuccessful 10-year blockade, the Greeks built a wooden hollow horse and disguised themselves, hid a force of about thirty select men. The Greeks pretended to sail away, and the Trojans pulled the horse into their city as a victory trophy. That night, the Greek force crept out of the horse and opened the gates for the rest of the Greek army, which had sailed back under cover of night. The Greeks entered and destroyed the city of Troy, ending the war.[55]

A Trojan horse could also be a person or thing planned clandestinely to destabilize or bring about the demise of an enemy or opponent.[56] Webster dictionary explains Trojan horse as a way intended to defeat or subvert from within usually by deceptive means as well. It is also seemingly useful and genuine computer program that contains designed concealed instructions which when activated perform illicit or malicious action hurting one.[57]

A Trojan horse could as well be explained as the Fifth column, an accomplice group within a country at war that are supportive to its adversaries. The one that looks like you, part of your army while it is not is the worst enemy to identify and defeat.

Trojan horses in our current context appear to care and love certain people by their words and actions. However, deep in the inside, where it matters most, they are about themselves but not the people they purport to care about.

HUBRIS EXPLAINED

Let us now look at the term hubris. Hubris is the lack of self-awareness, characteristic of excessive over confidence or arrogance, within a person which leads one to believe that they can do no wrong to oneself and to others. Hubris can cause short-sighted, irrational, or harmful behavior since one does not stop to examine their behavior or consider the opinions of or effects on others when behaving.[58]

Encyclopedia Britannica describes hubris as the intentional use of violence to humiliate or degrade. It came to be defined as overweening presumption that leads a person to disregard the divinely fixed limits on human action in an ordered universe.[59]

Hubris' personality quality is of extreme or foolish pride or dangerous overconfidence is often in combination with arrogance. "Arrogance" comes from the Latin "adrogare" and it means feeling a right to demand certain attitudes and behaviors from other people. Hubris, arrogance, and pretension are related to the need for victory (even if it doesn't always mean winning) instead of reconciliation, as would be made by "friendly" groups.[60]

Hubris know not that they do not know. This is arrogance. What does the Bible say about hubris? The Book of Samuel says, "Do not keep talking so proudly or let your mouth speak such arrogance, for the Lord is a God who knows, and by him deeds are weighed."[61]

The Supreme Court decided in favor of the liberals. That, court ruled that gay and transgender people were protected against employment discrimination based on sex. Remember that hubris and arrogance are related to the need for power and victory.

This ruling was a big hit for Donald Trump's voters and a victory for Barack Obama. Trump lived entire past of his life, and working among same-sex marriage proponents, it meant nothing to him. However, since he is running on a conservative agenda either by a conviction or for the sake of the voters, he ought to voice his dissatisfaction with the ruling.

Upon the ruling, Obama tweeted a message of optimism in which he wished the country a "Happy Pride Month." He tweeted a picture of the White House lit by rainbow colors, with the message: "Today reminds us that progress might be slow. It might take decades. But no matter what things might look like today, it's always possible. Happy Pride month, everybody."[62]

On what is so called Pride Month June, Trump's administration tells U.S. embassies that they can't fly pride flag on flagpoles; for which The U.S. embassies in Israel, Germany, Brazil, and Latvia are among those that requested.[63] The LGBTQ does not represent the wishes of all Americans: it should not be displayed as a sign of America. Imagine what would have happened with President Hillary Clinton or President Joe Biden?

LGBTQ people are human beings, God loves them as everybody else. The author disagrees with their lifestyle but loves and prays for them. God created woman for man and vice versa.

In religious usage, hubris means a transgression against God,[64] of which the Devil is the Chief of all hubris. The Devil has been cast down to the earth, for the arrogance of character as noted: "You said in your heart, I will ascend to the heavens; I will raise my throne above the stars of God; I will sit enthroned on the mount of assembly, on the utmost heights of Mount Zaphon. I will ascend above the tops of the clouds; I will make myself like the Most High. But you are brought down to the realm of the dead, to the depths of the pit".[65]

Trojan hubris is prevalent in the World. In the USA, it manifests itself in Democratic, Republican, and Independents operatives. Prophet Isaiah disapproves the people who take advantage of the disadvantaged. He states, "Scoundrels use wicked methods, they make up evil schemes to destroy the poor with lies, even when the plea of the needy is just".[66] Should there be a real case let "We the People" and "We the World" work to improve the suffering of the poor, and not take advantage of the disadvantaged.

Chapter Four

"Destiny is not a matter of chance; it is a matter of choice. It is not a thing to be waited for, it is a thing to be achieved."

— WILLIAM JENNINGS BRYAN

GOD USES THE LEAST EXPECTED

There are countless evidences that God used the least expected to fulfill his purpose. Here are some of them:

THE SLAVE GIRL

Often, God use the least expected options to achieve greatness. These days, far much worse than it used to be, honesty is not considered as the best policy. People would do anything to get

money.

The author is reminded of a story of an encounter where two men called Paul and Silas were walking on a visible and hostile environment. Once when they were going to the place of prayer, they met a slave girl who had a spirit by which she predicted the future. She earned a great deal of money for her owners through fortune-telling.

As Paul and Silas walked, she followed them shouting, "These men are servants of the Most High God, who are telling you the way to be saved." She kept this up for many days. Nobody was able to discern her problem. Finally, Paul became so annoyed that he turned around and said to the spirit, "In the name of Jesus Christ I command you to come out of her!" At that moment, the spirit left her, and she was a free woman able to think for herself.

Here comes the trouble: her owners realized that their hope of making money was gone, and they could no longer benefit from her, they seized Paul and Silas and dragged them into the marketplace to face the authorities.

The accusers of the duo said, "These men are Jews, and are throwing our city into an uproar by advocating customs unlawful for us Romans to accept or practice." Here what one could observe is that the owners of the slave girl were not native Jews. They were foreign country hubris interested not in the wellbeing of the Jews, but for themselves. They were Trojan hubris, riding on the back of the slave girl. The agitators did not care about Jewish traditions or the freedom of the slave girl who gained her human dignity which should have been audacious to rejoice about. Not at all. All they cared about was the money that they would no longer benefit from her.

People would do anything to fight a leader of the free world or organization that would threaten their financial gains. Consequently, they used their cunning method to attack the deliverers. The crowd without discerning the fact joined in the attack against Paul and Silas. The magistrates ordered them to be stripped and beaten with rods, which they did not deserve. After they had been severely flogged, they were thrown into prison, and the jailer was commanded to guard them carefully. When he received these orders, he put them in the inner cell and fastened their feet in the stocks. But God intervened and set them free from the prison,.[67] There is God's promise to the people that serve Him: "The righteous person may have many troubles, but the Lord delivers him from them all; He protects all his bones, not one of them will be broken".[68]

THE DEMONIAC MAN

Just like the masters of the slave girl, people in general do not like when others become productive citizens with a right mind. A story is told of a man who got delivered from possession by 'a legion of demons. In the Roman army a legion was a division typically numbered between 3,000 and 6,000 soldiers, so a legion is a considerable force.[69]

The man lived in the tombs, and no one could bind him anymore, not even with a chain. For he had often been chained hand and foot, but he tore the chains apart and broke the irons on his feet. No one was strong enough to subdue him, but Jesus did. There is power associated with the Name 'Jesus Christ.' It is to the same name that even the winds and waves obey. He rebukes them to be completely calm and they do so.

The name Jesus still heals, restores, provides and you name it. Should you be in any situation just call Jesus and you shall see the salvation of the Lord. Amid a crowd, touching his cloth brought healing to a woman who had bleeding problem for more than a decade that doctors could not treat.

Night and day the demoniac man was among the tombs and in the hills, he would cry out and cut himself with stones. When he saw Jesus from a distance, he ran and fell on his knees in front of Him. He shouted at the top of his voice, "What do you want with me, Jesus, Son of the Most High God? In God's name don't torture me!"

For Jesus had said to him, "Come out of this man, you impure spirit!"

Then Jesus asked him, "What is your name?"

"My name is Legion," he replied, "for we are many." And he begged Jesus repeatedly not to send them out of the area. A large herd of pigs was feeding on a nearby hillside. The demons begged Jesus, "Send us among the pigs; allow us to go into them."

He gave them permission, and the impure spirits came out and went into the pigs. The herd, about two thousand in number, rushed down the steep bank into the lake and were drowned. Those tending the pigs ran off and reported this in the town and countryside, and the people went out to see what had happened. When they came to Jesus, they saw the man who had been possessed by the legion of demons, sitting there, dressed and in his right mind; and they were afraid. Those who had seen it told the people what had happened to the demon-possessed man—and told about the pigs as well. Then the people began to plead with Jesus to leave their region.[70]

The people cared more about the demons, their culture, and the pigs than for the person who gained his human dignity by the Kingdom of God. The Gerasene who saw the deliverance of that man could have benefited to change their lives using that juxtaposition, yet they did not. It is to such kind of dead brains that Jesus rebukes, "For this people's heart has become hardened; they hardly hear with their ears, and they have closed their eyes. Otherwise they might see with their eyes, hear with their ears, understand with their hearts, and turn, and I would heal them".[71]

Just like the Gerasene, several State Attorney Generals, House Representatives, Mayors, and Governors do not want police presence in the riot areas, but in their houses. The leaders could not handle the chaos in their cities yet were against governments' intervention to the cities that were out of control. One could guess governments' intervention is for the sake of the voiceless, peaceful citizens who have been economically hurt by the protest.

As did others in multiple cities, Seattle City Council passed an ordinance which bans the use of "less lethal" tools such as tear gas, rubber bullets, bean bags, pepper spray, flashbangs, ultrasonic cannons, water cannons, and other tools used to break up crowds following complaints from protesters about "police misconduct."[72]

Police officers as well as civilian protesters have been injured or much worse killed in one way or the other. According to the author, if the Seattle protesters use lethal weapons to protest and fight the police, the police have a right to use proportionate methods to defend themselves, protect property that is being looted and destroyed indiscriminately. The blame goes to both sides, that is the violent protesters and the violent police that use disproportionate force to deal with the protesters.

The main thing is that there is a law. A lawbreaker, that is, police misconduct as well as protesters' misconduct should be dealt according to the law, no matter who one is. Everyone has the right to peaceful protest, but no has the right to destroy property that belongs to others who invested years of their lives for it.

The city council hubris preferred lawlessness over order; chaos over peace. It is to such kinds of leaders and followers that Jesus would say, "Leave them; they are blind guides. If the blind lead the blind, both will fall into a pit".[73] American inner cities are in ruins because of such poor leadership. That is why their inhabitants are prone to poverty, and disease. Communities suffer endlessly economically and educationally with K-12 failing school systems. At the end of the destruction, just as Minnesota Governor did, they ask the federal government to bail them out to repair the destruction inflicted by uncivilized looters, vandals and rioters that should not have happened in the first place.

There is a feeling that the federal government abandoned the black people. The government did not provide support to them in the first place providing with better schooling and infrastructure to begin with? It is not the duty of the federal government to address every issue affecting each county in every State. The States should take responsibility not only for handling but also overcoming issues such as infrastructure and education that can be dealt with locally.

A U.S. State is a country within a country. The federal government's responsibility is to regulate interstate and foreign commerce, declare war, set taxes, determine and oversee spending, and enact other national policies guided by the 435-member House of Representatives and the 100-member U.S. Senate that represent the 50 states; then the ultimate decider is the President to either sign the passed bills into law or reject with a veto.[74]

THE SAMARITAN WOMAN

Contrary to the Gerasene who pleaded with Jesus to leave their region, the Samaritans' benefit resulted in Jesus' encounter with one of their own. In the well-known story, as an outcast, a Samaritan woman had six unsuccessful relationships with men who could not satisfy her. The seventh encounter with Jesus had a different outcome. Each encounter one experiences with another person is not predictable to have the same outcome. It should be treated with an anticipation of having a better result.

Just one encounter, Jesus transformed the Samaritan woman's life inside out! Right after the encounter, she went into the town, Sychar, and told her people to come and see Jesus. They did and saw Jesus for themselves and loved him. Consequently, they urged him to stay with them, and he stayed two days. And because of his words many more became believers.

Later, they said to the woman, "We no longer believe just because of what you said; now we have heard for ourselves, and we know that this man really is the Savior of the World." A woman who did not have a stable family, someone considered uncountable in the Jewish culture, brought good news to her people. The Samaritans embraced the invitation that came through the woman, and so they benefitted having a transformed life for all eternity.

THE LEPERS IN SAMARIA

In another instance, presumed outcasts of a community became the reason for the end of severe famine in Samaria. The outcasts were lepers who lived in isolation, endless quarantine that they were not allowed to mix themselves in the community. They were the untouchables, unspeakable, and target groups for all forms of systemic attacks and abuses. However, for God, whether one is a leper or not, all are treated the same. Jesus touched the untouchables and healed the unhealable.

The lepers were afraid that they would die of starvation if they did not act. They discussed among themselves, "If we say, we will enter into the city, then the famine is in the city, and we shall die there: and if we sit still here, we die also. Now therefore, come and let us fall unto the host of the Syrians: if they save us alive, we shall live; and if they kill us, we shall but die."

It is better to try and fail than not to try at all. It is by trial and error people get to their destiny.

By divine providence, they went to the Syrian camp and found plenty of food. After they had enough for themselves, they said to each other, "What we're doing is not right. This is a day of good news and we are keeping it to ourselves. If we wait until daylight, punishment will overtake us. Let us go at once and report this to the royal palace."

The lepers were so concerned about the clean people that did not like them, that put them in unending seclusion. The same night they reported to the royal palace, and in the morning, there was plenty of food for the nation. The outcasts saved their people from starvation to death. The detailed story can be found in.[75]

THE BOY WITH FIVE LOAVES AND TWO FISH

Right after the death of John the Baptist, Jesus went to a solitary place. A crowd followed Him. He wanted to feed them, but it could take more than a half-year's wage to buy enough bread for each one to have a bite! Moreover, there was no place to buy food. The only food they could find was just five small barley loaves and two fish from an insignificant person in a Jewish culture, a boy. The disciples were skeptical about how far the food at hand would go among the crowd. By divine providence, Jesus then took the loaves, gave thanks, and distributed to those who were seated as much as they wanted. He did the same with the fish. When they all had enough to eat, He said to His disciples, "Gather the pieces that are left over. Let nothing be wasted."

The disciples gathered them and filled twelve baskets with the pieces of the five barley loaves left over by those who had eaten.

Good, deliverance, provisions, and healings have come to the people in need at a time when they need it; from the uncountable, the untouchable and the insignificant. If they accept it, they will benefit from the miracle. If they do not, they will suffer the consequences.

INFERENCES FROM THE ABOVE

Donald Trump got elected and became the 45th USA President (detail in the next chapter). He was the least likely to be the USA President. President Obama had the same perception. During the election year of 2016, he said, I continue to believe Mr. Trump will not be president. And the reason is because I have a lot of faith in the American people. And I think they recognize that being president is a serious job.[76] Trump got elected because the so-called good Democrat and Republican Presidents failed the American people and he promised to fix that.

To hate or love a person there must be a reason. However, the Office of the Presidency ought to be respected by all citizens. There are Trojans that hate Trump for no reason because the Trojan handlers and the dangerous hubris said he is bad. Nevertheless, the people that worked with him and covered his story do not see what people accuse him of.

Liz Crokin, an award-winning author, an entertainment journalist, political pundit, and an advocate for sexual assault victims has her own take on Donald Trump. She rebuffs the perception that Trump is a racist, bigot, sexist, xenophobe, anti-Semitic, and Islamophobe. The left and the media launch these hideous kinds of attacks at Trump every day. Yet, nothing could be further from the truth about Trump. She tells of how she had the opportunity to cover Trump for over a decade. She says, all her years covering him she never heard anything negative about the man until he announced he was running for President as a Republican.[77]

When Trump announced he would run for political office, just as Corkin did, all his cronies who loved and knew him not only parted from Trump but also turned against him. If Trump is as bad as how the media portray him to be why did they not tell the world about that before he declared his intent to go as a Republican? For Corkin, the main reason for parting with Trump was not a political or personal issue, it was about where she was making money from.

She speaks her motive "Keep in mind, I got paid a lot of money to dig up dirt on celebrities like Trump for a living, so a scandalous story on the famous billionaire could've potentially sold a lot of magazines and would've been a "huge" feather in my cap. Instead, I found that he does not drink alcohol or do drugs; he is a hardworking businessman and totally devoted to his beloved wife and children. On top of that, he's one of the most generous celebrities in the World with a heart filled with more gold than his $100 million New York penthouse.[78]

Jesus did not do many miracles in His hometown, a prophet is not honored at home, because of their lack of faith. That is why Trump once said that he would leave his birth city, New York after the Presidency. Let people give him a chance the way they did with other Presidents to finish his term. The more detractors detract the man, the more he is likely to win the second term. There are things that have nothing to do with Trump. Such as burning the Bible, burning church, burning, and looting businesses, wasting time, and painting BLM murals by his house. It would have been more productive to spend the money on the needy or volunteer and help children.

The main reason why the author, who chose not to vote for 2016 presumptive nominees, yet wants to do this project is to say, 'enough is enough.' If people keep on harassing him, chances are he will not give America his best. There is much to be done at his hand, let him focus on his job not on a relentless fight with the hubris who lost their income because of Trump.

When the invisible pandemic was invading the USA and the World, Democrats were obsessed with an impeachment hoax; and Trump, with defending himself. It was too late to stop the spread of the Covid-19 pandemic. Although Trump was the first leader to suspend flights from the hotbed of the virus. he was called a racist for doing so. Yet still passengers were travelling from China to Canada and make it to the USA. Months or weeks after the leader Trump, other countries followed and suspended flights from China.

Chapter Five

"If we lose freedom here, there is no place to escape to. This is the last stand on earth."

— PRESIDENT RONALD REGAN

UNREST IN THE USA

The main reason for the unrest in the USA is "We the People," collectively or individually we have deserting God's principles. A person ought to have peace with God, then by extension or in

return, God makes every valley of life raised up, every mountain and hill of life made low; the rough ground of life become level, the rugged places a plain. This is a promise written in the Word of God "When the LORD takes pleasure in anyone's way, He causes their enemies to make peace with them."[79]

When the LORD takes pleasure in anyone's way, He causes their enemies to make peace with them."
The Bible

There are individuals and organizations that are responsible for the unrest we have seen over the past four years in the USA, since the election of Donald J. Trump, the 45th US President. Trump did not attain the Presidency by a donation of Russians or other people group. He worked diligently and earned the position. During the campaign, Trump travelled to the forgotten people of the mid states who lost their livelihood due to excessive regulations of the Obama administration on productive companies. His opponent, Secretary Clinton, was talking about gay marriage equality, LGBTQ+, abortion as woman's right, and letting children choose their gender and bathrooms of their choice in the metropolitan cities, which is not a priority for Americans.

Trump's fulfillment of promises, creating jobs, could be one reason for the unrest by the agitators who want to see Trump failing the American people. Hayet remembers a relative, who is a Democrat voter that lived and worked for years in the mid states. He was working for a processing company, that imports suppliers to USA wholesale customers. However, the company, just like many others, was shut down due to environmental regulations under the Obama administration. The relative sold his house and had to move.

Due to the closing of the plant, people lost their livelihood; they had no jobs to take care of themselves and their families. Consequently, many families' income went in shambles. It is at this time, the people who lost their jobs intersected with candidate Trump who promised to reopen their manufacturing and other plants and bring jobs back to the USA (companies that left due to high taxes or excessive regulations).

While Trump was focusing on jobs, Clinton was focusing on gender bathrooms and promising to carry on Obama's legacy, which Americans resented and that eventually would become the reason for the demise of Secretary Clinton's Presidential aspirations. If Biden keeps allegiance with Obama, he may have to face Clinton's fate.

Trump won the election and fulfilled his promises, incentivized companies to reopen their plant. The former employers contacted all employees; including Hayet's relative to return, the company is currently fully operational.

Upon a call to return, Hayet's relative replied, "I cannot come."

"What can we do to make you come?" The company asked. He gave them his priority list and they agreed, and he moved back. Now he says, next time he will vote for Trump's reelection.

Jealous groups have been igniting and engulfing unrest among Americans. First, TVCNN. TVCNN is an acronym that refers to Trump Vulture Cunning News Network. Frequently, the author shall be using TV for Trump Vulture. What does the description of vulture in this context refer? "If you describe a person as a vulture, you disapprove of them because you think they are trying to gain from another person's troubles."[80]

This is not the first time Hayet is feeling such a sentiment. Over the years the USA has also seen Obama Vultures (OV), Bush Vultures (BV), Clinton Vultures (CV), etc. During the days of the Obama administration, Hayet felt as indignant as he does now when Democrats as well as Republicans acted as OV's and would not let him do his job, criticizing every turn he made. Such treatment of a President was wrong then, is wrong now, and is wrong for a president yet to come.

As a conservative U.S. citizen, the author disagrees with every decision Obama made that directly affects religious groups. Hayet wished a conservative leader to come after Obama and did not vote on 2016, because both presumptive nominees did not meet the basic requirement. Instead, God gave America and the world, an outsider, Donald Trump running as a Republican.

PEACE WITH GOD

The most important thing people should do is to have peace with God by accepting Jesus Christ as their personal Lord and savior. If not, people would fight with themselves and with others. The most important people and nations should do is to have peace with God by accepting Jesus Christ as their personal Lord and savior. If not, people would fight with themselves and with others. If you make peace with God, "The LORD will grant that the enemies who rise up against you will be defeated before you. They will come at you from one direction but flee from you in seven."[81] If you do not have peace with God, you keep on fighting with yourself and with everybody.

If you choose not to have peace with God, "The LORD will send on you curses, confusion and rebuke in everything you put your hand to, until you are destroyed and come to sudden ruin because of the evil you have done in forsaking him." If you choose not to have peace with God, "The LORD will cause you to be defeated before your enemies. You will come at them from one direction but flee from them in seven, and you will become a thing of horror to all the kingdoms on earth."[82] And you keep on blaming others for your defeat., Chastising Secretary Clinton and her voters as well as the TVCNN Senator Schumer said that, "When you lose to somebody who has 40 percent popularity, you don't blame other things — Comey, Russia — you blame yourself."[83]

By ignoring to have peace with God, you keep on changing places and procedures, and still you cannot be successful. Eliphaz the Temanite told Job what he needed most is, "Submit to God and be at peace with him; in this way prosperity will come to you. Accept instruction from his mouth and lay up his words in your heart. If you return to the Almighty, you will be restored: If you remove wickedness far from your tent and assign your nuggets to the dust, your gold of Ophir to the rocks in the ravines, then the Almighty will be your gold, the choicest silver for you."[84]

When Democrats had the majority, "Senate Majority Leader Harry Reid, D-Nevada, pushed through a controversial change to Senate rules Thursday that will make it easier to approve President Obama's nominees but threatens to further divide an already polarized Congress. The change reduces the threshold from 60 votes to 51 votes for Senate approval of executive and judicial nominees against unanimous GOP opposition."[85]

For the unmediated decision, "Republicans warned that it would not only tear apart cross-party relationships in the Senate, but it will come back to haunt Democrats if they return to the minority. "You will no doubt come to regret this, and you may regret it a lot sooner than you think,"[86] Senate Minority Leader Mitch McConnell, R-Kentucky, warned Democrats.

Now the Democrats have no majority, they cry over the decision they made. They are proposing to change the Electoral College. By doing so, they think it is going to be for their favor and are demanding to abolish it. That is not all. They are demanding that the number of Supreme Court Justices increase to 13 from the current 9 Justices.

When it comes to filling a vacancy in the Supreme Court the politicians and the justices know that it must be filled as soon as possible. In the past, President Obama, Hillary Clinton, Joe Biden, Justice Ruth Ginsburg were in favor of the mandated constitution filling the vacancy. Now, the situation is not in their side, they speak otherwise.

Now that the Democrats see that the Supreme Court is not going to be in their favor, the House Representatives will introduce a bill that will limit the occupancy of U.S. Supreme Court justices to 18 years from current lifetime appointments, in a bid to reduce partisan warring over vacancies and preserve the court's legitimacy. Every President to nominate two justices per four-year term.[87]

If you do not have peace with God, "In the morning you will say, If only it were evening!" and in the evening, "If only it were morning!"--because of the terror that will fill your hearts and the sights that your eyes will see.[88] The author is not saying that the Republican is God fearing Party. But at least they acknowledge God.

WHY IS TRUMP FACING BARRAGES OF ATTACK?

In his lifetime, Hayet has known a few American Presidents. These are: Donald Trump, Barack Obama, George W. Bush, Bill Clinton, George H. Bush, Ronald Regan, and Jimmy Carter. Out of all these Presidents, nobody has been faced with relentless barrages of attacks real or perceived the way President Donald Trump has and even more so, survived them all. To mention few of the attacks, 25 women have accused him of sexual assault, accusations from Stormy Daniel, Russia collusion on the 2016 election, Ukraine phone call, impeachment, and so on.

When it comes to President Trump's phone call to Ukraine's President Zelenskyy, Trump was accused of quid pro quo (this for that). Democrats thought that Trump would not release a classified document they always dreamed of, to create a case for a lame impeachment. Imagine to be impeached for 'I would like you to do us a favor though.'[89]

While the following statements from Biden has a visible and audible quid pro quo, according to Trump haters:

The Ukrainian prosecutor was investigating Biden's son and his company was fired at Biden's request after threatening to withhold $1B in aid. Biden wanted the prosecutor fired. He told Ukrainian President Petro Poroshenko; we are not going to give you the billion dollars if you do not fire the investigator (prosecutor). "We are leaving (Ukraine) in six hours. If the prosecutor is not fired, you are not getting the money, SOB. He got fired.[90]

The prosecutor was fired, the money was given. This is the real quid pro quo not 'I would like you to do us favor though.' Be fair and speak fairly.

Trump, a businessman, has been a buddy of the group that is attacking him for decades. He loved what they love and hated what they hate. He was one of the major Democrat donors. The Democrat leaders loved his money. In every major Democratic as well as some Republican fund raiser for a Presidential or any political office election, Trump was there. Why the relentless attacks on Trump then?

The latest attack, Trump's tax return, and how much he paid. The tax return of a citizen how much people paid or did not is nobody's business, but IRS. A businessperson would or should use all legal resources to pay as little tax as possible. Other than the IRS anyone who leaks a person's tax is a warmonger. This is not going to be the last attack. As the judgment day (November) gets nearer, the battle and attacks from the same groups will be uglier. However, be patient and stand firm because the Lord's coming is near to reveal all hidden schemes.

Trump is the first US president to allow 12 weeks (about 3 months) maternity leave for federal employees.[91] What else can he do to make Americans happy? It is too sad to see people complaining and whining about Trump! He has done more what the liberals claim to care. He does not deserve the relentless harassment. It looks it is not about the wrongs that Trump committed, it is about the loss of profit from the major donor and turning the establishment political arena upside down. It is understandable also there are people who do not need financial help but have personal disagreements as well as some other forms of economic losses or policy disagreement.

Some of the attacks are self-inflicted as a candidate as well as, as a President whereby his voters, cabinet, and in general people associated with him on the edge, doing damage control. There are also people who have an issue with his violent and bigoted rhetoric that enables some racist bigots and provides them with a platform to voice their opinions. I think it is important to not forget these people and the fact that their criticisms and outrage come from a very real place.

Sometimes, he may have said so to defend himself when there was no justification for that. He has said words that the author or any politician would not say. Here is the difference, the politicians tell you what you want to hear so that they get elected. For example, in 1970's when white voters asked Biden whether he was in favor of school segregation or not, he told them he was in favor of segregation and they voted him in. On the other hand, businessmen tell you what it is, sometimes it may be painful to.

Trump is on his way to fulfilling what the politicians did not, and he out-done his predecessors. Trump competed against the noble establishments, dynasty of presidency and defeated them in the ballot. They are so annoyed for that instead of being happy for the good of the USA.

Trump achieved what other presidents believed should be done yet did not do! There are endless examples one can talk about:

The black people, Native Americans and Latinos that have been facing mass incarceration due to Biden's criminal bill begged for changes in the harsh dealings of minor offenders. Clinton, Bush, and Obama they appeared to care for the black people. They even sing Black Lives Matter. Yet did nothing to change what is needed most, the Prison Reform and Redemption Act, First Step Act, and Criminal Justice Reform. Guess who signed the bill. It is Trump, the Man referred to as a racist, bigot, xenophobic, and you name it.

Biden as well had been given five long decades to show. Yet he did not. The USA is being shown what Biden has been doing for the for fifty years in politics and what he is going to do if he gets elected. The inner cercle people that worked with him should testify. Former Defense Secretary Robert Gates says of Vice President Joe Biden tells Biden has been wrong on nearly every major foreign policy and national security issue over the past four decades, with very murky lines of communication on military issues.[92] Imagine, a man with gloomy lines of communication on military matters leading the military! No wonder, no police force has endorsed him! Had Biden been good to the military personnel, they would have been overjoyed of his coming and would have endorsed him overwhelmingly.

With the Trump administration except for the social services area, (which makes people dependent all their life), military, police, VA, NASA, border patrol, and other government agencies are overfunded and well equipped. While with Obama and Biden administrations they were not.

Do you think he is going to change in the next four years? This is what the author would not trust. The common proverb proves it: Cheat on me once, shame on you. Cheat on me twice, shame on me. Trump has proved himself: Promises made, promises kept for the good of American people.

Trump's predecessors admitted of a crisis in the Southern border and planned to make a barrier. In 2006 in the Secure Fence Act, Senator Obama offered praise for the border control legislation, authorizing a barrier along the Southern border passed into law with the support of 26 Democratic senators including party leaders like Hillary Clinton, Joe Biden, and Chuck Schumer. That legislation would become the basis for one of Donald Trump's first acts as President.

"The bill before us will certainly do some good," Obama said on the Senate floor in October 2006. He praised the legislation, saying it would provide "better fences and better security along our borders" and would "help stem some of the tide of illegal immigration in this country."[93] President Bush was offered with the legislation to go ahead and build the wall or fence, yet he did not. As a President Obama as well, he did not achieve the Secure Fence Act. Instead he was involved in deporting illegal immigrants. The fact is, President Obama has deported more people than any other President, about 3 million between during his term.[94]

Deportation is lower under Trump administration than Obama. While the Obama administration deported 1.18 million people (about the population of New Hampshire) in his first three years. The number of deportations has been a little under 800,000 so far under Trump in a similar time frame.[95] Compare the deportations by Obama who claims to care for immigrants and Trump portrayed to hate immigrants.

Even when one looks at the deportation rate when the government first stated the removals, back in 1892, Democrat Presidents have deported more illegal immigrants than Republican Presidents; of whom President Obama is known as the Deporter in Chief. Here is the detailed fact: "From 1892–2018, Democratic presidents were in power for 60 years and removed about 4.6 million people for an average of 76,635 per year. During the same time, Republican Presidents were in power for 67 years and removed about 3.7 million people for an annual average of 54,670."[96]

Even when it comes to the DACA or the DREAM (Dreamers), there was a time when the Obama administration had the majority Senate and House votes that could have given the immigrants citizenship. However, they did not do. Unlike the proposed DREAM Act of George W. Bush, Obama's DACA does not provide a path to citizenship for recipients. Obama just did a renewable two-years extension, protection from deportation, putting the DACA recipients in a limbo.[97] When there is an extension of a provision a time will come either for another extension or ending the provision.

Now, Democrats appear to care for the immigrants on every legislation stashing the immigrants as a means of bargain and negotiation. If you claim to care for me, show it in a time when you are able and capable to do so, not when you have lost the power. The leader's pretention to care resembles to an Ethiopian proverb that says, *Jib kehede wsha chohe* when the hyena was killing the livestock, the dog was silent. But when the hyena left doing all the damage, the dog barked.

According to the Associated Press, Michelle Obama on her DNC speech assailed President Donald as the wrong President for our country. He has had more than enough time to prove it, he didn't. Perhaps she should use the same words on Biden, you have had 47 years to prove it, you didn't.

The premise for her such conclusion is, 'Trump has been ripping migrant children from their parents and throwing them into cages,' picking up on a frequent and distorted claim made widely by Democrat leadership. She is right that was Trump's now-suspended policy. However, it is hypocrisy, what she did not say is that the very same "cages" were built and used in her husband's administration, for the same purpose of holding migrant kids temporarily.[98] Friedrich Nietzche has a quote that says, "I'm not upset that you lied to me, I'm upset that from now on I can't believe you."

The cages are chain-link enclosures inside border facilities where migrants were temporarily housed, separated by sex and age. The enclosures/cages made for the child's safety. At the height of the controversy over Trump's zero-tolerance policy at the border, photos that circulated online of children in the enclosures generated great anger. But those photos — by The Associated Press — were taken in 2014 and depicted some of the thousands of unaccompanied children held by President Barack Obama.[99]

BLM did not start under Trump, it did under President Obama and beyond. The war on Police force did not start under Trump, it did under Obama and beyond. The American racial tension did not start under Trump, it did under Obama and beyond. Trump inherited whatever the Democrats and Republicans accuse him off that has been hurting people for hundreds of years. These politicians and their Trojan hubris hide the very thing that they did which Trump is doing yet magnify Trump's stories while obscuring their own deeds.

It is to these kinds of people that Jesus rebuked "Why do you look at the speck of sawdust in your brother's eye and pay no attention to the plank in your own eye? How can you say to your brother, 'Let me take the speck out of your eye,' when all the time there is a plank in your own eye? You hypocrite first take the plank out of your own eye, and then you will see clearly to remove the speck from your brother's eye".[100] Still the same leaders "Pile heavy burdens on people's shoulders and won't lift a finger to help. Everything they do is just to show off in front of others."[101]

BOB MARLEY'S WARNING

For generation, the black Americans have been enslaved, used, and abused by the politicians of both parties. More so by the Democrats. For how long will that continue? People should say enough is enough and woke out of such systems, think and work for themselves. The politicians make several promises during election, they get elected and do not fulfill their promise cheating and fooling their voters. The cycle continues every election year.

To be able to catch a fish, trap a rat, a bird, a cockroach, or any other target, one must have live bait or lures. For animals that are not edible, people use poison with the bait or the lures. The anglers, fishers' trap, bait, or lures (poison), noose is designed to bamboozle, persuade, fool, and trick the target and benefit the fisher. In the Eritrean culture for such acts there is a proverb that says *"Mehegosee Asha."* The literal meaning is making the fool happy by showing them what is not real. The targets are not aware of the brain behind the bait or lures. They come looking for what they see being fooled and tricked. They eventually get under control or get killed that one cannot escape from.

Whatever the Democrats, the Republicans, the BLM, the Antifa, and you name it, who claim to care for the people of color, immigrants, Muslims, minorities in general, they really do not. They care about themselves. The Democrats use the baits or the lures, the Republicans use nothing because they do not need much minority votes, the BLM and Antifa use protest to promote what benefits them. The minorities, bamboozled, lured, by the *"Mehegosee Asha,"* tricked, threatened to go for one or the other. Enough is ENOUGH! The people of color should think for themselves, work for themselves, fight for themselves.

The Bible warns readers to beware of baits, lures and persuasion that come on our life journey. There are unruly and defiant people with crafty intent. Their feet never stay at home, now in the street, at every corner lurking for a prey.

A story is written on how a woman dressed like a prostitute subdued a man: "With persuasive words she led him astray; she seduced him with her smooth talk. All at once he followed her like an ox going to the slaughter, like a deer stepping into a noose till an arrow pierces his liver, like a bird darting into a snare, little knowing it will cost him his life".[102]

This is how the easily lured, tricked, "His feet thrust him into a net; he wanders into its mesh. A trap seizes him by the heel; a snare holds him fast. A noose is hidden for him on the ground; a trap lies in his path"[103] get caught. The people who use you and abuse you may give you a bread, but there is a poison on it. A poison that keeps you bound as a bondservant, a person in a permanent role of service.

The masters may give you free or subsidized housing. Very few people understand that is indirect slavery. You live in such housing, your children will do the same, your grand and greatgrandchildren will also live in the same place. say enough is enough and break yourself from the gripe of the people who use you for their advantage and you will see what God can do for you. But, God's plan for you promise is, "'For I know the plans I have for you,' declares the LORD, 'plans to prosper you and not to harm you, plans to give you hope and a future.'"[104]

Bob Marley on his song 'Could you be loved,' song he warned people to beware of dishonest people. The main message of the song is:

Don't let them fool ya,
Or even try to school ya! Oh, no!
We've got a mind of our own,
So go to hell if what you're thinking is not right!

(The road of life is rocky, and you may stumble too,
So while you point your fingers someone else is judging you)
Love your brotherman!

Don't let them change ya, oh! -
Or even rearrange ya! Oh, no!
We've got a life to live.

Don't let them change ya, oh! -
Or even rearrange ya! Oh, no!
We've got a life to live.[105]

It is time to be woke. *Enough is ENOUGH!* Stop being, bamboozled, used, and abused.

Of course, each President is elected by God for the good or for the bad of the country. The former president's services ought to be appreciated; they all have achieved one thing or the other, regardless of whether one agrees with them, with or without accomplishment. Thank you, all Presidents, and elected leaders, for your service.

TRUMP'S MAJOR SIN

It is unbelievable to grasp the reality of truth until your eye opens. However, with the Trojan horses who have eyes yet cannot see who have head but empty vessel unable to think, they keep on doing unthought off deeds on harming America and Americans.

What opening of one's eye means is having a special revelation that cannot be had otherwise. There are so many instances in which people received special revelations when their eyes were opened.

There was a time when the Egyptian slave lady called Hagar fled from her mistress Sarah; she was in a desperate need of water. God opened her eyes, and she was able to see water right in front of her.

Trump's major sin is, he flipped on Democrats, running as a Republican. If he had run as a Democrat and won, he never would have had all the unrest going on in the USA. The other sin is that he kept his promise and outdid his predecessors, and they are jealous of that. Eight years of Obama's presidency did nothing to the very people that propelled him for the office. There were many things he could and should have done yet he did not. He put more efforts to advance on gay agenda taking it even to the UN, funding and exporting as well as threatening to withhold aid from countries that do not appear receptive to his agenda. This is quid pro quo.

Archived research reveals that, "Since taking office, President Obama and his Administration have made historic strides to expand opportunities and advance equality and justice for all Americans, including Lesbian, Gay, Bisexual, and Transgender (LGBT) Americans. From major legislative achievements to historic court victories to important policy changes, the President has fought to promote the equal rights of all Americans — no matter who they are or who they love.[106]

DOUBLE STANDARD

Donald Trump's case appeared before judicial panels of the Congress and Senate several times. The accusers are not going to speak the truth before the court of law for justice.

In the story of the slave girl, the Jews brought Paul and Silas before the magistrates, invented a story. The real problem for the accusers was economic loss because of the deliverance of the girl through the power of Jesus Christ. Yet, the accusers brought Paul and Silas before the magistrates a story that supported their narrative.

In the same manner, how many times have people invented story after story to hurt President Trump? For example, let us look at the USA PATRIOT Act that was signed into law by President George W. Bush.

The PATRIOT Act is an acronym that stands for Uniting and Strengthening America by Providing Appropriate Tools Required to Intercept and Obstruct Terrorism It was enacted by the United States Congress, a month or so after the 09/11 terrorist attack, of which World Trade Center in New York is one.

The premise of the Act is, to expand abilities of law enforcement to surveil, including by tapping domestic and international phones.[107]

Senator Obama, became so popular for opposing, condemning the PATRIOT Act for violating the rights of American citizens. He argues that the Act allowed government agents to perform extensive and in-depth searches on American citizens without a search warrant. He also argued that it was possible to secure the United States against terrorist attacks while preserving individual liberty.[108]

He based his opposition on "Hearing concerns from people of every background and political leaning that this law didn't just provide law enforcement the powers it needed to keep us safe, but powers it didn't need to invade our privacy without cause or suspicion."[109] However, as President, he did not abolish it. Instead in 2011, he signed a four-year renewal, supported U.S. National Security Agency (NSA) mass surveillance programs done secretly which was exposed by Edward Snowden.[110] The very thing that he opposed as a Senator: he was in favor as President. He used surveillance, wiretapping to spy on candidate Trump, Trump Tower, and his team to hurt the candidate and then President Trump. Under his administration, James Comey's FBI the senior leadership used fraud and doctored documents to investigate and undermine the Trump campaign and Presidency.

Under the title Democracy Dies in Darkness, the Washington Post indicates two main threads to the accusations of spying: contacts by FBI-linked operatives, under the leadership of James Comey, with George Papadopoulos, a young Trump foreign policy aide, and federal court surveillance of Carter Page, using the false Dossier as the basis for a secret warrant, George Papadopoulos — set up by an FBI agent posing as a Cambridge professor's assistant.[111]

The Obama surveillance team brought to light the entire set-up scheme and some of Trump team members were fired from the interim positions including General Michael Flynn. Thus, the Obama team used an illegal set-up plan to imprison Trump's team. In return Trump team revoked the illegal prison sentence by another illegal revoking. Thank God, Trump is the only courageous antidote of liberalism. An antidote is a medicine taken or given to thwart a particular poison[112] in a body.

DEMOCRATIC RELIGION

There are so many good people in the Democratic party. However, for the leadership in the midlevel or the media operatives, Democratic political party is like a religion. Honestly speaking, far much worse controlling than a religion, a communist government or like imprisonment.

In the creed of the jealous millionaire and billionaire liberal Democratic religion, leadership they presume America is for the rich white Republicans. They hate, discriminate the rich and do all they can to punish them, yet they love their money. This is a communist and socialist spirit.

Thus, a Democratic religion member, AOC suggests the rich should be taxed as high as 70% to cover the cost of her insanity. This is hubris characteristic. To be fair, if the rich pay 70% tax, she should also do the same. First you tax yourself 70% and then you can tell others to follow your example.

The wealthy should not be punished for being one, their success should be celebrated. If the liberal millionaires and billionaires using their Trojan horse politicians pick a fight on the rich, have the right to defend themselves and their wealth. They can at least flee to places that are friendly states.

As New York faces $2.3 billion tax-revenue shortfall, Governor Cuomo warned that the loss of revenue could not be made up by continuing to tax the wealthiest New Yorkers — the top 1 percent of whom already contribute 46 percent of all government revenue — at increasingly higher rates. "I don't believe raising taxes on the rich. That would be the worst thing to do. You would just expand the shortfall," he said. "God forbid if the rich leave."[113]

With the swelling budget holes because of the coronavirus pandemic, and the state's governor is concerned the state's financial situation may get worse if the city's wealthiest taxpayers leave for good.[114]

The same applies to California wealthy people.

There is still favoritism and discrimination of people in hiring for job positions, on the streets and in the Churches as well. However, since there is no legislation to support that, there is still fare share chance for whoever is willing to put more efforts and tenacity to break those barriers. More so, for Democrat, one is considered as a property, a slave, or an owned machine.

A property, slave or a machine has no voice and no choice to make but to serve in the interest of the owner. The party is considered as god, nobody has the right to question, challenge, leave, or criticize. Whoever dares to apply the freedom of choice, freedom of conscience, or freedom of voice would be in considerable danger, worse than deadliest the tsunami, injurious tornado, or lethal earthquake. After living as one of them, the presumed Democrat, Donald Trump exited, and he must face the wrath.

The Democrat plantation appears to hate and demean an independent thinker who is not governed by the rules of the plantation. In early 2019, Howard Schultz, former Starbucks CEO, who identifies himself as a lifelong Democrat declared his intent to run for president as an independent. Schultz said that Trump was not qualified to be the president, at the same time blamed both Democrats and Republicans for not doing what's necessary for American people."[115]

Schultz's running as independent was an abomination to the Democratic plantation. Thus, Democrats sounded especially alarmed at what they view as a spoiler candidacy. In a statement, Tina Podlodowski, Chair of the Washington State Democratic Party, slammed Schultz's ambitions (to run independent) as selfish.

Further, Podlodowski said, "Howard Schultz running as an independent isn't about bringing people together. It's about one person: Howard Schultz." That is not all, Julian Castro, the former Secretary of Housing and Urban Development who announced a bid for the Democratic nomination as well said that if Schultz did run an independent campaign "it would provide Donald Trump with his best hope of getting re-elected."[116]

Responding to the concerns of the Democratic plantation and criticism in his interview with The Seattle Times, Schultz responded saying, "nobody wants to see Donald Trump removed from office more than me. I am not entering this race to be a spoiler. This is not about vanity."[117] Yet nobody would accept Schultz's view. Eventually, his ambition to run for presidency got crushed by the Democratic plantation Feudal zealots.

It is imperative to admit that in the two major American political parties, there are good Democrats and good Republicans. Good Democrats and good Republicans go for elections voting. When one party or candidate wins, the loser concedes, and congratulates the winner. They forget issues and battles fought about that election and keep working together for the betterment of America while preparing strategies to win re-election next time. However, that is not so with a Democratic or Republican religion.

In fact, it is worse in a Democratic religion. When Democrats win, they rejoice; when they lose elections, they cry and keep on whining. As a religion, Democrats should not and cannot lose an election or a vote to Republicans. The result of 2016 election are a testament for the relentless attempts to overthrow President Trump. Four years after the election, Madam Secretary Clinton has not yet conceded, still blaming others for her loss. She is not running on the 2020 election but behind the show trashing candidate Senator Bernie Sanders campaign, still holding hostage her 66 million voters (about twice the population of California) instead of encouraging them to work with the winner.

Democratic religion is a must to be accepted by the constituents unquestionably. One cannot say, "I will check; I will see, I still have time to hear candidates and decide on the issues one cares about such as the economy, religious freedom, education, social issues, the Supreme Court, other political offices, environment, and healthcare."

It is assumed that Biden and the Democratic party are a better choice than Trump and the Republican party when it comes to black and minority votes that the Democrats take the black votes for granted. It is as simple as that.

On May 22nd, 2020, Biden had an interview with a black radio host Charlamagne Tha God. After talking over several issues, the interviewer stated that Biden needed to come back on the show because "We got more questions (until November)."

"You got more questions. If you have a problem figuring out whether you're for me or Trump, then you ain't black'," Biden responded.

In a straightforward way, what the Democrat Biden means is that, if you are black voter there should be nothing to figure out between Trump and him, who created legislation that is still affecting the black people. Blacks should automatically vote for a Democrat.

Emphasizing as one team to work together on his inaugural address JFK informed Americans, "So let us begin anew--remembering on both sides that civility is not a sign of weakness, and sincerity is always subject to proof. Let us never negotiate out of fear. But let us never fear to negotiate.[118] In these days of shaming and intimidating, people cannot negotiate honorably.

JFK further stated:

Let both sides explore what problems unite us instead of belaboring those problems which divide us. Let both sides, for the first time, formulate serious and precise proposals for the inspection and control of arms--and bring the absolute power to destroy other nations under the absolute control of all nations. Let both sides seek to invoke the wonders of science instead of its terrors. Together let us explore the stars, conquer the deserts, eradicate disease, tap the ocean depths, and encourage the arts and commerce. Let both sides unite to heed in all corners of the earth the command of Isaiah--to "undo the heavy burdens and let the oppressed go free calls out for the unity of political leaders.[119]

Just as JFK mentioned in his speech, it is obvious that people have different political views during a political campaign. Let the difference be buried with the end of the election of the winner, no matter who wins. A person should have the right to run or vote for their party of choice without any repercussions from family, friends, or co-workers. Let us keep on working together for the good of the country and setting up an example for the World for which Americans are known.

Before he immigrated to the USA, Hayet always loved and envied America for the peaceful transfer of power from one party to the other. For example, the most recent presidents, President Bush lambasted President Clinton during election campaigns. Clinton was forgiving and gracious during the transfer of power. President Obama lambasted President Bush during the election campaign. Bush was forgiving and gracious to Obama during the transfer of power.

President Trump lambasted President Obama during the election campaign. Obama was forgiving and gracious to Trump during the transfer of power. The same should apply for the coming generations. That is a sign of maturity. Although there are some people who want to abolish the mention of God on the pledge of allegiance altogether, until then, let "We the People," say "I pledge allegiance to the Flag of the United States of America and to the Republic for which it stands, one nation, indivisible, with liberty and justice for all."

RESHAPING THE COURT SYSTEM

The court system is one of the three branches of the American government, known as the Judicial body, that interprets the law according to the constitution. Its judges are appointed by the President to represent the views of the party of the appointing President. In most cases their decision is a patrician issue. "Donald Trump has appointed, and the Senate has confirmed 197 Article III federal judges through June 1, 2020, his fourth year in office. This is the second-most important Article III judicial appointment through this point in all presidencies since Jimmy Carter (D). The Senate had confirmed 228 of Carter's appointees at this point in his term."[120] Hopefully given the second term, he would unapologetically appoint another 197 such judges or so.

Although Hayet disagrees with Democrat elected Supreme Court Justices on matters of faith and abortion related issues, he loves them in general for being loyal on their representation of the President that nominated them. They come as Democrats, vote as Democrats, retire, or die as Democrats. On the contrary, when Republicans become Supreme Court Judges, they become wishy washy.

Justice Roberts has not been faithful to represent the values for which he was appointed to represent. He is known as having a swing vote. He has been acting as a wild card that can be used in place of another card or a Joker card on a standard deck. A Joker or wild card can be placed in front, in the middle, or behind becoming a deciding factor for being beneficial or harmful. Justice Roberts has become unpredictable on what he would vote for. If he knew that he was going to behave the way he has been doing, he should have told President Bush 'no thank you.'

Vice President Mike Pence criticizes Justice Roberts for being a disappointment to conservatives in a handful of recent decisions on disputes that have come before the Supreme Court.[121]

Just in June 2020, in two weeks' time he voted three times with the court's four liberal justices to assemble a majority in favor of a liberal result that closed the cases. The cases included protecting gay and transgender workers, protecting young immigrants Dreamers, and a Louisiana abortion law. He also dissented in favor of Obama Care, dissented in the case that legalized gay marriage, dissented in the case that found executing an intellectually disabled person to be unconstitutional, and dissented in the case that affirmed that California must reduce its overcrowded prison populations, to name but a few examples.[122]

Calvary Chapel Dayton Valley in Dayton, Nevada, argued that the State treated houses of worship less favorably than it did casinos, restaurants, and amusement parks. Those businesses have been limited to 50 percent of their fire-code capacities, while houses of worship have been subject to a flat 50-person limit.[123]

In Nevada, it seems being in the entertainment business has more freedom than those exercising constitutionally protected right to worship. Amid the COVID outbreak, the State has limits on the capacity of certain locations. For churches, it is no more than 50 people. For everything else, from movie theaters to casinos, it is much more than that. It seems a bit unfair. The standard makes no sense, but it is perfectly logical for Chief Justice John Roberts who sided with the liberal wing of the Supreme Court in the case of a church which challenged this unfair standard that ruled 5-4 against the church.[124]

Even the recent ruling about discrimination in the work-place using as a pretext for the 1964 Civil Right Act that prohibits employment discrimination based on race, color, religion, sex, and national origin, the term sex refers to being biologically born male and female, not to the people who choose a gender for themselves.[125]

HAMSTRINGING TRUMP

President Trump has been treated unfairly by the Congress, Senate, several Americans, and the World, more than any other President! They would not let him enjoy the privileges other presidents have. Whatever he does is considered as bad and wrong.

For example: President Obama pardoned, commuted, or rescinded the conviction of 1,927 people. President Trump has pardoned and commuted 36 people in total including, former Chicago's Democrat governor, Rod Blagojevich.[126] Look at the unfairness with which Trump is being treated. Just at 36 pardons, he cannot get the privileges that other Presidents got. Pelosi is profoundly and negatively overreacting and plans to limit pardons.[127]

Even if Trump describes or uses the same words other American leaders', Presidents used, it is deemed racist.

Referring to Ferguson destructive protesters President Obama referred them as 'Thugs.' Referring to the Minneapolis destructive protesters, President Trump called them 'Thugs.' For saying so, Trump is regarded racist, Obama is not. The double standard coming from the media and leftists is not going unnoticed. This is clear war and hatred on the president. It has got to stop.

Chapter Six

"You have to treat yourself like you matter. Because if you do not take care of yourself, you become vengeful, cruel. You take it out on people around you. And you are not a positive force, none of that is good. So, you suffer more and so does everyone else around you."

—DR. JORDAN PETERSON

ORIGINS OF BLACK LIVES MATTER and BLM MOVEMENT

The NPR's Mary Louise Kelly hosted Ryan Mac of BuzzFeed a reporter who untangled interviewing the BLM founder, an organization that is profiting off the BLM name.

Many people have been moved by the protests on the wake of George Floyd's death against what is called police brutality - moved to join in, to show and to donate. Among the recipients of the people's charity is the Black Lives Matter Foundation. It has raised several million dollars in the form of small gifts from individuals, well-intentioned employees of big corporations, including Apple, Microsoft, Google, big stores such as Walmart, Target, Home Depot, and many others.[128]

Wealthy organizations have been donating money to the BLM and nobody knows where the money goes. While receiving donations in the name of black people, no black person has benefited from the donations. At least one BLMGA (Black Lives Matter Greater Atlanta) leader has been exposed for misusing donated funds. Sir Maejor Page, 32, was arrested after authorities said he used donations for the social justice movement on tailored suits, guns, and a home in Ohio. On one official photo he appeared with the former Atlanta Mayor, Kasim Reed.[129] Nevertheless, the Black Lives Matter Foundation is not connected in any way with the Black Lives Matter movement.

BLM organization is a registered 501(c)(3). It has been around since — 2015. It was registered, shortly or a couple of years after the beginning of the Black Lives Matter movement. Founder Robert Ray Barnes is a 67-year-old music producer who lives in Santa Clarita He is the one and only paid employee of the organization, an African American man. He has been affected by many things, including the LAPD killing of his wife's ex-husband. He started this foundation to kind of build relationships between communities and the police.

He has this large mission statement of things that he wants to have such as annual dinners with cops, and he wants to have community-funded coffee meetings with cops. Yet, there has been no kind of expenditure of the money towards that kind of relationship building that he wants. It is kind of all just a figurative plan. The founder's professed goal is to create unity between the community and the police, which is kind of directly opposed to what the current Black Lives Matter movement is right now pushing for, to defund and abolish the police.[130] The author does not think it is the wish of people of color to abolish the police force, their only means of protection, but that of the Trojan handlers.

There is a real problem of crime, inequality, injustice, and unfairness based on race and gender. The BLM movement started as a legitimate cause for the right of the black people. To begin with when a black person kills another black person. That is called crime, and everyone wants crime to end of course. Black Lives Matter is talking about how black people are disproportionately killed by police than white people are. Also, police brutality in general is bad, and people who support BLM are advocating against police brutality against all races as well. Nevertheless, it appears that it has lost the source; the beginning point has been hijacked and is being Trojan horse of the leftist hubris communist, Marxist agenda promoting the gay plan in sighting hate on patriarchs.

Mr. Barnes declares that he has no connection and nothing to do with the BLM movement that has received about 4-million-dollar in donations.[131]

This means that the BLM movement that we have now is not the original organization It is hijacked and serving as a Trojan for the enemies of America. Black Lives Matter co-founder Patrisse Cullors said in a newly surfaced video from 2015 that she and her fellow organizers are trained Marxists. We are super-versed on, sort of, ideological theories. And I think that what we really tried to do is build a movement that could be utilized by many, many black folks.[132] Out of curiosity by who, how and where did they get trained?

What black folks need is not an ideology that cannot feed its own adherents, but Biblical truth, which is good for all.

BLM describes its philosophy as "an urban experiment", uses grassroots organizations to "focus on Black and Latino communities with deep historical ties to the long history of anti-colonial, anti-imperialist, pro-communist resistance to the US empire."[133]

The very group describes their intent to the opposition of the USA government. Unlike the French, the British, the Italians and other colonial and imperial powers, who had many countries under their rule, the USA had only the Philippines. It is not fair to describe America as the US Empire by an American citizen. Such a designation and name calling from American enemies is understandable, but not from American people. It is undeniable that we have internal problems and foreign policies that are not fair and just. Let us discuss and solve our issues.

White American boys and heterosexual married have become the main targets of this onslaught. Throughout this discussion, BLM shall be addressed as BLMS; 'S' stands for 'seasonal,' a movement that has been hijacked from its origin. BLMS comes out only on a season where a white police officer kills a black person. However, when a black person kills black person unjustly, or when white police kills a white person, BLM cares less. All human life unjustly killed should matter. Let us see how Dr. John MacArthur describes the current BLM.

JOHN MACARTHUR ON BLM

Dr. John MacArthur has a say on the current diverted manifestations of the BLM. He is an American Pastor and an Author known for his internationally syndicated Christian teaching radio program "Grace to You." He has been the pastor-teacher of Grace Community Church in Sun Valley, California, since February 9, 1969. He is also the chancellor emeritus of The Master's University in Santa Clarita, California, and The Master's Seminary in Los Angeles, California.[134]

He says that the people in the BLM movement are disruptive, they are radical, they are anti-authority, they are Marxist, they are atheistic. First, it is proper to look at how the #BlackLivesMatter started and what it stands for. Alicia Garza is known as one of the founders. She begins by telling "Black communities deserve what all communities deserve — to be powerful in every aspect of their lives."[135] They already have. In the USA, if you want to get anything, you work for it and earn it.

There are some obstacles but in general there is nobody and nothing can hinder black people from being powerful in every aspect of their lives. If there is a will, there is a way. However, before going long she diverts from caring for the black people to lesbian group not the general black population.[136]

"What is BLM's guiding principle?" asks MacArthur. In their documentation, he says that they say, "We make space for transgender siblings to participate and lead. We are self-reflexive and do the work required to dismantle cisgender privilege and uplift Black trans folk, especially Black trans women who continue to be disproportionately impacted by trans-antagonistic violence." They are transgender upholding. According to Deuteronomy 22:5, transgender behavior is an abomination to God. According to the word of God, man is the head of the woman as God is the head of Christ. The man has the responsibility of leadership. That is an anti-God idea.

MacArthur says BLM are queer affirming; "we gather to free ourselves from a tight grip of the belief that all are heterosexual. We gather to put an end to the notion that everybody needs to be heterosexual." In Leviticus, the Lord says "I am the Lord be holy Do not have sexual relations with a man as one does with a woman; that is detestable. Do not have sexual relations with an animal and defile yourself with it. A woman must not present herself to an animal to have sexual relations with it; that is a perversion (Leviticus 18:22-23). Leviticus 20:13 also tells exact the same thing, "If a man has sexual relations with a man as one does with a woman, both have done what is detestable. They are to be put to death; their blood will be on their own heads" Romans 1:18-32 as well.

Here is another quote from MacArthur, "We are intentionally amplifying that the experience of violence that black queer transgender, gender non-conforming women and intersex people face, there can be no liberation for the black people if we do not fight for these people." Any organization or any person advocating for what is ungodly practices is a devil's agent. One ought to ask what God' plan for me is and follow that path without creating a counterfeit plan. He says, "This is an organization designed by Satan. To use the suffering of some people (the black people) to destroy.[137]

Having seen the agenda of BLM, where is the plight of the poor black people suffering in the inner cities being discussed and improved? The main problem of the BLM is the absence of fathers in a family. This could mean that there is no presence of a father in the house or even the present father does not take the leadership in the family. BLM want to dismantle the very prevalent problem in our black communities.

"Pope John Paul II has been quoted saying, "As the family goes, so goes the nation and so goes the whole World in which we live." This, finding the diagnosis of the national and global challenges, and fixing family relationship brings solutions on the nation and on the whole World.[138] The more people keep silent, accommodating such abnormal behaviors, the more family and country get destroyed.

Chapter Seven

"People who have no purpose in their life are embittered by the difficulties of their life. And they become bitter first, then resentful then revengeful, then cruel. There are plenty of places to go past cruel. That is just where you start if you are leaning on a downhill path."

—DR. JORDAN PETERSON

BLAMING DAUGHTER-IN-LAW

There is a common proverb in the Eritrean culture that says, 'Instead of blaming their son, mothers love blaming their daughter in-law.'

Lil Wayne on Fat Joe chat pertaining George Floyd's death said this:

"It's actually learning about it," he said. "What we need to do is we need to learn about it more. If we wanna scream about something, know what we are screaming about. If we wanna protest about something, know what we are protesting about. Because if we wanna get into it, there is a bunch of facts that we think we know that we don't know. We scream about things that, sometimes, they really ain't true."[139]

Before one discusses what people have been talking regarding police brutality in the USA, there is a Eritrean saying that translates, 'Instead of blaming their son, mothers blame their daughter in law *n-we-den key ham-ya — n-se-bey-tee we-den*. The main message behind the saying is, let the person who made the mistake be blamed for their mistake. Do not cover up people's wrongdoing. For any wrong that goes in the family, it is the daughter in law that gets the blame, including when the wife gets pregnant every year.

Between the years 2004 and 2020, Hayet has been pulled over, stopped, or asked by police to show his ID many times. The pulling over has nothing to do with his race. It is a usual procedure for any driver's wrongdoing.

The police do not care how many times a person done what is right. They care and are on the lookout only for wrongs. If Hayet had done what is right, he never would have been pulled over. The first pull over was for speeding and an illegal crossing, entering the HOV lane. Hayet was driving on I-85 North, near Jimmy Carter Blvd in Atlanta. It was about 10:30PM on a six lanes expressway, next to the HOV lane.

A black car ahead of him was rolling over at about 55 MPH, the posted speed limit. Seeing that the car does not appear to increase its speed. He crossed the solid HOV illegal lane to overtake. When he reaches on the side of the black car, Hayet discovered it was a police car. The shimmering blue light signaled for Hayet to pullover. He signaled right turn and managed to do so carefully maneuvering the heavy and dangerous traffic all the way to the right, safe zone.

It was dark, varied sizes of automobiles flying like bullets. While expecting for the officer to come over, Hayet kept on staring through the rearview mirrors. The officer was doing routine check, while Hayet was nervously waiting in the car. At last, the officer cautiously approaching him from the passenger side.

"Please I need to see your ID and proof of insurance. Do you know why I ordered you to pullover?" asked the officer peeking via the passenger side automatically and cautiously rolled down window fearing for his life.

This mentality is the problem: police officers irrationally fearing for their lives that leads to the deaths of several innocent people. The officer is right for being cautious, it is part of their training. It is with such encounters where more police officers get killed.

"It is for illegal HOV crossing" replied the terrified Hayet.

After another few more tension-filled minutes, "This is your first offense. I will give you a ticket only for speeding.' For crossing over the HOV solid lane illegally, you ought to get another ticket and pay about $400 fine. I will just give you a warning for cooperating. Please drive safely and take care of your family," stated the officer as he handed over the ticket, ID, and the insurance card.

The incident happened when Hayet was on his way home at the end of the day, after his first job in the USA. The fine is more than what Hayet could handle, $130.00, more than half of his weekly earnings. He was so indignant of the painful fine he had to pay. *I cannot afford and should not get any more ticket, by following the rules*, he pledgee.

That is not all. Hayet has had a few other pullovers. Two not-at fault accidents, two random checks on certain streets, and three at fault mistakes; making a total of seven.

First ticket he got in 2004, the last in 2020. He went to the court date to challenge it, but he finds out the system made it easy to pay the fine rather than to challenge it. Anyway, he had to pay another $130.00, this time he could afford but was not comfortable wasting the money.

Hayet could have avoided the ticket by apologizing to the officer, but he would not do so. The officer was so professional, respectful, relaxed, unlike the first incident, expecting some sort of apology, verbalizing repeatedly, which Hayet did not. He regrets refusing to apologize. In all incidents there was no altercation or argument with the police officers. Hayet cooperated with what the police officer ordered.

Upon going to pay the fine at the courthouse, knowing that tickets drop off after seven years, "This is my first ticket," he said.

"This is not your first, you had one in 2004," replied the clerk.

Hayet was so shocked to find that the 2004 ticket still existed in the police records seventeen years later. That does not seem to be fair. It is commonly said that violations drop off after seven years. This is not only one seven years, past two sets of seven years plus three had passed.

The more violations one has, unpaid fines for people who could not afford to pay the fine or other civil violations that show up as a criminal citation, the more likely one gets blocked from getting employment opportunity. This is a terrible hinderance to the livelihood for people who have committed such violation. It must be changed and abolished. This is what needs to be abolished, not the police force.

Months before Rayshard Brooks was shot by a police officer outside of a Wendy's in Atlanta, he was granted an interview with a company called Reconnect which works to fight the incarceration crises in the USA. He spoke about his struggles with life after incarceration and how hard it is to get employment because of past criminal conviction and incarceration records. He admitted that if one does wrong, one ought to pay for it; but the severity of the mistake is not easy to bear. It affects people mentally, hindering them from employment to provide for the families, getting one's life back on track, being taken away from the family.[140]

Legislation on easing the burdens of minor offenders should be made. The do-nothing Democrats, Biden's group who jail people for jaywalking and other rich people who benefit from the prison system cannot ease that burden. President Trump may be able to do so, should one talk to him. The do-nothing Republicans as well. They, lament for not having the majority in the Senate and in the house. When American people give them the majority, what they asked for, they do not do what they promised, and they prove their do-nothingness.

Singer Jamie Grace, in her song "Live About it," being weary of the do-nothing people said,

I don't wanna hear a song about it
If we can't live about it
No we can't sing about it
No we can't write about it
If we don't do something about it
Don't want no songs about it
If we can't live about it
If we can't live about it.[141]

A couple of things to note: any black or white or in between person who would not cooperate to what officers ask could be in a great danger of injury or even death. When police officer pullover, each situation is risky, they do not know what to expect. Each situation should be treated as dangerous. In the year 2019, FBI's statistics show 89 law enforcement officers were killed in the line-of-duty. Demographically 45 were male, 3 were female, 40 were whites, 7 were black African Americans, 1 was Asian.[142]

Since police officers are being attacked either as a fight or flight of the suspect, they have the right to defend themselves and approach each incident as the last day of their life. Remember, police officers, like suspects are humans who have family members.

Hayet also has a friend who has had about 20 to 30 at-fault pullovers and arrests. Because the suspect respectfully cooperated with what the officers ordered, he never had any injury. In general, although there may be a few exceptions, most of the tragic incidents happen when the suspect refuses to cooperate with the police officer's orders. The chance of a police officer shooting a person for no apparent reason is almost non-existent.

To avoid from being shot, one should not make a sudden movement, run away, because police dogs and radio communication can overtake a person. One should not fight, argue with a police officer on the street exposing oneself for injury or much worse death.

Hayet experienced a pullover in early 2020 in Atlanta. He did what was right and safe driving in front of the officer to make a left turn. However, the officer was offended and pull him over. He was a black police officer. Hayet has choices to make. Either argue (saying I did what is right and waste time), resist, run away or apologize and cooperate. As Mark Twain is quoted saying, "Never argue with an idiot. They will drag you down to their level and beat you with experience."

The people that Twain refers idiots are those who have the authority to do with what they want to do with you using the law (the experience). They can set you free or make you pay a fine up to a couple of thousands.

Should you get caught up in a situation by a person, plead, apologize and be respectful. By doing so, one can avoid unnecessary killing.

Depending on how respond to a person in charge, be it a police officer, a teacher, a manager they can use the authority they have to hire, fire, injure, kill, or heal you. Do what is right to stay alive.

"I am sorry officer," Hayet quickly apologized while handing over his ID. The officer came right back and returned the ID without any ticket. If Hayet chose the road of resistance, arguing, being disrespectful he could have been jailed, injured, dragged off the car, or much worse, dead. Although there are some unavoidable situations, when people have encounter with the police, they determine the outcome of the encounter. The police respond depending on how people respond.

DOING WHAT IS RIGHT

There was a time whereby Adam's sons; Abel and Cain offered sacrifices before the Lord. The LORD looked with favour on Abel and his offering, but on Cain and his offering he did not look with favour. So, Cain was terribly angry, and his face was downcast.

Then the LORD said to Cain, "Why are you angry? Why is your face downcast? If you do what is right, will you not be accepted? But if you do not do what is right, sin is crouching at your door; it desires to have you, but you must rule over it."

Cain had a warning and a time to control himself and do what is right and acceptable. However, he refused to heed to the warning. Instead, he said to his brother Abel, "Let's go out to the field." While they were in the field, Cain attacked his brother Abel and killed him.

Then the LORD said to Cain, "Where is your brother Abel?"

"I don't know," he replied. "Am I my brother's keeper?"

The LORD said, "What have you done? Listen! Your brother's blood cries out to me from the ground. Now you are under a curse and driven from the ground, which opened its mouth to receive your brother's blood from your hand. When you work the ground, it will no longer yield its crops for you. You will be a restless wanderer on the earth."

Cain said to the LORD, "My punishment is more than I can bear. Today you are driving me from the land, and I will be hidden from your presence; I will be a restless wanderer on the earth, and whoever finds me will kill me."

But the LORD said to him, "Not so; anyone who kills Cain will suffer vengeance seven times over." Then the LORD put a mark on Cain so that no one who found him would kill him. So, Cain went out from the Lord's presence and lived in the land of Nod, East of Eden.[143]

A couple of points to note here are, first Cain did what was wrong, and he did not admit it. Second, he voluntarily went out from the Lord's presence, cutting relationship with God. Two wrongs will not make a right.

In response to Jacob Blake's shooting in Kenosha, Wisconsin, LeBron James tweeted, "I know people get tired of hearing me say it, but we are scared as black people in America. Black men, black women, black kids, we are terrified." In May 2020 also he tweeted, "We're literally hunted EVERYDAY/EVERYTIME we step foot outside the comfort of our homes."

Is this the normal way to make your voice heard? It would have been more productive to tell the so-called victims to do what is right and follow directives of police officers or anybody else who have the means to hurt them and fight legally.

By the way, where are James' fair tweets in response to the LA County police officers shot in ambush for no reason, Hayet was expecting something like, "Police officers are literally hunted EVERYDAY/EVERYTIME they step foot outside the comfort of their homes."

The worst part is that BLM protesters showed up at the hospital and hoped the deputies die. A BLM activist in Portland also while her group burning the American flag, said she is not sad a f***ing fascist died.[144] Hayet's Bible tells him, "Love your enemies and pray for those who persecute you."[145]

The person who died was a patriot prayer backer, not one involved in Burning Looting and Mayhem. Feeling not sad over the death of a person? That is cruelty, a slavery plantation mentality. In the slavery plantation, people were programmed to act like a machine, not to have sympathy for others, but for their masters. The slaves were consistently on the move. They cannot grieve the death of their family member; they keep on moving as if nothing happened. If they do, they could get punished by their masters. That is what is going on with America's Trojans. That is why we see black people killing blacks in their neighborhood and feel nothing. *Enough is Enough!*

In the same token, referring to Frederick Douglas' autobiography, Candace Owens tells, "He felt nothing when his mother died. He felt nothing when his sisters died. Because the system of slavery was consistently moving the slaves around. One of the things that held the system together was the breakdown of the family."[146]

If you condemn police officers for killing your demographic population, you should also condemn when your side kills police officers. Do not do to police officers what you do not want them to do to you. Or else it will be 'For with whatever judgment you judge, you will be judged; and with whatever measure you measure, it will be measured to you.[147] One evil won't get even with another evil.

Hayet as a black man is and has never been terrified of being hunted by anybody. In fact, he feels more secured in the USA than in his birth country or continent. The reason is that he has nothing to be terrified or be afraid off if he does what is right. That is why Holy Bible says, "The wicked flee though no one pursues, but the righteous are as bold as a lion".[148]

Sports columnist Jason Whitlock accused James of bigotry and promoting racism, demonizing a group of white people based on the behavior of a few. Bringing his own input and how to avoid being shot Whitlock argues, how he is a black person, and is not, scared, or terrified. Neither is LeBron James. He's lying. He and the political activists controlling (Trojan horsing) him want black people to immerse themselves in fear. Fear is a tool used to control people. If you comply with police instructions, there is virtually no chance of an American citizen being harmed by police.[149]

Several sports teams some sit-in; others walk off the field in protest for the so-called police brutality. But not the Kentucky Derby and few other teams. The office was pressured to walk off, by the 'No justice, no Derby,' masters or Trojans. However, they chose to go ahead not to politicize the sport. The truth as Dr. King has stated is, "Injustice anywhere is a threat to justice everywhere."

The killing of any person for no reason is wrong, as is the killing of a police officer by any person. We have lost enough people, be it civilians or police force. We must learn how to avoid any more killings. Enough is enough.

We feel sorry for the dead, but we have more people that are alive, and we must find a way how to steer clear of the dangerous situations.

The Bible says, "Anyone who is among the living has hope -- even a live dog is better off than a dead lion!"[150] The deceased brethren may have been lions, yet a living dog is better off than a dead lion. Because the figurative dog could grow and be a lion one day.

To fight with the police, manage to defuse the situation at hand and fight it at the court. However, sometimes it cannot be denied that the heartless police officers can take advantage of their power and harm innocent people before they reach the court of law. The World cannot afford the loss of life in vain. Especially in the days of Covid-19, there is a high possibility that cases such as that of Rayshard Brooks and George Floyd could have ended after a day or so in jail.

Regarding resolving issues smartly with an opponent, the Bible tells us, "Settle matters quickly with your adversary who is taking you to court. Do it while you are still together on the way, or your adversary may hand you over to the judge, and the judge may hand you over to the officer, and you may be thrown into prison. Truly I tell you, you will not get out until you have paid the last penny."[151]

In Georgia, Peter Mallory, who was sentenced to 1,000 years in prison on child porn charges, was released on parole after serving seven years of his sentence. So, please for the sake of God and not to give the Devil a chance of blood shed one should not resist an arrest. For minor offense, spending a night in jail is not the worst thing, dying on the street is.

LESSONS FROM PHILEMON

Philemon is one of the books of the Bible that the Apostle Paul wrote to Onesimus' employer called Philemon. Onesimus a former slave, stole property from his employer (master) and was taken to prison. While in prison, he met with Paul, got his life transformed, and became a believer. Paul is appealing to Philemon that,

> "Formerly he was useless to you, but now he has become useful both to you and to me." I am sending him—who is my very heart—back to you. I would have liked to keep him with me so that he could take your place in helping me while I am in chains for the gospel. But I did not want to do anything without your consent, so that any favor you do would not seem forced but would be voluntary. Perhaps the reason he was separated from you for a little while was that you might have him back forever— no longer as a slave, but better than a slave, as a dear brother. He is very dear to me but even dearer to you, both as a fellow man and as a brother in the Lord. So, if you consider me a partner, welcome him as you would welcome me. If he has done you any wrong or owes you anything, charge it to me."[152]

Prison is bad and shameful but sometimes good people such as Joseph in the Bible and others who refused to follow instructions and the law, that could be the place where they encounter their destiny. People reach to their destiny sometimes running, walking, or crawling. To get a liquid from a wet sponge people need to squeeze the sponge. The more the sponge is squeeze the more liquid is produced. The only reason Hayet became an author is that he got laid off from a job.

There are several people who met their destiny in prison. For example, Joseph in the Bible, Malcom X, Stanley Tookie Williams, Curtis Carroll and many more. Mainly the people that come out of jail with a transformed mind ought to get more chances, recommendations from people Paul like and acceptance by Onesimus like employer and by the society, they could repay back. Should people face what threatens or disrupts their peaceful existence, they should do all that is possible to deescalate to escape from death at that moment. Go to jail if need, open your heart and search what is God's original plan for your life.

Sometimes life could be filled with cruelty of injustice, unfairness, discrimination, and you name it. God is greater, better, wiser and knows how to change bad into good for whoever is willing to work for Him and with Him.

As much as possible be blameless. The first thing police officers do when they pullover a person is, check who you based on your vehicle's tag. Daniel was blameless, the king knew it, but because of corrupt system he let him be thrown into the lion's den. However, God sent His angel, and He shut the mouths of the lions. They have not hurt him, because he was found innocent in God's sight. Nor has he ever done any wrong before the king. Sometimes as in the case of Joseph, being blameless may not work, for a time being. But in all things, God works for your good.

Steve Harvey's TV Show was cancelled after he said Rich People Do Not Sleep Eight Hours a day. Explaining the incident, "Sometimes man we don't jump. Sometimes we get pushed. See God is fair. When He wants you to do something else and you won't do it, He will bring about a set of circumstances that will cause you interruption. So now, there's obviously something that you should be doing instead of what you were doing."[153]

Using the cancellation experience to show how one needs to keep having a positive attitude waiting to see what God would open he states, "You gotta understand how it works. Your life ain't nothing but a book. I happen to be 62 years old," Steve explains. "In this 62nd chapter, I got my finger on the corner of the page. All I am doing is about to turn it. I can't wait to see what God has for me on that other page."[154]

GEORGE FLOYD, WHO IS TO BLAME?

The USA is home of and welcomes every race. People attach every success or failure, murder, or homicide with the race of the offender. Americans should place focus on one people of one nation not on a race. However, in the real World, since in one way or the other racism, favoritism affects us all, it is necessary to discuss it.

Just as in the time of any previous Presidents, during Donald Trump's time in office, people have seen several murders and homicides. An FBI report shows, in 2018 there were an estimated 1,206,836 violent crimes. In 1999 also, there were 1,426,044 the same crimes. Of the 2018 crimes, there were 16,214 murders and homicide in the nation.[155] Still in 2018, the highest murder crime city was St. Louis MO, with 60.9 incidents while the lowest was in Irvine, CA with 0.0.[156]

Since the law says suspects are innocent unless proven guilty, all murders should be treated as a criminal case. It is sad to see whenever a white police officer hurts a black person no matter what the crime is, it is the officer who get the blame. That is not fair. One should be able to see the process before coming to a hasty conclusion. It cannot be denied also there is police carelessness that is more prevalent when dealing with black people.

The death of George Floyd at the hands of Minneapolis police is a tragedy, he did not deserve to die the way he did. It is a senseless death, a sign of pure evil within a human being. The officer intentionally wanted to kill him. There is no way one could take the knee of about a half of man's weight on someone's neck for about nine minutes.

When a lion or tiger catches their prey, they hold them by the neck, which is the main part of the body that controls the flow of the air. The only time they let up the neck of their prey is when they are sure that the prey is dead, and no longer a threat. That is exactly what officer Derek Chauvin did. A handcuffed person laying on the ground cannot be a threat to about four fully armed officers.

Now, to be able to administer a fair conclusion or justice, one should be able to look at both sides, or at least the timeline that led up to the fatal tragedy.[157]

After any death of a black person at the hands of police all the blame goes to the officer not to the suspect. Referring to who to blame. Lil Wayne said that "We have to actually get into who that person is. And if we want to place the blame on anybody, it should be ourselves for not doing more than what we think we're doing."[158]

Between the fatal day and George Floyd's last imprisonment, it is said that there was about five years gap, without any trouble. A good sign of improvement. He was trying to improve his life. Police officers and the law do not care about how many billions of right things a person does. What they care and get dispatched to a scene for is when one makes a wrong. An incorrect 911 call about a fake $20 bill resulted in the death of George Floyd.

Ms. Ayaan Hirsi Ali who is a Somali-born Dutch American activist, feminist, author, scholar, and former politicians who works for the Hoover Institution and the American Enterprise Institute and is one of the Wall Street Journal people has a message. She tells, the best way for any race to reduce or avoid violence or death at the hands of police officers is that the police wouldn't use guns so often if criminals didn't carry them so often.[159]

At a time when individuals, families, our country, and the World at large is ravaged by the coronavirus pandemic, it is time not to fight one another but work together for the common good of all.

This is not the time to fight and fulfill the desires of the enemy. We do not need Democrats, we do not need Republicans, we do not need Independents. What we need to live is Jesus. Because he lives, we shall live.

Jesus told Peter who was in a verge of denying him three times before a rooster crows in a few hours, "Simon, Simon, Satan has asked to sift all of you as wheat. But I have prayed for you, Simon, that your faith may not fail. And when you have turned back, strengthen your brothers."[160]

Ms. Ali perceives, there's even time for the candidates to debate the challenges we confront—not with outrage, but with critical thinking, we Americans were once famous for, which takes self-criticism as the first step toward finding solutions.[161]

To reduce police misconduct there are two ways. It depends on the police and the people they are supposed to protect and serve. A few years back when police used to be considered as a service rather than a job, there were more restrictions and qualifications to hiring a police officer. Now, with the decline of people wanting the police job, the recruiters are hiring people that are not qualified, or do not have reasonable qualification for the job. Hire the best of the best. Let there be also accountability of unlawful wrongdoing of a person no matter who.

The other solution is that, mainly black or minority parents should not train their children to fear, fight, and hate police officers. If the suspect grows up with such a negative attitude toward police, no matter how courteous the police are, they may be nervous during a police encounter because of the mentality that brought them up, for fear of being hurt any way.

Patents should tell their children that they can be anybody they would want to be if they put an effort. This is the only way to alleviate yourself from poverty.

Chapter Eight

"Let us not seek to satisfy our thirst for freedom by drinking from the cup of bitterness and hatred"

— REV. DR. MARTIN LUTHER KING JR.

WHAT IS MARXIST IDEOLOGY?

Growing up in a Socialist Ethiopia during the period of 1974-1991, there were three persons on billboards advertised more than all other advertisements combined. These were: Vladimir Lenin, Karl Marx, and Friedrich Engels. People used to regard them as political trinity. Now, what is Marxist ideology?

Marxism is a body of doctrine developed by Karl Marx. It originally consisted of three related ideas: a philosophical anthropology, a theory of history, and an economic and political program.[162] In a simple layman's term, Marxism deals with the haves and the have-nots and how to neutralize the economy for the common good of all rather than a few individuals who own the wealth. Key Marxist concepts are the opposite to capitalism, people of faith. It has created a divisive mentality of a society that is very much a 'them vs us' one. This means, Marxist ideology from American perspective instead of talking as 'We the People' it focuses on two distinct groups or classes based on wealth and race.

According to University of Hawaii's report, A class is defined by the ownership of property. Such ownership entrusts a person with the power to exclude others from the property and to use it for personal purposes. In relation to property, there are three great classes of society: the bourgeoisie (who own the means of production such as machinery and factory buildings, and whose source of income is profit), landowners (whose income is rent), and the proletariat (who own their labor and sell it for a wage).[163]

The ideas between these two classes or groups. These are: the haves and the have-nots. One is privileged the other is not. One is rich, the other is poor. One is powerful, the other is weak. One is the perpetrator and the other is the victim. According to the current American Trojan horse that appears disguised it includes one is male, the other is female; one is black, and the other is white; or to generalize, white people and the minorities. That is, white people are the oppressors and minorities are the oppressed.

OPPOSING CLASSES IN MARXISM

Marxism is based on hatred than in love. In addition to the economic opposition, there is also a gender class advanced by Marxist Feminism that considers women oppressed. Here one ought to know what feminism is. Feminism is the advocacy of women's rights based on the theory of political, economic, and social equality of the sexes.[164]

Stanford research also describes feminism as a political movement in the United States and Europe and a belief that refers that there are injustices against women, though there is no consensus on the exact list of these injustices.[165] In the Western world, particularly in USA, legally, men and women are entitled to the same right, what feminism claims to demand. However, much more needs to be done.

In 1963, President Kennedy signed the equal pay act into a law. For professional jobs, it is necessary that employees get the same pay for the same job performed by male or female. A 22-year-old media personality, Kylie Jenner, happens to be the highest paid person in the World. Kylie Jenner made $420 million more than the second person, Kanye. It is what one brings to the business that determines the pay, not gender. The Equal Pay Act is a promising idea in theory. Once again, the problem is that this is just a theory. Unfortunately, there still is a pay gap between genders regardless of President Kennedy's signature. Additionally, there may be areas where equal pay may not apply like in the sports area where one gender brings more money.

What the World may be facing now is "The radical feminist attempts to move towards a new and more universal analysis of domination that can encompass both class and gender oppression."[166]

Marxism's claim to provide a wide-ranging theory of human history and society is imperfect by its sidelining of experiences and aspects of life traditionally associated with women. It presents the concept of (re)production to argue that domestic, procreative, and caring activities and relationships should be part of the material basis of society.[167]

"Feminist and anti-racist economists need to work within the Marxist theoretical framework to realize their feminist and anti-racist goals. Next it argues that feminist economists should also be anti-racist"[168] All these claims are contrary to what America stands for.

The Red Terror killed about 200,000 Russians. There was a land reform, farmers were given an allotment of land by the government. But the lands were filled with corpses instead of crops.[169]

Under the communist leadership 'We the People' have no power, no say. The government decides on every sphere of life. Even if the government's decisions are leading the country to a wrong direction, one cannot object. There is no freedom of expression, no freedom of worship. It is the government that ought to be worshipped.

A communist regime is like whitewashed tombs, which look beautiful, caring, and concerned on the outside but on the inside, it is full of the bones of the dead and atrocities and uncleanness.

The communist countries of the past failed in leadership and in economy. They cannot be a solution to the suffering people of the World.

COMMUNISM, SOCIALISM, MARXISM AND FAITH

Communism, Socialism and Marxism are some of the Trojan horses of the devil. Their goal is to eradicate faith and religion. Several religious groups of Muslim and Christian faith have been and are still persecuted. A few that escaped the ethnic cleansing have been accepted as refugees in Western countries.

One may help the Communists to come to power. But at the end, they come after those that brought them into power and kill them. The survivors are left miserable. In the communist countries, people of faith; Christians have been persecuted, imprisoned, killed, survivors escaped to the USA and a few other places. The Trojan horses disguising as Communism, Socialism or Marxism may appear care for the community until they get power.

Cuban Fidel Castro was good until he got into power. So are the other Communist, Socialist, and Marxist States. Once they solidify the power, they come after everybody, be it Muslims, Christians and other religious or non-religious groups that helped them to come to power in the first place.

One cannot be a Christian and a Marxist. One cannot hold unequal views simultaneously,[170] argues Dr. Jordan Peterson referencing one who said they are so. Marxism and Christianity are diametrically opposed. Marxism is based on hate of one group and love of the other. To bring unity, the hated group must be abolished or eradicated. Whereas Christianity instructs that people have obvious differences, but all are one in Christ. One is not better in anyway than the other. The Communist countries have tortured and imprisoned people of faith just for their faith.

> One cannot be a Christian and a Marxist. One cannot hold unequal views simultaneously
> Dr. Jordan Peterson

Communist China's authorities have been accused of detaining hundreds of thousands, perhaps a million, Uyghurs, Kazakhs, Kyrgyz and other ethnic Turkic Muslims, Christians as well as some foreign citizens such as Kazakhstanis, who are being held in secretive internment camps which are located throughout the region[171] for reeducation purposes.

The worst part is that the UN Human Rights accused China of harvesting thousands of human organs from its persecuted religious minority groups. China denied the large-scale harvesting of organs but acknowledged of doing so using executed prisoners' organs.[172]

The Communist Spirit is so dangerous and merciless. When people of God rise up and pray, it will disappear.

PROBLEM OF MARXISM

American foot soldiers, the nobles, and the feudal operatives that capitalize and come in the form of BLMS or other Trojan hubris are not aware of the problem of Marxism. The problem that comes with Marxism is tyranny much worse than the perceived problem at hand. It is universally tyrannical in nature of all hitherto existing Marxist regimes. It increases the sum of human misery by increasing political oppression. Some have argued that the social and economic benefits of Marxism outweigh the political misery it causes.[173]

Communist and Islamic governments consider themselves as having the solutions for every problem. How come citizens of such countries flee in search of freedom? It should also be clear that some citizens of the repressive regimes either do not see the misery a regime cause or do not want to admit it. The deaths caused by Communist regimes that the Soviet Union created and supported—including those in Eastern Europe, China, Cuba, North Korea, Vietnam, and Cambodia—the total number of victims is closer to 100 million. That makes communism the greatest catastrophe in human history.[174]

"The inherent violence within Marxist theory itself is the exact same genocidal goal between Marxism and Nazism (the blanket generalization of an entire class of people who need to be exterminated regardless of their individual innocence).[175]

The Communist, Marxist countries are more oppressive and repressive than the state or the system they appear to oppose.

SHAMING AND INTIMIDATING

In the past, mob justice was followed by intimidating crowds of the Ku Klux Klan. Today the mob justice is followed by intimidating and shaming militant crowds of Antifa, BLM, and their Fifth column factions.

On one rally Representative Maxine Waters in an MSNBC interview spoke of how she does not honor and respect President Trump and would fight every day until he is impeached before they found no ground to do so.[176]

Waters is not the only one proposing impeachment. Representative Jerry Nadler, Congressman Adam Schiff, politician Julian Castro few among many as well who are impeachment obsessed voiced, "we cannot depend only on the election for our Democracy. If we do not impeach Trump he is going to get elected." Really! The Trojan masters behind the Democratic Party know that Trump is doing well, by doing so exposing the do-nothing politicians. The only way to stop Trump is to impeach the man.

The U.S. Democratic Representative Al Green who made three attempts to impeach Trump is quoted saying "We can't beat him, so let's impeach him!"[177] Bryson Gray on related theme song said, "You want to impeach him I guess that's what you do when you can't beat him."[178]

This is the world the USA is in, disrespecting a rightfully elected President. It should not be tolerated.

You want to impeach him
I guess that's what you do
when you can't beat him.

Bryson Gray

These are acts of the outrageous behavior of abuser engaged in shaming or humiliating the victim are hubris character.[179]

In America, it is right to disagree and solve the differences peacefully. But it is wrong to dehumanize each other as people fight for justice. It is not acceptable to go on the street and make a fellow human being to feel guilty for their religion, race, and origin of geographical location.

She also spoke to her audience, "If we cannot protect the children, we cannot protect anybody. If you see anybody of that cabinet in a restaurant, in a Department store, at a gasoline station, you get out and you create a crowd and you push back on them, and you tell them they are not welcome. People must turn on them, protest and absolutely harass them until they decide they are going to tell the President they cannot associate with him.[180]

This is a coward way of fighting. Real men and women fight on the ballot. Maxine's on-sight hate-shaming and intimidating government officials does not go in line with American value. Americans have a right to free speech and right to have their own opinions, go wherever they want to go freely. Because of such hatred, many Republican officials and even journalists who are not trojan horses of the Democratic plantation have faced multiple protesters heckling them in public places.

Waters mentioned enforcing shaming of her enemies. Shaming and intimidating are not the proper American way of doing life and governance. It is the actions of weaklings who know that they could not win in the real American way of fighting. The question is, how would she feel if someone would do the same to her? Take a note that the scripture informs believers, "For in the same way you judge others, you will be judged, and with the measure you use, it will be measured to you."[181]

Should one have issue with the governance, they should deal with that Office. Going to the residence and heckling an official in the way Maxine Waters advocates for is immature and dishonorable to the US Representative Office!

The Democratic shaming intimidators would not save even one of their own. When Mayor Jacob Frey didn't support abolishing the police department, his stance got him booed off the street by activists who demonstrated outside his house.[182]

Amazon's Jeff Bezos donated $10 million to organization supporting justice and equality of which Black Lives Matter is one. Yet angry protesters did not spare Amazon, from looting and damaging.[183]

While attempting to embarrass and shame constituents who donated to President Trump, Texas congressman Joaquin Castro appears to have overlooked the fact that some of the very people that he named Trump donors also donated cash to him and his twin brother, a Democrat 2020 presidential contestant Julián Castro.[184] A donor has a constitutional right to donate to whoever they want, but not in the Democratic plantation field. A person should expect to be indebted to Democrat.

Eric McCormack and Debra Messing declared a war on Trump's major donors ahead of planned fundraiser for the President wanting his supporters to be blacklisted.

Chastising their endeavor Whoopi Goldberg states, "Your idea who you don't want to work with is your personal business. Do not encourage people to print out list (as Julian Castro was). Because the next list that comes out your name will be on, and people will be coming after you. In this country people can vote for who they want to that is one of the great rights of this country. You do not have to like it. We do not go after people because we do not like who they voted for. We do not go after them that way. We can talk about issues and stuff. But we don't print out lists.[185]

Ayaan Ali, a writer at the Wall Street Journal, in relation to bringing solution and police force work, states, "The problem is that there are people among us who don't want to figure it out and who have an interest in avoiding workable solutions. They have an obvious political incentive not to solve social problems, because social problems are the basis of their power. That is why, whenever a scholar like Roland Fryer brings new data to the table—showing it's simply not true that the police disproportionately shoot black people dead—the response is not to read the paper but to try to discredit its author."[186]

Chapter Nine

"Many of the issues my father has championed are not historically Republican priorities, yet where Washington chooses sides, our president chooses common sense. Where politicians choose party, our president chooses people."

—*IVANKA TRUMP, 2020 RNC SPEECH*

MARGARET SANGER

It has been known that the USA government (the Democrats and Republicans alike) direct hundreds of millions of dollars every year to Planned Parenthood clinics in the USA and all over the world.

President Trump promised and is working to cut those funds domestically or globally. The political outsider elected Republican President, believes every child has a right to live, while the so-called religious Obama and Biden do not believe the same.

It does not come as a revelation to find out that the Planned Parenthood organization celebrate its founder.

The Smithsonian Museum portrait gallery recently opened a new federally funded display according to the museum's curator to celebrate women who challenged and changed America over the past century. Included in the list is the dishonorable for some, honorable for others, such as Mrs. Clinton, feminist Margaret Sanger. The national portrait gallery website provides a brief description of Sanger as a concerned crusader who fought with a courage of a wounded tiger for the promotion of birth control. What the Smithsonian exhibit fails to mention however is that Margaret Sanger founded the largest abortion chain in the country now known as the Planned Parenthood.

What the exhibit also does not clarify is the racist ideology behind Sanger's promotion of Birth Control. Many people do not know what the term "Eugenic" is, one of the Sanger's main ideals. It is a means of control of who should have children and who should not. She speaks about how charities should be eradicated, and sterilization should be legal to avoid the "no needs," targeting the black race which she called the "Negro problem." She aimed to control who should not procreate, and she wanted to exterminate those she considered undesirable.[187]

Before one discusses Margaret Sanger, and how her work affected the world, one needs to know who she is. Margaret Higgins Sanger (born Margaret Louise Higgins, September 14, 1879 – September 6, 1966, also known as Margaret Sanger Slee) was an American birth control activist, sex educator, writer, and nurse.[188]

Her stated mission was to empower women to make their own reproductive choices. She did focus her efforts on minority communities, because that was where, due to poverty and limited access to health care, women were especially vulnerable to the effects of unplanned pregnancy.[189] The mission statement does not appear to be a harmful idea on the outside. It is on the inside detail, practical applicability of it targeting certain people where the problem comes.

Margaret Sanger's slogans were: Birth control: to create a race of thoroughbreds and more children from the fit, less from the unfit, advocating and giving genetically inferior groups in our population their choice of segregation or sterilization. Sanger invited Hitler's racial advisor Eugen Fischer to lecture in the USA. One of her advisors even travelled to Germany to meet Hitler.[190] This is the first step to knowing that Hitler was the Democratic Party ally.

One should admit that some slum mothers who begged for information about how to avoid more pregnancies transformed her into a social radical. She joined the Socialist Party, a political Party that believes the government should own and distribute all goods, including requiring couples to submit applications to have a child. She was also part and began attending radical rallies.[191]

Encyclopedia of World Biography describes Sanger as a woman evil to the core. Yet some insist on polishing her image & publicizing her as some hero because of birth control. She says, "The most merciful thing that a large family does to one of its infant members is to kill it."[192] This is who she was.

The racist Margaret Sanger killed the minorities in the womb by means of abortion. For the survivors of abortion, people whom she referred to as 'human weeds,' she sterilized. For the people who survived abortion and sterilization she used to kill by her army the Ku Klux Klan (KKK). Juneteenth in Tulsa Oklahoma is a witness. She had made a speech to the KKK, the enemies of the minorities. Look at the title of the article and how her audience salute her. It is a salute debuted in Nazi Germany in the 1930s to pay homage to Adolf Hitler. It consists of raising an outstretched right arm with the palm down. Here is Sanger's speech to local KKK women:[193]

SANGER DELIVERS BURNING SPEECH
LOCAL KKK GALS HANG ON EVERY WORD

On Juneteenth, an eyewitness account states "From his office window, attorney Buck Colbert "B.C." Franklin could see planes circling low overhead Greenwood, the thriving African American district in Tulsa, Oklahoma, in the early morning hours of June 1st, 1921, and they were growing in number. Moments later, he heard "something falling like hail upon the top of my office." The planes were dropping bombs."[194]

The people who survived the bombing also had another fate ting positioned in place: In a 1931 manuscript, Franklin vividly described what he witnessed during those horrifying hours, when thousands of white citizens brutally attacked the African American community of 15,000 situated within 35 blocks surrounding the corner of Greenwood Avenue and Archer Street, just north of the railroad tracks that divided the city's black and white sections. Homes and businesses were set on fire, raided, homeowners who remained to defend their homes were shot and their property looted. Franklin's is one of many first-person accounts that chronicles one of the worst acts of racial violence in U.S. history."[195]

SANGER'S ALLEGIANCE WITH THE KKK AND HITLER

It is not Republican's policy, but Democrats that are in favor of Hitler and the KKK. Democratic party supports and admires the Eugenic, abortionist, racist Sanger, it is the Democrat's policy. Hillary Clinton admires Margaret Sanger's tenacity and vision of the woman involved in a selectively breeding out the unfit and forced sterilization of humanity at clinics as well in prisons. What was Sanger's vision? To eliminate the poor, minorities, blacks, Jews, Asians, lower class white people as well. It is not Trump's Republican Party; it is academia, celebrities, Clintons, Obamas, and the Democrats who support a woman who wanted to exterminate people she referred to as "weeds." Democrats have had minorities vote for generation It is the very people that hate them. The minorities have an obscured enemy.

Ms. Sanger is Hitler's role model; he followed her sterilization method. She is not Trump's role model. She is Hillary Clinton's role model. She gave a speech to the domestic terrorist group known as the KKK who have killed thousands of black people.

In fact, in October 2015, when Obama was in the Oval Office, Republicans led by Senator Ted Cruz requested that this racist woman's bust be removed from a historic museum. They, (U.S. Senator Ted Cruz (R-Texas) and U.S. Representative Louie Gohmert (R-Texas), along with 24 House Republicans) "sent a letter to the Director of the National Portrait Gallery Kim Sajet, calling for the immediate removal of Margaret Sanger's bust from the Smithsonian's National Portrait Gallery. The bust is on display in the Gallery's "Struggle for Justice" exhibit.[196]

What Justice did she struggle for? Is believing in using contraceptives to control the population of minorities, or people she deemed as 'undesirables'; the work of an avowed advocate of eugenics and the extermination of groups of people specifically blacks a struggle for justice? How unable are the voters of Democrat leaders to see and identify their real haters?[197]

EUGENICS

Eugenics is a movement that is aimed at improving the genetic composition of humans. Historically, eugenicists have advocated for selective breeding to achieve these goals. Margaret Sanger was a powerful anti-Semite who actively participated in the immigration restrictions keeping Jews out of the United States. She actively opposed the free maternity clinics that would have given Sadie Sachs (a Jew) the care she needed to bring her child into the World.

Margaret Sanger was against every form of social welfare program because they would help the poor survive. Most of all Sanger hated the Roman Catholic Church whom she feared would destroy humans by encouraging the poor to defend their God-given right to have children. Sanger called the Catholic Church tyrannical while she was demanding compulsory birth control and sterilization for millions. Hitler used eugenic principles to justify the atrocities he committed.[198]

Eugenics is a way or a method of selective breeding of individuals who have "desired traits." In 1883, Sir. Francis Galton used the term eugenics, meaning 'well-born. People deemed to be unfit more often came from families that were poor, low in social standing, immigrant, and/or minority.[199]

To fulfill her objective of exterminating or reducing the birth of the no 'needs,' abortion clinics are located primarily near lower-class settlements. For example, in the county where Hayet lives, there is an abortion clinic located in a walking distance. There are more apartments located where the abortion clinic is situated. There is one college nearby too.

In 2019 and early 2020 until Covid-19 disrupted the entire system, on weekdays Hayet drove by the abortion clinic on his way to work. The only protesters one could see are white folks. Are the minorities ignorant of the very system that is designed to exterminate them? Or are they comfortable with it?

Ms. Sanger was intentional on her work of extermination and wanted to hide behind appearing as a good person. Quoting one of her provocative letters to Dr. C. J. Gamble, Senator Cruz on his letter to the curator said, "We (the Planned Parenthood group) do not want word to go out that we want to exterminate the Negro population."[200] It is to such a person that Secretary Clinton favorably speaks how enormously in awe she is of Ms. Sanger.[201]

"Colored people are like human weeds and need to be exterminated."

- Margaret Sanger

PLANNED PARENTHOOD AND ABORTION FOR PROFIT

Planned Parenthood was founded by a racist ideology of a white woman called Margaret Sanger who wanted to exterminate certain groups of people due to unwanted personality traits. Of these traits that do not deserve to procreate include children born out of marriage and people who have been to jail, some whites, minorities, and the black people.

The Alan Guttmacher Institute (AGI) describes abortion, to put it plainly, as a very lucrative business that offers the opportunity to get rich quick. What makes it quick rich is, it takes less time to perform it. For all human history, the praise of wealth has led many to rationalize career choices that they would never otherwise dream of.[202]

In abortion services, there may be a few genuine cases to care for the wellbeing of the mother. However, many of the services behind abortion are based on profit making, although it is legally registered as a non-profit entity. It is a quick money-making scheme. Yet, this business enjoys tax exemption. "Tax-exempt refers to income or transactions that are free from tax at the federal, state, or local level.[203]

Abortion continues to be "subsidized" by federal tax exemption of organization income and donor deductions. Thirty-one percent of the nation's abortion clinics and thousands of non-profit hospitals providing abortion and abortion counseling (in addition to the usual range of health care services) currently enjoy tax-exempt status under Internal Revenue Code § 501(c)(3).[204]

FUNDS AND FEES FOR ABORTION PROVIDERS

Abortion providers receive government grants and contracts annually for, the dollar amount moves well past $1 billion.[205] After receiving such big amounts of money, if abortion services were out of compassion it should have been free. Yet, this business makes money from their desperate customers.

Just as in any business there are salespersons, abortion clinics are not exempt. The main purpose of a car, gold, computer, or service provider is to make customers purchase. A salesperson makes sure the customer makes a purchase. The salespersons are mean, merciless sharks who have no concern for the customer's financial struggle. All they care about is how to entice, bewitch, and cheat the   into purchasing. They use discounted sweet-talk, saying, "low interest, no payment for months, payment plan, provide with their own or other easy access credit card" and many more. There is also a threat and intimidation on the desperate, "If you leave now, there is a high risk the price could change." Customers get forced to decide 'now.'

Abby Johnson, a college student got pregnant while in school. She went to the abortion clinic and acquired her first credit card to pay for the service. Since credit card companies and banks are beneficiaries of the abortion services, they will keep on supporting any politician that advocates for abortion. The abortion sales would pressure one to purchase the service, and they would not want the customer to leave the clinic without making a financial commitment to the service.

While abortion sales try to expedite the abortion for their profit, Pro-life counselors beg mothers not to abort their baby. A good number of the abortion survivors have become great influencers in the community. Pastor James Robinson is one such survivor.

His 40 years old mother, who had no child was working as practical nurse caring for an elderly man. She got approached, raped by an alcoholic son in the family and got pregnant. She went to a doctor and asked for an abortion, out of deep conviction, he refused. Later, she prayed about it and thought that she should have the child. She gave birth to a son and gave him up for adoption.[206] What if he had been aborted? The world would have missed the unwanted and unexpected child who turned out to be a great man.

The base fee even for the abortion pill is $435, and the highest could be $3,000. Of the 1.21 million annual abortions performed in 2005, each year in the U.S., the abortion industry brings in approximately $831 million through their abortion services alone.[207] Plus the one billion government grant, it is about two-billion-dollar business industry a year.

Of the 1.21 million abortions, 37% are obtained by black women. The 37% of 1.21 million is about half million a year. This is the vision of Margaret Sanger wanting to exterminate the Negro population in action.

When a car gets totaled, it is taken to car junkyard. The car junk handlers love this commodity because they do not pay for it, yet they make profit off it. There, one by one the useful parts are sold to customers. It is legitimate to do so to reduce duplicate production. Likewise, in addition to government grants and abortion service fees, abortion clinics make money by selling body part remains. The people who purchase these body parts that remains in the name of research as well do make profit from abortion. The more abortion clinics profit monetarily from the service, the more abortions they would perform.

Abby Johnson spoke of how her supervisor told her team that they should increase abortions. The demand to increase by doubling or tripling abortion was a red flag for Johnson, *if we are trying to help women why are we told to increase abortions?*

An undercover video shows how Planned Parenthood Federation of America, while under investigation in 2015, told Congress that its Gulf Coast affiliate in Houston had an undercover proposal to sell fetal livers for $750 per liver and $1,600 for liver/thymus pairs, earning them as much as a quarter million dollars just from one clinic.[208]

Abortion clinics attempted to cover-up the fact but failed and it was exposed, "Two Southern California companies admitted of being guilty for selling body parts from Planned Parenthood Orange and San Bernardino Counties against the law in a $7.8 million settlement with the Orange County District Attorney."[209]

Several undercover videos show the abortion clinics allow technicians to come and harvest the parts they need from children born alive with a healthy heart beating outside the womb.[210]

Although the law such as 18 U.S. Code § 1958.Use of interstate commerce facilities in the commission of murder-for-hire forbid such murderous practices, it still goes on in the USA in the abortion clinics.

On the contrary, the pro-life people would never make profit by extorting the pregnant women that are in crisis who need help. If the pregnant women choose to give birth, pro-life people help with taking care of the child, finding one who would adopt the survivor babies without a charge.

GOVERNORS THAT SUPPORT ABORTION

There are several Governors that are in favor of abortion at any time during the time of the pregnancy. Virginia Governor Northam, a Democrat is positioned to remove abortion restrictions for what Virginia Delegate Kathy Tran, said in a committee hearing that it would technically allow abortion until the point of birth, even if the woman is dilating, about to give birth.

Governor Northam was asked about Virginia House Bill 2491 in a radio interview about what would happen if a child was born after a failed attempt at abortion, he said, "the infant would be resuscitated if that's what the mother and the family desired, (if the parents do not want they let the American baby die) and then a discussion would ensue between the physicians and the mother. Some took Northam's comments as an endorsement of infanticide.[211]

In support of Governor Northam's perspective, "Professor of obstetrics, gynecology and reproductive sciences at the University of California, San Francisco Dr. Daniel Grossman told The New York Times in February that, "in very rare cases of an infant being born alive after an attempted abortion, If it seems unlikely that the baby will survive, the family may choose to provide just comfort care — wrapping and cuddling the baby — and allow the child to die naturally without extreme attempts at resuscitation." [212]Not taking care of a baby born alive is medical malpractice and pure murder.

On one of his campaigns in Wisconsin, Trump informed the crowd that their Governor, Tony Evers, would veto the born alive legislation brought to him by the Republican legislators. Sure enough, he did and on his lopsided justification he stated, everyone should have access to quality, affordable health care, and that includes reproductive health care. Politicians shouldn't be in the business of interfering with decisions made between patients and their health care providers."[213] Although he said, 'everyone should have access' his veto discriminates one over the other by allowing the abortion clinic to let 'the born alive American children' die without care to children many of whom could survive on their own outside their mothers' wombs.

The North Carolina Governor, Roy Cooper (D), also vetoed the same 'born alive bill' emphasizing the cruelty of the infanticide.[214] The Democratic Governors that veto the born alive bill are committing a silent genocide of Americans and should be stopped.

The Conservative Supreme Court choose to advance the liberal Justices. Thus, "The Supreme Court on Monday June 29, 2020 struck down a Louisiana law that required doctors who perform abortions in the state to have admitting privileges at nearby hospitals. This was the first major abortion case before the Supreme Court since President Trump added two new conservative justices to the bench."[215] Adam Liptak who covered the court provided the context to the decision was surprised. There was no good reason to think the court would uphold the Louisiana law restricting abortions in the state because we have two new justices appointed by President Trump since the last time the court addressed the issue in 2016.

Chapter Ten

"When an election was over, in the past, I think we were more inclined to work together then and fix the problems in the past. Today we seem to be in a constant divide-and-conquer mode."

— GENERAL JAMES MATTIS

RESISTANCE GROUP

There are several reasons one could resist a person or a group. Some are justified, others not. The election of Donald Trump has revealed the real color of American enemies. Whatever the resistance group blames Trump, be it police misconduct or discriminations, it has been there for about 500 years, 50 years of Joe Biden's politics and about 20 years of Barack Obama in politics. What is the hullaballoo now as if it is something new?

MICHAEL MOORE

Who is Michael Moore? According to Wikipedia, Michael Francis Moore was born April 23, 1954. He is an American documentary filmmaker, author, and activist worth about $50 million. His works frequently address the topics of globalization and capitalism, a critic of Republican governance.[216]

Millionaire Michael Moore predicted that Trump would win over Clinton in the 2016 election and he did. His prediction was based on resentment to Trump. He also predicted that Trump might not go on to serve out his four years term on Seth Meyers show. To prove his prediction, he said that Trump is not President until he is sworn by the Chief Justice of the USA, at noon on January 20 of 2017. He said so in early December 2016 that's more than six weeks before the inauguration. Additionally, he emphasized saying, "Would you not agree, regardless of which side of the political fence you are on, this has been the craziest election year? Nothing anyone has predicted has happened. The opposite has happened. So, is it possible that in these next six weeks something else might happen, something crazy, something we are not expecting?"[217]

Moore predicted that Trump might have decided to quit before he even took office. Several people at some point in their life on the first day of their job knew they had taken the wrong job, did not proceed with the new job.[218] That was and is Moore's wish, but it did not happen, and hopefully will never happen. This very unfulfilled prediction is one that has been fueling hate and all sorts of demonstrations against the then candidate and now President Trump, including the Woman's March and Black Lives Matter Movement. People may argue that these movements are not specifically against Trump. They have their own ideals and goals and should not be minimized to a march "against Trump." However, the fact shows that all oppose Trump.

MOORE'S 10-POINT ACTION PLAN TO THUMP TRUMP

In his article 'The 10-Point Action Plan to Thump Trump," Moore writes in number 4 that he joined certain groups. All the groups that he joined were fake, lopsided, and clandestinely intended to hurt families, faith groups, black people, minorities, and the USA at large. Let us look at some of the groups Moore is a member of and what their origins are.

In his wish to stop Trump's Presidency, Moore proudly speaks of his other militant wing of the comedians, "Our beautiful Army of Comedy – with its Platoon of Satirists led by Alec Baldwin and Melissa McCarthy – is killing it! The devastating impersonation of White House spokesman Sean Spicer by McCarthy has Trump fuming to the point where he has considered getting rid of Spicer."

It appears Moore is excited to see that his militant wings are in motion engaged in the so-called peaceful protest yet disintegrating America, "So the momentum is with us right now — and if we all just take a little time to do the Action Plan below, I'm convinced we'll succeed in halting the dark force that is Trump. We can tie him up in knots at every turn, and eventually, we can bring him down," on the following action plan.

Here is the list of the militant ideology of Michael Moore's 10-Point Action Plan to Thump Trump plan:

1.   The daily call: You must call to Congress, two US Senators, local State House/Assembly Representative, every day. The goal is, "Remember — A call a day keeps Trump away."

2.   The monthly visit: To add even more pressure, SHOW UP! Do both of your U.S. Senators.

3.   Have your own personal rapid response team: You and 5 to 20 friends and family members must become your personal rapid response team. Each of the 5 to 20 team members forming their own local rapid response team. (NB. Moore's team is not volunteer for natural disasters but to oppose Trump's agenda)

4.   Join! Join! Join! Join some of our great national groups. Moore speaks that he joined Planned Parenthood, ACLU, Black Lives Matter, Democratic Socialists of America, Equal Rights Amendment Action. Moore says once you join, they will keep you informed of national actions and fight for us in court.

5.   The women's march never end. Moore speaks of how women's march on Washington on January 21st in the US and in the World was record breaking.

6.   Take over the Democratic Party: the old leadership must go. God love 'em for their contributions in the past, but if we don't enact a radical overhaul right now, we are doomed as far as having a true opposition party during the Trump era.

7.   Help form blue regions of resistance: Show the rest of America what it looks like when Trump is not in charge! (Disobedience to authority? Scripture tell us to obey and respect authority even if they do not deserve. Such leadership creates a defiant, disobedient generation who would not be willing to obey police officer's directive and end up being shot during a scuffle)

8.   You must run for office: if we keep leaving the job up to the dismal, lame, pathetic political hacks who have sold us all down the river, then what right do we have to complain? (Moore tells others to run for office, but he would not do so for himself. He tells of how he ran and was elected when he was 18, about 48 years ago. If he is a man (brave person) he should have done against Trump). Joe Biden is running for Presidency at the age of 77; In four years, Moore will be 72 years old and could try for 2024.

9.   You must become the media: find the media who are doing a good job and then start your own "media empire" by sharing their work and your work on the internet.

10.   Join the Army of comedy: Trump's Achilles heel is his massively thin skin. He cannot take mockery. So, we all need to MOCK HIM UP![219]

This ten-point plan appears to tear down and hemorrhage America not to build it. When one looks at the groups Michael Moore joined and he encourages others to join, 'Planned Parenthood, ACLU, Black Lives Matter, Democratic Socialists of America, Equal Rights Amendment Action' most of them appear to be enemy of what family values, faith groups, specifically what Christianity stands for.

Michael Moore, who supports police defund wishes unrest plays out like movie where 'heroes swoop in and kill the murderous cops.' Then the superhero would rain fire down on Police HQ & the audience would stand & applaud! White, Black, and Brown - the entire audience would scream YES! Thank God it is just a movie.[220]

Here, the question is who are the heroes who rain fire down on Police HQ and who are the murderous cops? Is this only a hypothetical movie or dream? Have we not seen Police HQ and several police vehicles burn as well and the entire audience would scream YES?

Unless there is a law and order leader who brings the perpetrators into justice, this is going to be the normal way of life. With the destroyers bailout politicians such as Kamala Harris by her support to the Minnesota Freedom Fund (MFF) that brought $35 million after she tweeted.[221]

Here are other groups that America loving should pay attention and say enough is enough.

AMERICAN CIVIL LIBERTIES UNION ACLU

The ACLU as an organization dares to create a more perfect union — beyond one person, party, or side. Their mission is to realize this promise of the United States Constitution for all and expand the reach of its guarantees.[222]

The ACLU lists the most pressing civil liberties issues of our time as the following: Immigration, LGBTQ Rights, Reproductive Rights, Criminal Justice, Security and Privacy, Voting Rights, Capital Punishment, Disability Rights, Free Speech, HIV, Human Rights, Juvenile Justice, National Security, Prisoners' Rights, Racial Justice, Religious Liberty, Smart Justice, and Women's Rights.[223]

Although the declaration of ACLU says, "The ACLU strives to safeguard the First Amendment's guarantee of religious liberty by ensuring that laws and governmental practices neither promote religion nor interfere with its free exercise."[224] Nevertheless, the organization defends everybody else but not the Christian faith and Christians. One may feel comfortable for being defended by ACLU for being a Muslim. But in the end, if one faith group is attacked and while another keeps silent, they will be next to be attacked. The purpose of such group is to silence all faith groups.

Perhaps the First Step Act may an exceptional where the ACLU agrees with President Trump. "Hailed by supporters as a pivotal moment in the movement to create a more fair justice system, endorsed by an unlikely alliance that includes President Donald Trump and the American Civil Liberties Union, the First Step Act is a bundle of compromises."[225]

The communists have divided people in variety of categories, bringing enmity one over the other, making one group not to trust the other. In the end, all groups become powerless; the communists take charge of all. In the current American context, if I keep silent when another religious group is attacked today, next will be mine. A German Theologian Martin Niemöller disapproved the silence of the majority when a faith group or certain peaceful citizens are attacked. During the days of Hitler, he told the religious organization to take care of their church while he takes care of the state. The church did not bother to criticize him, because he did not touch them. He subdued the people he wanted to subdue, imprisoned some and kill the groups that he wanted to get rid of. After learning nobody was coming to help him, from his personal experience he stated:

"First, they came for the Socialists, and I did not speak out because I was not a Socialist.

Then they came for the Trade Unionists, and I did not speak out because I was not a Trade Unionist.

Then they came for the Jews, and I did not speak out because I was not a Jew.

Then they came for the Catholics, and I did not speak out because I was not a Catholic.

Then they came for me, and there was no one left to speak for me."

There is no gift or a pass from the devil. One must pay for it directly or indirectly.

DEMOCRATIC SOCIALIST OF AMERICA (DSA)

Communism and socialism are umbrella terms referring to two left-wing schools of economic thought; both oppose capitalism. In a simple term, Communism and Socialism are two sides of a coin.

Just to begin with, the people who advocate for Socialism are those who really do not know what it entails. In the Socialist States is there is no consistent electricity and water supply. The government is in control and without any notice, the basic supplies could be cut indefinitely.

Communism is the extreme form of socialism. First, let us look at the differences and similarities of communism and socialism. The key difference between socialism and communism is the means of achieving them. In communism, a violent revolution in which the workers revolt against the middle and upper classes is seen as an inevitable part of achieving a pure communist state. The property and the resources are owned and controlled by the state rather than the individual. Socialism is a less rigid, a more flexible ideology, all citizens share equally in economic resources as allocated by a democratically elected government.[226] Whereas in a capitalist economy one works for oneself and make wealth out of it.

Alexandria Ocasio-Cortez and Rashida Tlaib, who were elected to the House of Representatives are just two joined members of the prominent elected officials. For most part, DSA stands against what the USA government stands for. The USA government supports Israel, while DSA on August 5, 2017, passed a motion to formally endorse the Boycott, Divestment and Sanctions movement (BDS). The DSA maintains it is an anti-racist and anti-fascist organization. It also aligns itself with the socialist feminist movement. The heart of the DSA members and leadership may be motivated by good intentions but it is not a good direction for America

Marxism, communism, socialism is not good for China, Russia, Cuba, North Korea, and other countries as well. The Americans who support DSA do not know what a socialist or communist country looks like. Millions have left those Socialist countries and come to the haven, the USA, or West countries in general. It is too sad that they want to take immigrants back to the states that they escaped from. In socialist countries, people cannot protest the government or a government official. People have no guarantees for tomorrow and are at the mercies of the government.

The people of these Socialist countries are always hungry and do not have human freedom. They cannot say anything that criticizes the government, for fear of imprisonment or death. Once a person is taken into custody, they cannot have the legal right to question the government for the imprisonment or for the death of loved ones. The government is always right, just as a god that nobody dares to challenge.

The author grew up in Socialist Ethiopia. The government controlled everything. There was extremely limited free market economy. The government purchased what they thought was good for the people and put it on sale through their local representatives' sales shops. The communist government controls and determines how many grams of bread should be baked and how much it should be sold. The price of everything is set by the government, there is no free market economy. The business that sells by adding any money to the set price of the bread or anything else would be in a big trouble.

People have migrated from Socialist, Communist, Islamic, Buddhist, Hindu, Christian and other traditionalist countries to the USA seeking what they could not find in their birth countries. The USA is a beacon of hope for humanity. That is why without exaggeration it could be said that there are immigrants from every tribe of the earth in the USA. People have come to taste and enjoy what made America, what it is. This ingredient is their fear of God and the Judeo-Christian values they upheld. Once they go against what made them, then they become like other failed countries.

The outcome of abandoning God in the name of religious liberty and so on is clear; "The LORD is with you when you are with him. If you seek him, he will be found by you, but if you forsake him, he will forsake you."[227] Yet, DSA appears to long to achieve to what caused many immigrants leave their countries of origin. Look at China, USSR, Cuba, North Korea, Venezuela, Vietnam, the Germans that united averted mass exodus, the same to many African socialist countries. While many immigrants would love to come to the USA to taste and enjoy what made America, it is sad to see the DSA leading towards what broke so many countries before.

TRUMP VULTURE CUNNING NEWS NETWORK (TVCNN)

TVCNN is an acronym refers to Trump Vulture Cunning News Network.

It appears there are two major traditional sources people get information from. These are: From TV Anchors (Newspersons) to (Radio Hosts) and Opinion talk Shows Hosts (Radio/TV personalities). A newsperson or a news anchor is a person whose main duty is to "work closely with reporters and will be responsible for gathering information, broadcasting newscasts throughout the day, and interviewing guests." Listeners should be able to follow current events and present news stories to audiences in an informative, interesting, and unbiased way.[228]

The author believes that American media should be free minded, non-partisan with justice to viewers, not biased or partisan, especially toward any political group. Media personality is a professional job. Friendship and belonging to one party should be different from viewing one person favorably than the other that could be classified as employment or workplace discrimination. It should have no place in American society. However, a partisan view from a media person's, Opinion Talk, or government owned media is at least acceptable.

The only thing TVCNN gets right is, the weather. For other partisan issues, the station cannot be trusted.

Chapter Eleven

"You Democrats (addressing black Muslims), you have been in that party for a long time. Answer me what did you get? You got a President who is worried about his legacy"

— MINISTER LOUIS FARRAKHAN

PRESIDENT BARACK OBAMA

President Obama was the 44th American President. Just like any other president he has done some good and some bad as well to America for which he will be remembered. Former Libyan leader Muamar Ghaddafi was happy that an African immigrant's son became the USA president. At the same time, he was skeptical and was afraid that "they" could use him and do Africans more harm than "they" did. Who are the "they" Ghaddafi is referring to? Eventually, what Ghaddafi feared came upon him; what he dreaded has happened to him, he died by the hands of President Obama. Libya is in a far much dangerous state to the World now. This happened after Obama's USA government's unauthorized intervention.

In reference to Obama, Minister Farrakhan was happy that he got elected president and voted for him. Yet he was skeptical that he could bring change to help black people. Like Ghaddafi's skepticism, President Obama was used by the white liberals in some areas to the point of vetoing to serve the interests of certain people, not black people.

Addressing people, Minister Farrakhan states to black audiences, "You Democrats, you have been in that Party for a long time. Answer me what did you get? You got a president who is worried about his legacy." Hayet would say, *enough is enough* time to change from what does not benefit you. Addressing to President Obama directly he had a message:

> I just want to tell you Mister President. You are from Chicago and so am I. I go out in the streets with the people. I visit the worst neighborhood; I talk to the gangs. While I was there talking to them, they said, "You know Farrakhan, the President never come. Could you get him to come and look after us?" There is your legacy Mr. President. It is in the street, but people are suffering. If you cannot go and see them, no worries about your legacy. The white people that you have served so well, will preserve your legacy. Hell, they will. But you did not earn your legacy with us. We put you there, you fought for the right of gay people, you fought for the rights of this people and that people, you fight for Israel. Your people are suffering and dying in the streets. That is where your legacy is. You failed to do what should have been done.[229]

On one of the final trips of President Obama as a president was Kenya, his father's birth country. Obama personalized the issue of gay marriage by comparing homophobia to racial discrimination that he had encountered in the United States. Never has such a powerful foreign leader challenged Africans so directly on their own soil.[230]

It is dishonorable and not dignifying to compare the inhumane discrimination what the African ancestors' slaves endured with his perverted sent agenda.

HOMOSEXUALITY AND LESBIANISM

The issue of gay agenda has been a part of human history since the days of Sodom and Gomorrah, ancient cities that were destroyed because of that practice. Democratic party leadership and people are for it, while the Republican leadership and people are against it. The difference though is that a Democrat tries to force everybody to accept that lifestyle while Republicans are free to choose should they choose that lifestyle; they just keep it for themselves.

Dr. Ravi Zacharias, a Christian apologist answers homosexuality and race comparison. For Dr. Zacharias, race is sacred. For Obama, the gay agenda is sacred.

Dr. Ravi was asked, "How do your respond to non-believers who accuse Christians of being hateful to people who support lifestyles that are not according to the precepts of our faith?"

In answering the question, he brought an example of a reporter who asked him the same question at Indiana University.

"I have a personal question for you," she asked. "I have a problem with Christianity. And here is my problem. Christians are generally against racism. But when it comes to homosexuality, they discriminate against homosexuals."

"I find your comment so interesting," he replied.

"In the first part of question it is an '-ism' you are talking about. In the second part you particularize it with individuals. I am fascinated about that, but it is okay. Here is what I want to say to you. The reason we believe that discrimination ethnically is wrong is because the race and ethnicity of a person is sacred. You do not violate a person's ethnicity and race. Because it is a sacred gift. And the reason we believe in absoluteness to sexuality is because we believe sexuality is sacred as well. That is why we make our choice that same way. You will help me if you will tell me why you treat race sacred and discretize sexuality."

She was quiet. "I have never thought in those terms," she replied.

"God gives you the most sacred gift of the prerogative of choice. But God does not give you the privilege of determining a different outcome to what the choice entails. The consequences are bound to the choice. If we go back to the book of Genesis, God told Cain 'if you do what is right will you not be accepted?' Sin stalks at your door; its desire is for you, but you must master it. So, when I see the sacredness of marriage, any change from it, from the Biblical point of view is a departure from the Biblical mandate.

At the same time, the Bible commands us to love even those with whom we disagree. Our responsibility as a church is never to hate the individual. Our privilege is to love. Only God can change the heart of a person. And God is the ultimate judge. In a pluralistic society let us, as Christians be both light and salt and learn to love one another. And let God be the judge over all of us. He is the only one pure in his judgments. We can make errors."[231]

The way Ghaddafi stated, Obama's liberal senders used him to say what ought not to say, that no other white leader has ever said in Africa, the gay agenda. He had a free pass for it because of his black privilege. He even threatened African leaders that if they do not uphold his gay agenda, they would not get American aid, one that most African leaders beg for. This is quid pro quo. LGBTQ+ rights are not an urgent pressing issue in Africa. The good thing is that President Kenyatta and President Museveni rebuffed Obama's pressure regardless of the outcome.

To the faith group, mainly to Christianity, Obama has been used as Trojan hubris to challenge and discredit American Judeo-Christian values like no other previous President.

HILLARY CLINTON LOST THE PRESIDENTIAL ELECTION

In American history Hillary Clinton became the first female presumptive nominee. Clinton, compared to Trump, had more extensive political experience after holding leadership positions as a First Lady of Bill Clinton, US Senator and Secretary of State.

On her bid for presidential election, Secretary Clinton focused on denouncing and attacking Trump supporters as bigots, irredeemable, and a basket of deplorables. She advocated for expansion and carrying on the legacy of President Obama's policies which would be detrimental for her election. She became the victim of President Obama's unfavorable mistakes.

Divorcing herself from Obama, which was unlikely, would have been a better choice. Most Americans and immigrants are traditionally religious. Thus, for Christians, Muslims, Hispanic, Far Eastern, Middle Eastern people, or other religious groups are traditionally conservatives; regardless, which they belong to. Obama's and Clinton's LGBTQ, equality of marriage for the same sex union, one choosing one's gender, freedom of using bathroom of one's choice outraged traditional family-oriented minorities and Americans in general. If Joe Biden refuses to divorce himself from Obama, which is unlikely, he will have the same fate as Secretary Clinton's.

All things happen or do not happen for a reason. Christians believe in God: there is nothing like a surprise, an opportunity, or a chance. For a non-believer it may appear so, but for God, it is not. Without God's will nothing happens. God is not surprised by what had happened over the 2016 election and by what did not happen in 2016 or by what will happen on the upcoming 2020 election or beyond. Religiously, there are two simple answers to man's problems. These are: for obeying one receives blessings; for disobeying one receives curses or punishment.

Pertaining to the shocking win of Trump for Presidency, a father once told his children "For my thoughts are not your thoughts, neither are your ways my ways," declares the Lord. "As the heavens are higher than the earth, so are my ways higher than your ways and my thoughts than your thoughts."[232]

There are two main reasons why Secretary Clinton lost the election. These are:

First, Secretary Clinton's supply of what did not interest Americans: though she won the majority vote by 2.87 million more votes than Trump did, he received the majority in the Electoral College. It is not fare for a winner to be determined by the Electoral College. However, it what it is. It was brilliant idea designed so by the Framers for all States to have equal representation in the country. Democrats are advocating to abolish it. When the law does not serve the interests of the Democratic Party, they change it to a way that can benefit them. Yet she is not the only one to have lost an election this way.

There is a total of five U.S. Presidents who lost the majority vote yet were elected by the electoral college. The Electoral College is a body of electors established by the United States Constitution, which forms every four years for the sole purpose of electing the president and vice president of the United States. The Electoral College consists of 538 electors, and an absolute majority of at least 270 electoral votes is required to win an election. Each state gets a minimum of three electoral votes, regardless of population, which gives low population states a disproportionate number of electors per capita.[233]

There are five American party presumptive nominees that took office without winning the popular vote, the majority vote. In other words, they won the Electoral College votes, not the popular vote. These were:

John Quincy Adams (Federalist) lost by 44,804 votes to Andrew Jackson (Democrat) in 1824. John Quincy Adams was elected by the House of Representatives after a tie in the electoral votes. Rutherford B. Hayes (Republican) lost by 264,292 votes to Samuel J. Tilden (Democrat) in 1876. Benjamin Harrison (Republican) lost by 95,713 votes to Grover Cleveland (Democrat) in 1888 George W. Bush (Republican) lost by 543,816 votes to Al Gore (Democrat) in 2000 Donald Trump (Republican) lost by 2,868,686 votes to Hillary Clinton (Democrat) in 2016.[234]

Secretary Clinton's campaigns and her extensive political experiences were not a secret for the American people. She denounced Trump and many of his supporters and capitalism and advocated the expansion of President Obama's policies, LGBT rights, marriage equality and women's rights. Advocating for marriage equality related issues is not favorable for Americans.[235] advocating for marriage equality related issues is not favorable for Americans.

Second, Secretary Clinton's allegiance with President Obama. During the last days of Obama's Presidency, he dumped trash on America. Under the administration of gay-rights, activist President said, "Religious Organizations Could Lose Tax-Exempt Status If Supreme Court Creates Constitutional Right to Same-Sex Marriage.[236]" This is a big threat for the faith group voters.

Chapter Twelve

"There are 86,000 seconds (about 24 hours) in a day. It's up to you to decide what to do with them."

— JIM VALVANO

MEET COREY KERRY

Four years after Trump was declared as the winner, the 45th President of the USA, Hayet spoke with a lady on the street an avid supporter of Clinton. Her name was Corey Kerry, a former college-mate, Corey is as white as a Cherokee rose amid the choicest flowers. Hayet has seen her every day taking a walk in the areas where he lives. Several times he passed by her, appreciating her tenacity to walk rain or shine.

Corey is the only child of her parents. Thus, her parents raised her up like an eagle that stirs up its nest and hovers over its young, that spreads its wings to catch them when they are about to be crushed and carries them aloft. She shared their food, drank from their cup, and even slept in their arms. For her parents, who paid more than she could ever imagine, she can make choices that would make them happy and proud of her.

Corey embraces teachings that come through hypocritical liars, whose consciences are seared as with a hot iron. These liars are not ashamed to hold other people to some higher standards than they hold themselves. They teach the purity of relationship ideals but fail to live up to them and engage in the same behaviors they condemn others for. The more Corey spends time with these hypocrites, the more she compromises with the godly influences that she loved while growing up.

When Corey first came to college, she lived holding her life accountable, a transparent and honest living, giving willful consent for her parents to access her academic reports, attendance, and of course financial records at any time even without her presence. Those days were the safest and best moments in her life, the days that she reported every happening to her parents as her teammates. Later, ungodly students began to taunt her for being *a dependent university student and Mommy's girl*.

Without regard to her accountability and integrity, she first hid a tiny and insignificant piece of information from her loving parents. Then, the mini and insignificant information hiding gave birth to more of the same as well as hiding about where she had been in the evenings and doing the same for all her grades.

At one time, she disallows the communication between her parents and the school. Giving full access of reports to her parents would have kept her accountable and safe, but she became foolish that she made the change.

Her old childhood song,

> O be careful little feet where you go
> O be careful little feet where you go
> There is a Father up above
> And He is looking down in love
> So, be careful little feet where you go.

The song eclipses from her mind. After experiencing friendship with ungodly people and making intentional mistakes, the guilty feeling distances her from the affirming fellowship. Eventually, she admits defeat and continues doing the same thing more often; it finally becomes an insatiable habit.

"Corey, I just want to let you know how I admire you that you take a walk every day. It is something that I would love to do but cannot."

"Thank you," she replies beaming a beam on her face."

She is trying to hide from the wind blowing dust. While clearing the dust, "Are you okay?" Hayet asks.

"I am okay, nothing is worse than Donald Trump becoming the president."

Why are you so indignant and furious spewing hatred that Trump won over election which took place nearly four years ago?

To calm her down, he says, "Is it right for you to be angry as such over an elected leader?"

"Yes, even to the point of death."

"Why?"

She adjusts her Atlanta Hawks hat and lifting her hand, she pauses for a minute or so.

"Why should I not be angry. I am worried for the next generation with a such leader in the White House. Look at what he is doing to our country!"

"It is because he cares for America."

"No, no, no, Trump cares only about himself."

"Tell me who else doesn't care about himself or herself. Your priority is always for yourself." Hayet presses further, "Tell me how much salary he earns by serving as a president?"

"Nada! He has the right to earn money out of the presidency, but he does not. He donates his salary."

"Why would you say then he cares about himself?"

"He doesn't care about my people, the poor."

"Do you own your people?" Hayet states with a smirk. "Why and what are the measurement of caring?"

"He proposed that he would make deep cuts to planned parenthood, safety net programs, affordable housing efforts, food stamps, and Medicaid."

"It affects me and my people. There are so many people that depend on it."

"So, what do you expect Trump to do to the social programs?"

"Keep on expanding."

"For how long and for what age group?"

"For as long as it is needed and to all age groups. Imagine how many people will be homeless because of the cuts, and how many kids will go hungry because of the cuts to food stamps, and how many patients will not be able to see a doctor because of the Medicaid cut? Is that not cruelty?"

"It's not cruelty."

"Why taking food from the mouth of children is not cruelty? You are as cruel as Trump."

"It's not cruelty, it is love."

"How could taking food from kids be love."

"Sometimes it is through painful or terrible experience people get to learn the reality of life which is good for themselves and for their families."

"What do you mean?" she states fretfully. Furthermore, "This is not a good take? Why should people have to suffer unnecessarily? It's not "character-building" or anything, it's just abusive," she cries.

"Every eagle is designed to soar high into the Sky."

"But not in a racist America."

"Why not?"

"Because the system won't let you soar. It is designed to work for certain people."

Hayet is furious. "Stop blaming the system. Will the system break your wing to make you unable to fly?"

"No!"

"To tell you the truth, the system is equally open for the 'certain people' that you refer as it is for the so-called victims of the system. The innovative hard-working take advantage of the open system, while the lazy and their Trojan horse agitators sing as in Mahalia Jackson's,

'Nobody knows the trouble I've seen,
Nobody knows but He knows my sorrow
Yes, nobody knows the trouble I've seen'.

While doing nothing, and they will not be able to discover their potential to soar."

"Wait a minute!" shouted Hayet as if he had a key point to make.

"Bring it on," smiled Corey anticipating hearing more while gesturing with both of her arms.

"Corey, I would say there is a system that would not let you fly with a good intention. If the eagle parents continue to feed their child, it will never be able to learn how to fly and fend for itself. By being unable to fly, there are people who take advantage of your victimhood. You understand?"

Corey did not want to admit there is a system that keeps on advocating and feeding adult eagles which would make them lame.

"No offense, but this is dumb. People are crippled by debt, struggling to survive, and straight up dying because of the terrible system we live in. Why should people have to struggle unnecessarily because the government is not providing basic services to them?" She yelled.

"Really," stated Hayet, "If that's what you believe I cannot change your mind. You cannot keep the birds of sadness from flying over your head, but you can keep them from nesting in your hair. Everyone can get sad from time to time, but you can find ways to overcome that sadness and prevent it from turning into something that keeps you sad forever."[237]

"If a mature eagle is not willing to fly sometimes the parent eagle will be forced to push it out of the nest. I strongly believe that a loving push out of one's comfort zone is a must to transform the weak into a mature person."

"But it is painful."

"I understand the pain of being pushed out of your comfort zone. I have also been pushed out. The pain is temporary, but its results are useful for you and for the generations to come. You remember the old saying, 'No pain no gain.' If one is not willing to face and endure pain, one cannot gain."

"I love the usefulness of pain for me and for the generations to come, but not its pain. For I have walked through the same painful shoes."

"Tell me about that."

"There was a time when people trampled on me, people discouraged me, and people vilified me for no apparent reason. Out of the anguish and pain I cried, O' God, who sinned, my parents or I that I have to go through such painful experience that crushes my bones?"

A wise man who knew my painful experience challenged me "Keep on walking because neither you nor your parents sinned. This happened so that the works of God might be displayed in you. As long as it is day meaning when you can work, when you can fly, you must do the works of God who brought you in to this earth. Night is coming when you cannot work."

'Wow!" replied Corey in amazement.

"It is at that time when one is kicked out of their comfort zone that they discover their ability to soar. If a mature eagle is not willing to fend for itself, then it does not deserve to eat its parents' food. It is at this point the eagle parents push out the mature eagle to fly by itself."

"I cannot believe it. Tell me how and why you advocate for Trump's cuts on social service funding?" she echoes, surprisingly.

"I do not advocate for Trump. I am speaking What is good for all Americans; what and how they should do to help themselves and their families. The Government is not and cannot be the solution for everybody and for everything."

"Listen brother! But it is SUPPOSED TO BE!! That is why so many people are dissatisfied. The government is literally supposed to provide for its people, who invest in their country."

"I am talking about the people who feel and believe that one is inherently deserving of privileges and special treatment from l government provisions," do you see my point, Corey?"

Hayet further explained from his personal experience. "For the people who cannot provide and help themselves, the government should provide not only enough, but more than enough. It is a righteous cause to do so. But for the people who do not want to work government should not. I came as an immigrant refugee to the USA."

"Who was the president at that time? A Democrat or a Republican?"

"It does not matter which party; what matters is that God opened a way for me and my family to come."

"Wow! I have a lot of questions to ask you."

"I would be willing to answer your questions."

"That is a powerful message."

"You know Corey," Hayet retorted a couple of steps backward. "Who thought that Trump would win, all polls were showing that Madam Secretary Clinton was leading up to the last hours of Election Day."

"That is what makes me angrier."

"Well, you have to cool down, learn to accept the reality and prepare yourself for the next election. As vigorous as you are, for not seeing what you hoped for, every vote count and even one vote matters. Did you vote?"

She started to fumble and stammer. "That is a personal thing I am not going to tell you."

You do not look like one who voted, Hayet whispered. "The reason why I brought the question is that, when the media personalities interviewed Secretary Clinton's supporters whether they voted during the election, a scores of them replied they did not vote.

"So, are you telling me that I did not vote?" she retorted angrily.

"It is up to you and you have the right whether to vote or not. What I am telling you is what the journalists reported interviewing Clinton supporters."

"What did the reporters find out?"

"Several of them did not vote."

At this point Corey calmed down. "Did you vote and who did you vote for?" she inquired with a fake smile.

"As you have just stated earlier, it is a personal thing I am not going to answer that question."

Hayet learned that she was not going to accept the reality that the USA has its 45th President Donald Trump. She acted as if we were going to have a presidential election tomorrow.

"To the arrogant the Bible says" Hayet began to explain.

"Are you calling me arrogant?"

"Not really. As a person of faith, I am just telling you what the Bible says about the arrogant hubris."

"What does it say?"

"Boast no more, and to the wicked, 'Do not lift your horns. Do not lift your horns against heaven; do not speak so defiantly. No one from the East or the West or from the desert can elevate themselves. It is God who judges: He brings one down, he exalts another. Leadership is from God."

"Maybe God brought him to punish the country," declared Corey

"Is that a just judgment for a woman of faith?"

"Maybe that is my prejudiced perspective."

"Nobody knows why God brought Trump into the Presidency. It could be for good or for bad. We shall see. All that one could say is that it is God who gives people the leaders." Well, I have to go I am freezing, see you next time," stated Hayet as he walked away from Corey.

Chapter Thirteen

"I'm going to support the policy over the person"

— ISAIAH WASHINGTON, ON LEAVING THE
DEMOCRATIC PARTY

WHO TO ENDORSE AND WHY?

A person has the right to endorse a candidate of his or her choice. If it is so, why such opposition to Trump from the very people who ought to be supportive of him? Whoopi Goldberg and her 'The View' team grilled Dr. Ben Carson, "why did you endorse Donald Trump?" Here is the main part of the interview:

"When I dropped out my first choice went with me. I was going to remain neutral. But then I realized that you know the political establishment was aligning to protect their turf. They do not like the idea people beholding to them who cannot be controlled coming to Washington DC. That was the main reason that they did not like me very much, but I was easier to get rid of than Donald Trump."

"Sir. I hate to ask this question. You have aligned yourself with a man who has bashed women, made countless racist remarks. You are Ben Carson why would you align yourself with that?"

"You know you have to look at the good and the bad. There is no perfect person. But what I think really the worst thing that threatens our nation right now is a political class, a ruling class and they are so threatened by anybody who is not beholding to them. They will do virtually anything to destroy that person."

"This guy, I am sorry is a racist. He is not good for the country. He did not denounce the white supremacist, you are Ben Carson, you are so much better than this."

"I am Ben Carson that is why I am doing this. I look at the big picture. Could I focus only or racial issues? Absolutely. Could I focus only on women's issues? Absolutely. I could look at any little thing and pick anybody per line. But right now, the nature of our country is at stake. We are determining what kind of nation we are going to be. Are we going to be a country formed by the people or formed by the government? This is the choice we are making right now."

"He said stuff about African Americans. He said you have a pathological disease" interjects Joy Behar.

"Well, if it were about me, I would be offended. But it is about America. We must save this nation."

"But he is a liar," questions Joy.

"Tell me a politician who does not tell lies?"

"Abraham Lincoln. I don't know."

"What I have to do is look at who is most likely to oppose the ruling class that is ruining our country? My main interest is to save this country particularly for the next generation. Right now, the programs that have been put forth by both Democrats and Republicans for the last few decades are doing nothing but creating more dependency. We have gone from a can-do nation to what can you do for me nation. It is not a good thing; it is not helping America. Again, the reason that I am endorsing him is because I recognize that we are heading down the same past that we have been on all along.[238]

Who would you rather trust? The liberal, the far-left politicians or Dr. Ben Carson? You have a right to choose. Dr. Carson's interview has influenced Hayet's choice.

For everyone willing to work and to bring change to the existing system, there are oppositions. Nehemiah, the builder had opposition groups who came in different group. Nehemiah's reply to the detractors was, "The God of heaven will give us success. We his servants will start rebuilding, but as for you, you have no share in Jerusalem or any claim or historic right to it."

For any purposeful person it is common to find the enemy within, as what Trump has been facing since his election. While everybody else was working, among the men of Tekoa, their nobles would not put their shoulders to the work under their supervisors. The nobles are the people who control the system, who make their earning and power off the poor.

The liberal media and the Democratic socialist and their instructors have been forcing their ideology in our learning institutions and indoctrinating our children. This is what has been going on in our country for decades, no leader addressed them and got us to the current state we are in. That is what got the least likely candidate, Trump, to get elected.

WHAT DID TRUMP SUPPLY?

Trump the candidate took advantage of the situation when there was a high demand for a leader who would defeat the indirect third term of Obama's Presidency. The demands included addressing and promising to solve illegal immigration issues which had been a problem for decades of years and which no president dared to bring a permanent solution to, for fear of political repercussions. Most American presidents including Clinton, Bush, Obama, and plenty of presidential candidates admitted of the need to build a wall on the Southern border. However, nobody took a real step to implement it.

When it comes to trade - be it with China, Mexico, Canada, and European nations the previous system allowed all other business treaties to benefit more than what the USA was gaining from those trade agreements. When it came to the defense agreement with Japan, Middle Eastern countries, the NATO, the USA was paying more than anybody else. Trump promised to get all members to pay their fair share. Trump advocated that the USA should not be paying other countries' bills.

When it comes to Israel, during the Bill Clinton era, it was noted that the US "Congress passed a law in 1995 mandating the U.S. to move its embassy to Jerusalem, even Clinton a long term an advocate of just such a move before assuming office - successfully pushed for a clause in the legislation that gave the president leverage in determining when the move would actually take place, effectively postponing the move indefinitely."[239]

Prior to Congress passing a law of 1995, in "March 1994, Vice President Al Gore reaffirmed the Clinton administration's position which recognized a united Jerusalem as the capital of Israel." However, three Presidents: Clinton, Bush and Obama would not implement the action. Trump promised he would move the embassy, and nobody believed that the political newcomer would implement that. There was also a high threat of persecution of Christianity and Judaism in the USA by the Obama administration. Trump promised to restore religious freedom.

The open abortion policy that was killing millions of children that Trump promised to reverse was another indignation toward the Democratic leadership. That is not all. On the last days of Obama, America was overwhelmed with homosexuality and lesbianism related bombardments on America that some of the citizens resented. It was at this time that Trump came and promised to reverse all that Obama planted. Let us look now at how and why Secretary Clinton lost to Trump.

WINNERS AND LOSERS OF 2016 ELECTION

It is stated that 2016 election was so unique, because of two unique candidates: Hillary Clinton the political elite who spent her entire life in public service versus Donald Trump, the politically inexperienced businessman.

The lamest presidential election battle in the USA history produced a President Trump, the unlikely candidate to win. Trump, the political novice, emerged as Republican presumptive nominee amidst about twenty-five major political geniuses who are also eloquent speakers and convincing debaters.

Trump was unapologetic for his love for America and Americans. His controversial nationalist campaign motto was "Make America Great Again." The ruthless, unique candidate Trump said what the eloquent politicians would not dare to say for the sake of political correctness. His boldness gave him millions of dollars' worth of free media coverage. Because of his offensive and merciless blunt, disrespectful verbiage on Mexicans, immigrants, Muslims, and women, while few regular voters got offended and refused to vote, yet he garnered voters who never or rarely voted in previous elections.

Here the author would like to point out two sides of Trump's Presidency. One is planned, the other one is opportunistic run and win.

The planned Presidency is that he spoke about running for President in 1999, about 30 years earlier with CNN's Larry King Live than the actual 2016 election.[240] That was the time when CNN was nonpartisan network, cared about the facts serving political party, every religion, every race equally. But no more nowadays. CNN has proved to be a militant wing of far left. Conservative views are not so welcome.

The other point is that one could say that Trump was an opportunist. An opportunist is a person who exploits circumstances to gain immediate advantage rather than being guided by consistent principles or plans.[241] Trump, the businessman knew the mentality of customers, what the consumers need and love, and he supplied. Does he believe on what he promised during the campaigns and after the election? Nobody knows Trump's sincerity and internal convictions, but he is walking a sincere walk.

Americans, immigrants or non-immigrants, Jews, Christians, Muslims, Hindus, Buddhists, and other faith groups are traditionally religious. They have faith in them. Anyone who attacks that unchartered territory, one who fails to provide what faith groups need and love is doomed to be unsuccessful. CNN's Don Lemon, who himself is gay wishing the gay agenda to be a governing factor in American society asked the following question to Rep. Beto O'Rourke, the ultra-extremist:

"Do you think religious institutions like colleges, churches, charities should lose their tax-exempt status if they oppose same-sex marriage?"

"Yes!" O'Rourke replied.[242]

That 'Yes,' became the fastest demise and funeral of his political campaign, RIP.

O'Rourke followed Obama's footsteps. The Obama Administration of which Biden had been part of for eight years was a threat to Religious Organizations. The Obama administration declared that religious leaders who refuse to serve (marry) gay couples Could Lose Tax-Exempt Status If Supreme Court Creates Constitutional Rights to Same-Sex Marriage.[243]

Should a person choose a gay lifestyle it is their choice. The problem comes when they legislate and force everybody to accept that lifestyle as the people of Sodom and Gomorrah did.

LESSONS FROM SODOM AND GOMORRAH

During the days of Sodom and Gomorrah, people were living gay lifestyle. It was legislated legally. Referring to their perversion Jude says, "Sodom and Gomorrah and the surrounding towns gave themselves up to sexual immorality and perversion. They serve as an example of those who suffer the punishment of eternal fire."[244]

The people of Sodom and Gomorrah did not ask or request about legalizing the issue. They forced anyone who came to their jurisdiction to be part of them. This is how it happened:

Two angels arrived at Sodom in the evening, and Lot was sitting in the gateway of the city. When he saw them, he got up to meet them and bowed down with his face to the ground. "My lords," he said, "please turn aside to your servant's house. You can wash your feet and spend the night and then go on your way early in the morning."

"No," they answered, "we will spend the night in the square."

He insisted so strongly that they did go with him and entered his house. He prepared a meal for them, baking bread without yeast, and they ate. Before they had gone to bed, all the men from every part of the city of Sodom—both young and old—surrounded the house. They called to Lot, "Where are the men who came to you tonight? Bring them out to us so that we can have sex with them."

Lot went outside to meet them and shut the door behind him and said, "No, my friends. Do not do this wicked thing. Look, I have two daughters who have never slept with a man. Let me bring them out to you, and you can do what you like with them. But do not do anything to these men, for they have come under the protection of my roof."

The hooligans were not interested on sleeping with women, but me. Thus, "Get out of our way," they replied. "This fellow came here as a foreigner, and now he wants to play the judge! We'll treat you worse than them." They kept bringing pressure on Lot and moved forward to break down the door. But the men inside reached out and pulled Lot back into the house and shut the door.

Then the two angels struck the men who were at the door of the house, young and old, with blindness so that they could not find the door. Eventually, Lot and his family, who were not practicing gay lifestyle were spared by exiting from the city. The Lord rained down burning sulfur on Sodom and Gomorrah—out of the heavens. Thus, he overthrew those cities and the entire plain, destroying all those living in the cities—and the vegetation in the land.[245]

The sin or wrong of Sodom and Gomorrah was homosexuality. In God's eyes, it was wrong at that time, it is still wrong currently no matter whether Congress, Senate, Parliament, or Supreme Court legislates it. Although God encourages believers to respect the law of the land, his Kingdom law supersedes man's law and will judge everyone accordingly!

What you do could be acceptable by the law of the land. However, God's law is the ultimate judge. The same law and judgment apply to all. People know what is right and wrong but choose to do what is wrong and darkness instead of the light.

Jude informs believers, "Though you already know all this, I want to remind you that the Lord at one time delivered His people out of Egypt, but later destroyed those who did not believe. And the angels who did not keep their positions of authority but abandoned their proper dwelling—these He has kept in darkness, bound with everlasting chains for judgment on the great Day."[246] If God did not spare the angels, He will not spare us too.

For years, Americans have been patient and have tolerated the intolerable in the name of tolerance. *Enough is Enough*. The nucleus of America, what made America the greatest nation, the Church, God, family, and country are under barrages of attack. If the attacks were to improve the love for faith, family, and country, one could tolerate. But all the internal and external attacks are on these fundamental values of America.

The more one tolerates the intolerants the more out of control it gets. *Enough is enough!* Rise up, Church, God, country, and family loving Americans and fight for your rights! If one is not willing to stand up, soon the land of the free and the home of the brave will have the fate of European Christians, spiritually inefficient. The EU nations have good as well as bad leadership not friendly to religious institutions.

President Obama has been the most liberal Trojan horse of the European Union thane serving the American people. The only way the EU or other nations bring America to their level where morality, God, and family have no say is through their Trojan horses.

> The more one tolerates the intolerants the more out of control it gets.

For example, when Obama started the war on Libya, there was no immediate threat directed to the USA. He consulted the EU and the Arab Union. He did not consult his counterpart decision makers in the USA; the Senate and the House of Representatives who is responsible to lead. The Democratic Socialist Trojan hubris will continue using threats and intimidation, shall not rest until people surrender their God given unalienable freedom, get silenced, defaced beyond recognition. This is what Jennifer Rubin said, "Washington Post columnist warns of need to 'burn down the Republican Party' to wipe out Trump supporters."[247] This is not about the Republican Party, which Hayet cares less. Both parties have contributed to the state we are now. It is less about the existence of the American republic.

Rubin further states, 'burn down the Republican Party' in the hope of extinguishing any trace of the enthusiasm for President Trump. Not only does Trump have to lose in 2020, but also there must be a purging of "survivors" who still support him. It is not only that Trump has to lose, but also that all his enablers must lose. We must collectively burn down the Republican Party. We must level them because if there are survivors -- if there are people who weather this storm, they will do it again,[248] She advocates.

This is the verdict on the conservatives if one does not fight. The people who supported Trump did not and still do not like his character. What people hated on the 2016 election was Obama's third term by extension. The same applies for the 2020 election the coming of Obama's failed policy behind Biden. Yet Trump's work is good for the country. It is such supporters who think what is good for the USA that are being targeted his and must be leveled. To level means to flatten and make even surface without slopes or bumps.

To defend America and American values one needs to turn their heart to God the healer! In regards to returning, God spoke to Jeremiah, "If you repent, I will restore you that you may serve me; if you utter worthy, not worthless, words, you will be my spokesman. Let this people turn to you, but you must not turn to them."[249]

People have come from every nation, faith, and tribe of the earth to the USA loving American's value of individual freedom. America should lead the way.

As it has been stated earlier, O'Rourke's belief is not new. On July 21, 2014, President Barack Obama amended two earlier executive orders to extend protection against discrimination in hiring and employment to additional classes. It prohibited discrimination in the civilian federal workforce based on gender identity and in hiring by federal contractors based on both sexual orientation and gender identity.[250]

This executive order hinders faith-based contractors from doing their religious duty to the Americans. Toward the end of his Presidency Obama introduced guidelines on how schools should handle transgender students and how students should be allowed to use bathroom of their choice. There have been no visible problems of such type in schools. However, with the intrusions of Obama's policy came floods of troubles in schools. Obama's policy and Clinton's promise to uphold his legacy became harmful to her political fate.

On the other hand, Trump promised the American people that he would protect religious groups and would reverse Obama's executive orders that targeted faith-based institutions.

THE CANDIDATE VERSUS THE PERSON

The candidate versus the person discusses two personalities distinctly. This comparison is between two things within a person. Example, God loves a sinner (the person) but hates a sin (done by the sinner). James describes a sin as if anyone knows the good, they ought to do and doesn't do it, it is sin for them.[251]

Any conservative organization that does not support gay lifestyle is deemed by the Livid infected as a hate group. What the conservatives hate is the deed not the person.

On June 12, 2016, a terrorist attacked Pulse gay nightclub in Orlando, Florida that killed and injured about sixty people. Chick-fill-A, which is deemed as gay unfriendly restaurant, opened their door on SUNDAY, they were supposed clos, but kept on serving meals for free for the affected people. Which liberal restaurant offered such services? Not Any! Chick-fill-A as an organization separates the gay person from the gay practice. That is why they volunteered to serve on their off day.

It is possible to not like the candidate but like the person or vice versa. To be fair, the author was so frustrated with how Democrats and Republicans on pre-election as well as post-election treated the eight years of President Barack Obama's presidency. Trump Vulture has treated Trump much worse than any other president since he won the election, and they have not relented.

Obama had his own OV (Obama Vulture or OVCNN) Democrat opponents, mainly Hillary Clinton and several Republicans alike used his father's or his stepfather's religion (Islam), his association with people his opponents do not like, and being of mixed race.

As a conservative Christian, there are several issues that the author disagrees about with Obama. The same extreme liberal issues are the cause for Secretary Clinton's loss. However, there are times when Obama ought to be defended from the Democratic and Republican OVCNN.

Here comes the question now. There are so many people who hate Trump the person and the candidate as they did Hillary the person and the candidate. Go and ask the protesters in Portland or other places, 'What is it that you hate Trump the person or the President? What did he do to you personally?'

They cannot give a sensible answer. By answering louder in a destructive way, they think they got the answer, but they know nothing. The main reason Michael Moore is being discussed in this section is that he has a role to play for the unrealistic stereotypical prejudices that resulted in some unrest in the USA.

Since his prediction that Trump may quit and not complete his term, did not come to fulfillment, he published "The Michael Moore Easy-to-Follow 10-Point Plan to Stop Trump" to stop Trump from completing his four years term. In the first few days of Trump's Presidency, people have seen that multiple Republican lawmakers have grown weary of holding local town hall meetings with their constituents.[252]

Every meeting gets stormed by angry hecklers, the kind of people Moore encourages to form a 'rapid response team.' They storm and clog local offices or meetings that they have no business with. On his Ten-point plan he is happy to see, not the rebuilding of America, which has been in ruin for decades at the hands of Democratic and Republican establishments, but the tearing down of the USA. He proudly states that, "Tens of thousands of citizens across the country have stormed Congressional District Offices and Town Hall Meetings to express their rage at the Trump agenda."

Let us face it. What is Trump's agenda? As for the author, Trump's agenda is to fulfill what other politicians voted for did not fulfill! To bring them back jobs that have gone out of the USA due to high taxes and government regulations.

Most of the protesters against Trump are organized under Moore's ten-point plan and reports show some of them are paid a decent amount of money per hour. Whereas Trump supporters are individual collections.

Chapter Fourteen

"Martha, Martha," the Lord answered, "you are worried and upset about many things, but few things are needed—or indeed only one. Mary has chosen what is better, and it will not be taken away from her."

— THE BIBLE

PROTEST IN THE USA

While taking a walk in the neighborhood street early morning, the birds chirping from among the pine trees, Hayet got to meet Corey in early July. She feels good about her body and keeps in shape. She is power walking, faster than she normally would in her day-to-day activities.

"Hi Corey, how have you been doing?" called out Hayet.

"I am so tired," she replied while cracking her knuckles.

"So am I. I slept late last night and woke up early this morning. I am working on a new book project. Did you work yesterday?"

"No! We have not been working since late March to avoid the Corona virus from spreading or from contracting Covid-19." *If you have not been working, then what made you so tired?* Hayet thought.

"Yesterday, I came home late. I have been protesting every day for the past thirty plus consecutive days going downtown Atlanta."

"Really!" stated Hayet distancing himself six feet plus from Corey.

"Indeed. You can join us today if you want. It is easy," she spoke.

"I do not join a protest for or against anybody, I pray," he replied.

"I also do pray and act."

"When are you going to end the protest?"

"As long as it takes. No justice no peace."

"Is it fair to protest against injustice by another injustice? I cannot afford to protest every day. I have to work."

Downtown Atlanta is so far and hectic. Hayet does not like going there unless he must. "Anyway, Corey. So, you drive about 40 minutes one way to go to protest and spend hours there every day managing all the heavy traffic?"

"Indeed! The traffic is not that bad, because people are not driving due to Covid-19."

"So, it is okay not to go to work to avoid spreading or contracting Covid-19. But it is okay to go to protest every day."

"Y-e-s!"

"I don't get it. It does not make sense. You are exposing yourself to coronavirus."

"May be for you! But for me it makes sense. I should no longer prioritize my personal safety from the coronavirus. The risk of catching Covid-19 is huge, for me and for my family, however the protests are worth it."

"I am not talking about you! I am talking about the droves of people that come to protest, at the end of the day each go home potentially spreading ten to twenty times more people than the protesters exposed to the virus. You are protesting over the death of one person which started because of a $20-dollar fake bill."

"I don't think the fake money was the real reason. And even if it were true, George Floyd would not have deserved to die for that. The point is, this is not the first or last time. There have been hundreds of cases like this and nothing has changed."

"I mean protesting one in every 1,000 black men that could die at the hands of unjust police officers while infecting tens of thousands is not proportionate."

"You do not understand how dire things are for black men."

"Well, it is your choice. Remember that I am also a black man and have black children and am related to many black families."

"Okay then, moving on from that. Tell me about your book project. What is the title of your book?"

"There could be a change or modification to the title. However, as of today, it is: *Enough is Enough! Trojan Horses and a Dangerous Hubris Exposed.*"

"O' my gosh! Don't tell me that you support Trump. He hates people like you. He will send you back to Africa."

"I am not afraid of Trump. What I am afraid of is, the Trojan handlers behind Democratic Party. Besides, it is the USA that I support."

"Do you have a sponsor for that?"

Hayet is so furious and does not know how to respond. Finally, "That is a dishonorable question from an educated person such as you." Furthermore, "You know that this is not my first book project. Nobody sponsored me for my past projects nor would I want a sponsor for my current."

"Really!" interjected Corey.

"Perhaps you should tell me if you have a sponsor to protest. I do not go and cannot afford to protest every day for more than thirty days. Even when Governor Brian Kemp ordered shelter-in place, I did not take off day. People who hate Trump follow a group or crowd mentality. I am just an individual who thinks about what is good for the USA."

"How can you prove to me that you are not for Trump?"

"I confess my sins to God. I do not have to confess to you. During the 2016 election, I did not vote for either presumptive nominee. Nobody influenced, and nobody told me not to vote. It was out of my personal conviction. I did not like the Clinton presidential candidate. I also did not like the person and the candidate Trump. Over the past four years, Trump has proved his credibility."

To prove his credibility, Jesus said about himself referring to his haters, "Do not believe me unless I do the works of my Father. But if I do them, even though you do not believe me, believe the works."

"So, what is the point?"

"I did not believe and did not trust Trump. However, after seeing his works, Trump Presidency is good for America and Americans, and he deserves a second term."

"You are sick, brother," concluded Corey.

"How?"

"You do not know who Trump is and what he does."

"I knew who Trump was form his past life and did not trust he could run as a conservative. That is why I did not vote. But now having read his conservative agenda, I will vote for the conservative values he stands for."

Shortly after Secretary Clinton lost election to Trump, on a CNN panel discussion Van Jones had passionate discussion over the victory of Donald Trump defeating the political elites, all that Trump stands for as a white lash against African American President.

This was a rebellion against the elites — true. It was a complete reinvention of politics and polls — it is true. But it was also something else. We've talked about everything but race tonight," he said. "This was a white-lash against a changing country. It was a white lash against a Black President, in part, and that is where the pain comes.

What Jones was not aware of is that people were against the idea that came with President Obama. Americans were not interested. Secretary Clinton promised to fulfill Obama's legacy, which the American electorate were not in favor. Next time when Trump wins 2020, who knows that Van Jones might say that this is a black lash.

IS THERE SYSTEMIC RACISM IN THE USA IN 2020?

To answer the question, it depends on which side to look at. That is from the victim, the oppressor, or the neutral fair personal judgment perspectives. Who determines the prevalence of systemic racism? First, it is important to look at the meaning of the word 'systemic racism.' Systemic racism has many ways of implementing it on voting, employment, property ownership, segregation in schools, etc. The main part is, it is a government protected system, legalized, institutionalized discrimination based on race.[253] In a country of systemic racism victims have no right to challenge the system that allowed the systemic racism.

So, do we have systemic racism in the USA supported by the government? Not really. We have racist people no matter which party, but not a systemic racism. Let us look at one example of systemic racism.

For example, in 1975, Biden made an amendment against school integration to segregate schools changing the previous Supreme Court ruling to desegregation. It was a move that followed the wishes of many of Biden's white Democratic constituents in Delaware. Biden's segregation ruling by the court was upheld. That is a systemic racism, reversing a case that ended legal school segregation 21 years earlier. He led the charge on an issue that kept black students away from the classrooms of white students.[254] That was systemic racism in education, because the government upheld Biden's segregation advocacy.

Over the wake of George Floyd's death, people have heard the word systemic racism like no other. The worst part of it is that systemic racism has been vocalized by the disobedient to authority; easily swayed, disrespectful, unrooted, emotional Trojan horses. White young women who speak against systemic racism appear to be a considerable number.

Abraham Lincoln hated slavery and considered it immoral. In 1862 he issued the Emancipation Proclamation. Enslaved people shall be henceforward forever free. He believed that, if the Negro is a man, why then while my ancient faith teaches me that `all men are created equal;' that there can be no moral right in connection with one man's making a slave of another?[255] One could also say that he didn't care about black people being enslaved. He only ended slavery in the states from the Confederacy because he believed it would lessen their economic power. He allowed slavery to be legal in states in the Union.

About sixty years after the Emancipation Proclamation, a heartless Democrat under the Jim Crow law institutionalized systemic racism on economic, educational, and social disadvantages for African Americans living in the South. Jim Crow laws and Jim Crow state constitutional provisions mandated the segregation of public schools, public places, and public transportation; and the segregation of restrooms, restaurants, and drinking fountains between white people and blacks. The U.S. military was already segregated. President Woodrow Wilson, a Southern Democrat initiated the segregation of federal workplaces in 1913.[256]

In 2020, there is no officially government supported law that favors one over the other race or gender. Since there is equal protection act for all American, there is undeclared racism but no systemic racism as some claim that it exists. What currently exists is compartmentalization of humanity, which is a modern form of slavery. To compartmentalize or compartmentalizing is basically an internal process of putting your feelings toward someone, or some experience, in a metaphorical box, and putting them on a shelf in the back of your mind to be forgotten, or stirred up when something reminds you that they're there.[257]

Compartmentalization is a subconscious psychological defense mechanism used to avoid cognitive dissonance, or the mental discomfort and anxiety caused by a person's having conflicting values, cognitions, emotions, beliefs, within themselves.[258] This is what has been happening in the USA for the past 50 years.

Although black Americans are as free to be successful like white people, the compartmentalization and marginalization belief holds them hostage from rising out of their current predicament. The worst thing one could do is, to make one believe that one is this or that while one is not. For example, making a person believe that are marginalized, poor, their fate is decided by others, making them believe they have no free choice, they cannot arise beyond the set limitations, making them believe that white police are out there to kill black men.

The controllers also make the victims believe if they do not vote for a certain party candidate they are doomed. This is the worst form of slavery, as what Kanye West would call it 'voluntarily mentally enslaved by choice, we cannot be mentally imprisoned for another 400 years' during an appearance on entertainment site TMZ.[259] It is hard to make a person with compartmentalized mind believe that one can do better than they are.

It is hard to make a person with compartmentalized mind

A matured adult elephant can be tied by a single childhood rope or chain for the rest of life. The elephants used to compartmentalization restrict themselves that they cannot move beyond the rope or the chain. They are not aware that they have strength, that they are the world's strongest animals that they can lift staggering weights of up to about 300 Kg (=660 Lbs.)[260] However, a compartmentalized elephant, person, or bird does not believe that they can go beyond the parameters that they are designed to stay in. One could say that systemic racism existing today is subjective. Paul once said, "To the pure, all things are pure, but to those who are corrupted and do not believe, nothing is pure. In fact, both their minds and consciences are corrupted."[261]

IS DONALD TRUMP A FASCIST?

Ronald Regan has once said, "If fascism ever comes to America, it will come in the name of liberalism." Before answering the question, one needs to know who is a fascist? First it is imperative to look at the characteristics of fascism before concluding. The Italian term fascismo is derived from fascio meaning "a bundle of sticks", ultimately from the Latin word fasces. This was the name given to political organizations in Italy known as fasci, groups like guilds or syndicates

Originally, Fascism is a form of far-right, authoritarian ultra-nationalism characterized by dictatorial power, forcible suppression of opposition as well as strong regimentation of society and of the economy which came to prominence in early 20th-century Europe. In 1917—in which Bolshevik Communists led by Vladimir Lenin seized power in Russia—greatly influenced the development of fascism. [262] Now, do we have a dictatorial power in the USA? Absolutely, not! Do we have forcible suppression, intimidation, shaming of opposition? Absolutely, yes! It is the antifa, BLM and other Fifth column henchmen that are acting fascists. The best way to avoid being called a fascist is be the first to refer other people fascists.

Fascist concepts include: the creation of a nationalist dictatorship to regulate economic structure and to transform social relations within a modern, self-determined culture, and the expansion of the nation into an empire; and a political aesthetic of romantic symbolism, mass mobilization, a positive view of violence, and promotion of masculinity, youth, and charismatic authoritarian leadership.[263]

Most scholars place fascism on the far right of the political spectrum. Such scholarship focuses on its social conservatism and its authoritarian means of opposing egalitarianism. However, Roderick Stackelberg places fascism—including Nazism, which he says is "a radical variant of fascism"—on the political right by explaining: "The more a person deems absolute equality among all people to be a desirable condition, the further left he or she will be on the ideological spectrum.[264]

One American party exhibits the characteristics of fascism while the other does not. Thus, a form of political behavior marked by obsessive preoccupation with community decline, humiliation, or victimhood and by compensatory cults of unity, energy, and purity, in which a mass-based party of committed nationalist militants, working in uneasy but effective collaboration with traditional elites, abandons democratic liberties and pursues with redemptive violence and without ethical or legal restraints goals of internal cleansing and external expansion.[265]

Fascism is commonly associated with Italian and German Nazi regime that came to power after the First World War. Which party members worked and invited Hitler's team? It is the Democrats.

One author asked some experts of fascism whether Donald Trump is a fascist. Roger Griffin asserts, Trump does not qualify to be a fascist. Because He does not want to overthrow the existing democratic system. He does not want to scrap the Constitution. He does not romanticize violence itself as a vital cleansing agent of society. He further states, "You can be a total xenophobic racist male chauvinist bastard and still not be a fascist." The experts said that fascism supports the revolutionary overthrow — ideally through violence — of the state's entire system of government as a necessary characteristic of it.[266]

Fascism expert Robert Paxton defines fascism as a form of political behavior marked by obsessive preoccupation with community decline, humiliation, or victimhood and by compensatory cults of unity, energy, and purity, in which a mass-based party of committed nationalist militants, working in uneasy but effective collaboration with traditional elites, abandons democratic liberties and pursues with redemptive violence and without ethical or legal restraints goals of internal cleansing and external expansion

Which American party exhibits such behavior? Paxton further clarifies; fascists were in favor of totally overthrowing the existing constitution, which was usually democratic and perceived as weak. This was wildly popular. We are not in that position today.[267]

The President of Greater NY BLMS, Hawk Newsome said if change does not happen, "If this country doesn't give us what we want, then we will burn down this system and replace it."[268] on Martha MacCallum interview.

This is real fascism.

Expert Stanley Payne as well notes that Trump lacks a connection to the pro-violence philosophy at the heart of fascism. That is not all, that violence is good for you, that it is the sort of thing that makes you a vital, alive, dedicated person, that it creates commitment. You make violence not just a political strategy but also a philosophical principle. That's unique to fascism.[269]

Thus, Trump cannot be called a fascist. Further, the experts say, Trump's views on violence simply do not follow in that tradition. "Trump is inciting prejudice, words do have consequences," Matthew Feldman says. "But that doesn't mean he's a fascist."[270]

At the conclusion of the expert's discussion, if Donald Trump is not a fascist, what is he? They ask. They came up with their conclusion that Donald Trump is a right-wing populist.[271]

The word populist refers to a person, especially a politician, who strives to appeal to ordinary people who feel that their concerns are disregarded by established elite groups.[272]

Populist may probably describe Donald Trump rather than fascist.

DEMOCRATIC PARTY AND BLACK PEOPLE'S VOTE

For decades, the majority of African Americans and the minorities have been Democrat voters and they remain poor. Think again. Enough is ENOUGH! This is the very party that openly discriminated black from voting in the America, with federal troops no longer present to protect the rights of black citizens, white supremacy quickly returned to the old Confederate States. Black voting fell off sharply in most areas because of threats by white employers and violence from the Ku Klux Klan, a ruthless secret organization bent on preserving white supremacy at all costs.[273] "Representative Elijah Cummings incorrectly stated Democrats were responsible for giving black people the right to vote during his 2016 Democratic National Convention."[274]

One-time Virginia Gov. Ralph Northam (D) acknowledged apologized appearing in a "clearly racist and offensive" photograph in his 1984 medical school yearbook that shows a man in blackface and another in a Ku Klux Klan robe.[275]

The truth is that, when Republicans were in favor of integration, Democrats were against it. In fact, it is during a Republican Presidency of Ulysses Grant that the US had the 15th Amendment. The U.S. Constitution amendment granted African American men the right to vote by declaring that the "right of citizens of the United States to vote shall not be denied or abridged by the United States or by any state on account of race, color, or previous condition of servitude.[276] The statue of the very President Ulysses, who fought and allowed blacks to vote was toppled in San Francisco by the angry Trojan horses' rioters!

It is sad that the minority and the black voters have not been able to identify their real enemy. For generations, it has been perceived that the Democratic Party is a champion party for black people and minorities, while Republican Party is black and minority unfriendly. Some have labelled Trump as heartless, does not care for the poor, systemic racist, white supremacist, KKK friendly, Nazi or Hitler friendly, and that the Republican Party that puts blacks in prison, forced sterilization, making people unable to have children in prison.

The truth is that the Democratic Party is the one responsible for millions of atrocities on blacks in the past and today. It is sad that Minorities and Blacks have not been able to see the reality, we are still slaves and subservient of the Democratic Party. This must be stopped. It is time to declare, "let my people go." This requires a radical person whose eyes are open to see what the blind subservient cannot see. The point Joe Biden stated on an interview 'if you're black and don't vote for me, you're not black' proves that point.

The most dangerous party for black minorities and the humanity in general is the Democratic Party! It has its own problems and those should not be overlooked, but the Republican Party is not the champion party for black people or minorities either, especially in recent years.

The Democratic leadership does speak the language of love and care but before one knows, it is gone. This refers to the bad Democrat leadership not the good and sincerely caring ones. The Trump Republican Party appears to be rude and rigid, although painful, they tell you what you need to hear not want you want to hear. Hearing what you do not want to hear gives you the opportunity to identify your enemy then you can choose either fightback or run away from what threatens your existence "The white conservatives aren't friends of the Negro either, but they at least don't try to hide it," tells Malcom X.[277]

As for the Democratic Party, they tell you what you want to hear in a sweet talk yet kill you - before you realize that you are being killed in slow motion. It is like a frog in slowly boiling water! The evidence is that if one puts a frog in boiling water, it will jump out right away. However, if it is set in water that is gradually heated, it will not realize the danger until death.

AMERICAN BLACKS THE FREEST PEOPLE IN THE WORLD

During Congressman John Lewis' funeral eulogy speech, Dr. Alveda King slammed Obama for his comparison of today's politics with that of Dr. Martin Luther King's time when segregation was still on the books and legal system and voting for blacks was not allowed. The speech was about division, not reconciliation.[278] President Obama's speech bringing postal service into the war front appears to be a behavior of crying wolf, calling for help when it is not needed, with the effect that one is not believed when one really does need help.[279]

Hayet has been working on elections for years counting mail in ballots and other duties related to elections. The possibility of cheating an election is unlikely. Every ballot is counted. However, there are some that get rejected for not doing the right way. Hayet believes it is wrong election procedure to count votes after the election day. It will fracture America. Voters should not be left in limbo for days or weeks after the election. That is how the dictators do elections as *"Mehegosee Asha"* meaning, making the fool happy showing voters fake voting, what is not real.

The crying Hillary Clinton has warned that President Donald Trump should not be allowed to steal the election. Trump did not steal the past election, nor will he steal the upcoming one. In fact, it is she who stole the election from Bernie in cooperation. The Democrats are known for that, they keep on changing rules believing it would benefit them. However, whatever they make up hurts them instead.

On the first 2020 Biden and Trump debate, Vice President Biden was asked about the Green New Deal. He said, "I don't support the Green, New Deal." Then later, when thy told him how expensive it is, he said, "The Green New Deal will pay for itself." So, what Biden does not support will pay for itself. With the conservatives, they tell you the answer whether you like it or not. With the liberals, yes could be no, and no could be yes and they do not feel ashamed for changing their word.

The author believes that Obama knows that VP Biden is not going to beat Trump. He is using every opportunity to cry from his inner frustration for not doing what he could have done and should have done yet did not do for the black people. In voting just as in all rules of life, there is a guideline for eligibility. The current voting rules are the same as we had during the eight years of Obama administration and beyond.

"I don't support the Green, New Deal."
"The Green New Deal will pay for itself."
Joe Biden

During the RNC 2020 speech, referring to the do-nothing Democrats and Republicans, Ivanka Trump said, "I've seen in Washington it's easy for politicians to survive if they silence their convictions and skip the hard fights. I couldn't believe so many politicians prefer to complain about a problem rather than fix it. I was shocked to see people leave major challenges unsolved so they can blame the other side, campaign on the same issue in the next election. How long are we going to get fooled by politicians that campaign for the same issue every year?" It is time to say *enough is enough*.

Dr. Voddie Baucham, Dean of Theology at African Christian University and former Pastor from California, believes today's social justice and anti-racism movements are venomous ideologies drenched in Marxist critical theory, which aim to redistribute justice to certain societal groups with no consideration for the individual. He argues that the left's narrative that Black Americans are the most oppressed than Black People in the world is not true,[280] which is advocated by Fifth column operatives.

The author is a black person, a refugee, and an immigrant. If he is willing to put effort and stay out of trouble, he can be whatever he would want to be and achieve whatever he would want to achieve. He does not deny the existence of racism and favoritism. However, he believes God is greater and bigger than racists, fascists, misogynists, and all other powers of darkness. What God has for him before the creation of the world, nobody can hinder, slow, or block it. It all depends on the individual.

Job of the Bible who saw God's hand in his life witnessed, "I know that you can do anything, and no one can stop you."[281]

When Dr. Baucham speaks from the perspective of where America was and where America is with race relations the uninformed people tend to think, he just does not have empathy, compassion, and does not understand how bad it is. He was born and grew up in drug and gang-infested, South Central L.A., raised by a single, teenage Buddhist mother.[282]

He is an American, an expat in a foreign country, who has been to dozens of countries in the world. He knows two things: One, Black People in America are the freest and most prosperous Black People in the World. Period. And the second thing is this: people outside of America just think that we are the most oppressed people in the world. People think that incidents like that of George Floyd are happening every day. He speaks of how it sickens and saddens him about the reputation Black People have, that somehow they are weak and impotent, and that they can't do or be anything unless White People do it for them, which he thinks is a racist idea.[283]

In line with Dr. Baucham, Ayaan Hirsi Ali, former Somali refugee, MP in the Netherlands speaks what it means to move to the USA abandoning her MP privileges. She speaks, like most immigrants, I came with confidence that in America I would be judged on my merits rather than based on racial or sexual prejudice.[284]

As a person who lived and experienced firsthand real racism in Africa, in Saudi Arabia and in Europe, she says, America is the best place on the planet to be black, female, gay, trans or what have you. We have our problems, and we need to address those. But our society and our systems are far from racist. We know that there is almost no difference in the unemployment rate for foreign-born and native-born workers—unlike in the European Union.[285] There are so many improvements needed to be done. We can advocate for more changes in America while acknowledging that it is better here than in other places.

Ms. Ali believes Americans were renowned for their can-do, problem-solving attitude. Americans traditionally solved problems locally, sitting together in town halls and voluntary associations. Some of that spirit still exists, even if we now must meet on Zoom. But the old question— "How can we figure this out?"—is threatened with replacement by "Why can't the government figure this out for us?"[286]

Dr. Baucham emphasized how Black Americans are some of the strongest people in the history of the world. We overcame slavery, and now we're bowing and scraping like we need someone to do something for us," he added. "Our individuality is at stake. Our self-pride is at stake. And our trust in God as the answer and solution to our problems is at stake."[287]

Chapter Fifteen

"I only cite these things to show you that in America the history of the white liberal has been nothing but a series of trickery designed to make Negros think that the white liberal was going to solve our problems. Our problems will never be solved by the white man. The only way that our problem will be solved is when the black man wakes up, clean himself up, stand on his own feet and stop begging the white man, and takes immediate steps to do for ourselves the things that we have been waiting on the white man to do for us. Once we do for self then we will be able to solve our own problems."

— MALCOM X

FIND THE PROBLEM AND WORK TO FIX IT

To be able to find a solution for any existing challenge, one ought to find the problem and work to fix it. Or else it would be insanity. Insanity is said to be doing the same thing all over again and expecting different result. One of the existing problems in America is fatherlessness. According to the 1938 Encyclopedia of Social Sciences, that year only 11 percent of black children were born to unwed mothers. As late as 1950, female-heads of households constituted only 18 percent of the black population. Today it is close to 70 percent. In much earlier times, during the late 1800s, there were only slight differences between the black family structure and those of other ethnic groups. Currently, the US Welfare System has encouraged young women to have children out of wedlock.[288]

A friend from Minnesota, referring to the area where George Floyd died said, Minnesota is the most generous Welfare State in the country. That is why people flood to Minnesota from other states. The state encourages single motherhood by giving incentives.

A woman gets more financial help and housing accommodation from government by divorcing her husband. Thus, a woman does not need a man. That is a feminist spirit. All a woman needs, is the government to substitute a father or a husband. The time she needs a man to satisfy her sexual need, she can get any one from the street, get pregnant again, get more money per child, the cycle continues. There are more fatherless children in those areas than anywhere in the US.

President Obama on one Father's Day message stated:

You and I know how true this is in the African American community. We know that more than half of all black children live in single-parent households, a number that has doubled – since we were children. We know the statistics – that children who grow up without a father are five times more likely to live in poverty and commit crimes; nine times more likely to drop out of schools and twenty times more likely to end up in prison. They are more likely to have behavioral problems, or run away from home, or become teenage parents themselves. And the foundations of our community are weaker because of it. How many times in the last year has this city lost a child at the hands of another child?"[289]

Jason Riley, an author, who works on Wall Street Journal editorial page states, "My beef with the black left is that they want to keep the focus on what government or Washington or politicians or white people in general can do for blacks, instead of what blacks can do for themselves."[290] The help might be with good intention, but it really does not help one to be successful. In his book Stop Helping Us: How Liberals Make It Harder for Blacks to succeed, tells how the Welfare System is a bondage for the black people.

Another problem for the black people is a group that calls themselves white liberals. Van Jones would call white liberal Secretary Clinton supporters are far much worse than KKK, they have no concern for the wellbeing of the black people.

During analysis on racial tension he said,

"It's not the racist white person who is in the Ku Klux Klan that we have to worry about. It's the white, liberal Hillary Clinton supporter walking her dog in Central Park who would tell you right now, 'Oh I don't see race, race is no big deal to me, I see all people the same, I give to charities,' but the minute she sees a black man who she does not respect, or who she has a slight thought against, she weaponized race like she had been trained by the Aryan Nation."[291]

If the Negro wasn't taken, tricked, or deceived by the white liberal, then Negros would get together and solve our own problems.
Malcolm X

In the same solidarity, Malcom X has identified it exclusively, "The worst enemy that the Negro is this white man that runs around here drooling at the mouth professing to love Negros and calling himself a liberal, and it is following these white liberals that has perpetuated problems that Negros have. If the Negro wasn't taken, tricked, or deceived by the white liberal, then Negros would get together and solve our own problems. I only cite these things to show you that in America, the history of the white liberal has been nothing, but a series of trickery designed to make Negros think that the white liberal was going to solve our problems. Our problems will never be solved by the white man."[292]

Malcolm X was right about the black people identifying our problems and finding solutions to our own problems. The most devastating problems that black people face today have absolutely nothing to do with our history of slavery and discrimination. The white liberals claim as if it is so. Even the people who when through the horrendous experience of slavery would not describe it the way these warmongers do.

Chief problem of the Black People is the breakdown of the black family, wherein 75 percent of blacks are born to single, often young, mothers. In some cities and neighborhoods, the percentage of out-of-wedlock births is over 80 percent. Actually, "breakdown" is the wrong term; the black family doesn't form in the first place. This phenomenon is entirely new among many blacks.[293]

Liberals have no real concern for others. Their actions speak louder than words. Letting a living and breathing child to die as propagated by Margaret Sanger and continuously being practiced by abortionists shows how inhumane they are. If they do not care for a helpless newly born child, the author does not expect any mercy from such people.

To bring solution to the problem we must let God be involved. The main problem in America and the World is a "sin problem." When people decide to deal with the sin problem, then the land gets healed and becomes a blessing to its inhabitants. If not, the land keeps on devouring its inhabitants. An American citizen killing other Americans, destroying American properties. This is the work of leviathan spirit coming in different names of organizations professing to care for human beings but working hard to destabilize the American republic. *Enough is Enough!*

Now, the question is who would you rather trust? A white liberal or Van Jones and Malcolm X?

SOLUTION FOR PEOPLE OF COLORS' PROBLEMS

The solution for black lives will never come from Democrats, who claim government can solve it all, nor from Republicans who call for individual responsibility. King David faced multiple near-death instances: from the paws of a lion and bear. Most of all, several times from the hand of King Saul, who deeply hated him. He lifted his eyes and hope to the mountains— (Democrats/Republicans) and he could not get help. After a season he concluded, "Cursed is the one who trusts in a man, who draws strength from mere flesh and whose heart turns away from the Lord." It took David a season to figure out that his help would not come from mere man (Democrats or Republicans), but from the Lord, the Maker of heaven and earth.

There was a great famine when Samaria was besieged. The siege lasted so long that a donkey's head was sold for eighty shekels of silver (about $24), and a quarter of a cab of seed pods for five shekels (about $1.5).

As the king of Israel was passing by on the wall, a woman cried to him, "Help me, my lord the king!"

The king replied, "If the Lord does not help you, where can I get help for you? From the threshing floor? From the winepress?"[294]

The same applies to the problem of the Black People. The solution does not come from a career politician or from businessman, but from the Lord. Demonstrating millions of times from being agitated by Livid-20 Trojan handlers has not brought and will not bring any solution either. At least the praying conservatives who prayed and helped the blacks to gain all the rights that we have can be trusted to help a little, but not the liberals who care about their kingdom not God's kingdom.

In the past, help for the Black People came in from the hand of the Lord through Christian abolitionists. Even today, Christians have a key role to play in the face of the white liberals that claim to care but do not show real care. Our guiding principle should be the God given knowledge of differentiating wrong from right. To solve the existing problem let us begin having peace with God and ourselves.

Referencing to the Trojan horses riding behind BLMS movement Ms. Ali states, "I have no objection to the statement "black lives matter." But the movement that uses that name has a sinister hostility to serious, fact-driven discussion of the problem it purports to care about. There will be no resolution of America's many social problems if free thought and free speech are no longer upheld in our public sphere. Without them, honest deliberation, mutual learning, and the American problem-solving ethic are dead."[295]

Joseph had some related experience of trusting in man which did not bring any fruit. One time he interpreted his fellow inmates' dreams. He told the one who got released, "When all goes well with you, please remember me, and show me kindness; mention me to Pharaoh and get me out of this prison. I was forcibly carried off from the land of the Hebrews, and even here I have done nothing to deserve being put in a dungeon." However, his memory froze, he did not remember Joseph; he forgot him. It is when God remembers a person that effective change comes like floods.

The Democrats of JFK started with good intentions of bringing solutions to American problems. However, it got cut short by the people who hated his principles.

Unlike the current and past Democrat political candidates who told voters "I will give you free education, free health-care, free or affordable housing and so on," JFK had a unique perspective on the American people. During the inauguration he emphasized, ask not what your country can do for you--ask what you can do for your country.

The very people who have been and who in disguise still are behind every black suffering cannot be the solution for black lives problems. A white liberal whom CNN's Van Jones states could pose a bigger threat to African Americans than the Ku Klux Klan cannot be solution for black problems.

The solution for the Israelites from Egyptian slavery came from their own person, from Moses. In the same manner about getting a solution and a deliverer from among their own, an angel told Joseph the fiancé of saint Mary that their own child would save his people from their predicament.

The worst part is that people are not going to accept, appreciate and respect a deliverer from among themselves. That is why the Trojans seek a solution for the black people's problem from the white people. In several instances the Israelites wanted to stone Moses for doing what was good for his people. There are house slaves of the same system that have no concern for the black people who pretend to care and help.

O'Rielly stated, "The reason there is so much chaos and violence in the black precincts is the disintegration of African American family. Raised without much structure, young black men often reject education; gravitate toward street culture, drugs, hustling, and gangs. Nobody forces them to do that, again it is a personal decision.

In 2013, long before BLM organization started, Don Lemon was caring for the people. Approving, responding, or emphasizing to Bill O'Reilly's presentation on black on black crimes Don Lemon mentions detailed realistic solutions for the black people's problems. "Black people, if you really want to fix the problem here are just five things you should think about doing:

1.   Number one, probably the most important. Just because you can have a baby, it doesn't mean you should. Especially without planning for one or getting married first. More than 72% of children in the African American communities are babies born out of wedlock. That means an absent father. Studies show that lack of male role model is an

express train right to prison, and the cycle continues. So black folks please pay attention to the hip-hop rap culture that glorifies everything that I just mentioned. Thug and reprehensible behavior are culture that is making a lot of people rich not just you.

2. Finish high school. You want to break the cycle of poverty stop telling kids that they are acting white because they go to school, they speak proper English. (By annual earning, High School dropouts average $19,000; High School graduates average $28,000; College graduates average $51,000). Over the course of career, a college graduate will make nearly a million dollar more than a high school graduate. That is a lot of money.

3. Respect where you live. Start small by not dropping trash, littering in your own communities. I have lived in several predominantly white neighborhoods, I rarely ever witnessed people littering. I live in Harlem now; it is historically black neighborhood. Every single day I see several adults and children dropping trash on the ground when the garbage can is just a foot away. Just being honest here.

4. The N word (no emphasis)

5. Pull up your pants.[296]

When Don spoke about these great points, he was pointing out what needs to be fixed. He never made a single point of a systemic or institutional racism. He asserted success is achieved by being intentional and being a focused person rather than relying on donation from government. Excellent job Don, that is the only solution to being successful for the black people.[297]

The Socialist and Marxist in disguise Trojan horsing the BLMS engaged in destruction, looting and defacing monuments are not the real people that are suffering in the affected cities. A friend from Minneapolis told Hayet that the people who are involved in destruction are not the local people. The local people work and live in the places that have been damaged and there is no way they damage their work. As early as the day after the death of George Floyd, people came from as far as New York. They did not spare even 'Black owned business,' hundreds of them were looted, burned, and destroyed.

People have no place to do shopping. The business owners may not rebuild their businesses for fear of more destruction. A person who does not learn from the past mistake will see the same mistakes repeated. Insurance companies would be unlikely to insure property in the areas where the local government is not willing to protect. Hence, the unemployment and poverty rates will be higher this time. Thus, "the high crime rates in so many black communities impose huge personal costs and have turned once-thriving communities into economic wastelands."[298]

The very community that the Trojan horses purport to help are harming, hurting, and suffering the most. The people who damaged the properties are gone to their respective places. The local victims remain with the aftermath ruins having no means of livelihood, leaving them in far much worse conditions than before George Floyd's death protests.

America's and Black People's enemies in guise, who are behind the Black Lives matter seasonal and other counterpart organizations want to drive Trump out of the Presidency which is the same purpose as that of Michael Moore since November 2016. They are holding the black people as a pawn to achieve anti-family, anti-authority, anti-God, anti-patriarch acts engaged in a destructive agenda.

Malcom X had observed that the Democrats and Republicans had been fighting each other for power and prestige, and the one that is the football in the game is the Negro, 20 million black people. A political football, a political pawn, an economic football, and economic pawn. A social football, a social pawn.[299]

Malcom X further clarified the most dangerous hubris for the black people and that Trojan horse is the liberal white people. Mr. X answered the 'how.' He stated, "The liberal elements of whites are those who have perfected the art of selling themselves to the Negro as a friend of the Negro. Getting sympathy of the Negro, getting the allegiance of the Negro, and getting the mind of the Negro. Then the Negro sides with the white liberal, and the white liberal uses the Negro against the white conservative. Because of being used, anything that the Negro does is never for his own good, never for his own advancement, never for his own progress, he's only a pawn in the hands of the white liberal.[300]

Enough is enough! The Black People should set themselves free from the gripe of the white liberals' poison, be able to think and work for themselves. If not, nobody cares about them.

Comparing the white liberals and the white conservatives Malcom X said, "The white liberals are more dangerous than the conservatives; they lure the Negro, and as the Negro runs from the growling wolf (conservative), he flees into the open jaws of the "smiling" fox (liberals). One is a wolf; the other is a fox. No matter what, they'll both eat you."[301]

Trump is in charge for four or at most eight years. What one would have to look at is the long-term solution for the black people. The BLMS leadership hopes and wishes that Trump gives in and leaves the office. Democratic leadership has been behind the injustices the black minorities have been facing for generations. It is time to expose the Trojan hubris and make the black people think for themselves.

Over the years we have seen one statue after the other removed. It all started with the removal of the Ten Commandment tablets from Court Houses and from schools. People did not protest because it was not a big deal for them, or they were not directly affected. Today, historic sites and statues that have done no wrong have become the targets of displaced aggression, anger, and vandalism. As parts of the protests, in different part of the US, schools that have nothing to do with politics have been vandalized and damaged.[302]

DISPLACED AGGRESSION

Displaced aggression is a way of releasing your anger over a thing or a person that has nothing to do that triggered or caused you to be angry. Businesses, buildings, and statues have nothing to do with the unrest that has been going on in the USA.

As the removal, defacing of historic monuments and statue progressed over the wake of George Floyd's death; several statues more have been defaced, destroyed, and vandalized. Now, it has come home, to what directly affects our Christian heritage.

The worst thing is that some of the very people engaged in the destructions of our history, never read a single book do not know who did what to help end slavery. Or who and what the statue represents. The BLM protesters did not spare Frederick Douglas' statue. It was hacked from its base in Rochester, New York and damaged beyond repair.

Where are the Democrat leadership? They did not condemn the act, President Trump did, saying 'these anarchists have no bounds.'[303] Such destructions are not for the blacks' cause, but anti-black and anti-America. Douglas was a former slave. He escaped slavery and helped shuttle slaves to freedom. Thus, he became an abolitionist and worked together with Christian abolitionists.

It was not the liberals or the KKK, it was Christian activists; Quakers who were the earlier leaders in abolitionism. They initiated and organized an abolitionist movement. Throughout Europe and the United States, Christians, churches, were to be found at the forefront of the abolitionist movements.[304]

The slave masters who come in the form of 'Planned Parenthood, ACLU, Black Lives Matter, Democratic Socialists of America, and Equal Rights Amendment Action let the dogs out. The house slaves keep on doing the interests of their slave masters.

The slave masters live in their fortified castles at least 100 miles far away from the inner cities, where poverty-stricken blacks and minorities live. That is where the worst education K-12 exists while the masters educate their children in private schools. The masters have their own private securities and securely gated neighborhood. Yet they call out to defund and disband the police who have no protection as they do.

In such cases, it is the minorities who have no private securities that suffer at the hands of lawless anarchists.

The current American liberal Taliban militants, when they see a white person's (in the case of Frederick Douglas, any) statue, that is a bad person and must be destroyed, spray painted, beheaded, toppled, and vandalized. The assumption of the angry protesters is that a lot of the statues and monuments are being taken down because they are of slave owners and people who fought for slavery during the Civil War. Several abolitionists' statues such as that of Abraham Lincoln, Matthias Baldwin, John Greenleaf Whittier, Ulysses Grant, and others, have faced one or the other form of vandalism. One of the toppled statues was that of Hans Christian Heg who was an abolitionist that died trying to end slavery."[305]

The protest that is going on is not about BLM; it is about planting a seed of hate for the American republic. They intentionally destroyed a statue of a person who helped the black people to be free from slavery.

The groups that Moore encourages people to join hate Christians and what Christianity stands for. The California Gov. Newsom would let tens of thousands of protesters sing, chant, and do all kinds of nuisances without any restriction, but when it comes to church gatherings, he set a number restriction to about $1/4^{th}$ capacity, and that people should stop singing and chanting. This is not about the Covid-19 pandemic; it is about hate for people of faith, mainly Christians.

After destroying our history, one of the far-left activists Shaun King said: "All images and statues depicting Jesus as a 'White European' should be torn down because they are a form of 'White supremacy. Always have been. In the Bible, when the family of Jesus wanted to hide, and blend in, guess where they went? EGYPT! Not Denmark. Tear them down."[306]

As further implementation what Mr. King has threatened, Boston Police are investigating after a statue of the Virgin Mary was vandalized, set on fire outside of a church in the city's Dorchester neighborhood. Police responded to a reported fire outside of St. Peter Parish on Bowdoin Street.[307]

On Friday June 26th, 2020, US District Judge Gary Sharpe issued a preliminary injunction on behalf of Catholic Priests and Orthodox Jewish congregants saying that Andrew Cuomo, Attorney general Letitia James and New York Mayor Bill de Blasio "exceed" their executive Powers by limiting worship services and condoning mass protests as the state continues reopening from Covid-19 restrictions. The restriction affects religious institutions only; they do not restrict looters, vandals, and protesters who are at a higher risk of contracting the disease.[308]

The more one caves into these Democratic Socialist affiliated American Taliban Trojan horsed guises, the more it gets worse. America should take a stand with a strong leader for law and order and say enough is enough. The perpetrators behind the unrest should be brought to justice. The president of Greater NY BLMS, Hawk Newsome said if change does not happen, "If this country doesn't give us what we want, then we will burn down this system and replace it. All right? And I could be speaking figuratively. I could be speaking literally. It's a matter of interpretation"[309] on Martha MacCallum's interview.

This is not about figurative speech; we have seen the practical applicability of his speech, private owned businesses burned, looted, and destroyed. Imagine if a white person made such terroristic threats, he would be in prison within 24 hours. This is a privileged black person. In America, if one wants to see a change, the way to go is to have a dialogue and vote but not burn whether it is yours or somebody else's property. What people are observing is a work of uncivilized destruction of democratic principles and not the American way of solving problems.

Newsom is not the only one to say so. Madonna the singer, as well said, "Yes, I'm angry. Yes, I am outraged. Yes, I have thought an awful lot about blowing up the White House, but I know that this won't change anything. We cannot fall into despair."[310] Don Lemon of CNN, also said, we are going to have blow up the entire system if Democrats win back the White House and the Senate. Jennifer Rubin said burn down the Republican party. Marshall University professor entrusted with teaching our children also wished that Trump supporters die before election.

The slave masters of BLMS purport to care for the minorities. However, the opposite is true of them as people see their fruit from being engaged in destruction and planting hatred for the very values the American republic stands for. A wise man in relation to identifying good from bad said,

> "Watch out for false prophets. They come to you in sheep's clothing, but inwardly they are ferocious wolves. By their fruit you will recognize them. Do people pick grapes from thorn bushes, or figs from thistles? Likewise, every good tree bears good fruit, but a bad tree bears bad fruit. A good tree cannot bear bad fruit, and a bad tree cannot bear good fruit. Every tree that does not bear good fruit is cut down and thrown into the fire. Thus, by their fruit you will recognize them.[311]

On the other side, one could see that Trump vows to protect the very thing that the anarchists want to destroy. Who would you rather have destroyers of our history or defenders?

To speak the truth, Jesus was not a European, on whom the anarchists want to place their displaced aggression. Jesus was a Jew, neither black nor white. Is it not enough destroying our national monuments? The action of destroying Christian monuments has already started. Hayet can confidently say that there is no way a black person could vandalize or burn a Bible or a Church. It is the BLMS in guise, communists who hate Christianity, who burned Saint John's Church in Washington.

This tragedy has not happened in Islamic or Communist countries, in the USA and nobody of the Democrat operatives condemned the vandals and the arsons during their DNC. Instead of condemning the burning of a Church, the hypocrite media Trojan horses, the foot soldiers, and their followers (who do not know the Bible) were so obsessed that Trump posed for a photo op with a Bible in front of the Church. That is not a big deal, people have the same rights. The big deal is choosing to be silent for the group that is causing BLM (Burn Loot and Mayhem).

There was a time when the Teachers of the Law and Pharisees saw Jesus eating with sinners and tax collectors, they asked his disciples: "Why does he eat with tax collectors and sinners?"

On hearing this, Jesus said to them, "It is not the healthy who need a doctor, but the sick. I have not come to call the righteous, but sinners."[312]

Be a judge please! Which one is worse? Posing for a photo holding a Bible, or burning and vandalizing a Church? Distinguishing right from wrong does not require a genius brain, but merely common sense.

Anti-freedom group in disguise hide behind BLM and continue spreading hate for America. BLM unveiled a policy agenda shortly after it was founded accusing Israel of being an "apartheid state," guilty of "genocide." Released in August 1st , the platform also calls for defunding police departments, race-based reparations, breaking laws, voting rights for illegal immigrants, fossil-fuel divestment, an end to private education and charter schools, a "universal basic income," and free college for blacks.[313] This is the same agenda as that of the DSA or the Democratic Party.

BETTER COMMUNITIES AND BETTER SCHOOLING

When it comes to schooling, Trump is for charter schools. Charter schools are public schools that give opportunities for minorities or people in general that cannot afford to live in areas where the rate of K-12 is of high quality. There is a school system that Hayet is familiar with. K-12 school ratings are 10/10. One must be a resident of the area to be admitted to the schools. If not, they cannot be admitted. Thus, to give high quality educational opportunities to parents, charter schools came in as an alternative to the failing public schools. The parents can take their children to high rated charter schools for better schooling.

Good schools are the products of good communities that is the combination of good families. Thus, the community makes good schools not the government. The government can build good school buildings for everyone with equal opportunities, teachers and all supplies related to that. Of what value is it if the communities and families do not take responsibility to take advantage of it?

Additionally, BLM is not as what it appears on the front, there is a guise agenda behind. With or behind or together with every BLM riot there is a gay agenda riding behind the legitimate cause perhaps not several people have paid attention to. The liberal for gay agenda is like ticks stashed or mutated secretly behind BLMS or any other group that Trump talks about dealing with. As Van Jones would call them, White liberal Secretary Clinton supporters are far much worse than KKK, they have no concern for the wellbeing of the black people.

By the help of White conservatives, Black People fought and made it thus far. The Ku Klux Klan couldn't sabotage chances for black academic excellence more effectively than the failing public school system are in most cities.[314] If they were genuine, they would have fixed the failing schools, and would have mentored the failing students. If they were for real, they would have raised their voices in the inner cities where there are more black on blacks' killings, specifically in Chicago. LGBTQ and BLM masters and their slaves show up only when a White Police officer kills a black person. They will not show up to local neighborhood initiatives and volunteer to help the suffering community in one way or the other.

In Flint, Michigan, a woman was formally charged in the fatal shooting of a store security guard who refused to allow her daughter inside because she wasn't wearing a facemask to protect against transmission of the coronavirus.[315]. Calvin Munerlyn, a black security guard, a father of eight, working for Family Dollar was shot after enforcing the order by the employer that customers had to wear facemasks report shows. His widow calls the killing 'senseless and stupid'.[316]

Both the killer and the victim are blacks. Where are the 'Planned Parenthood, ACLU, Black Lives Matter, Democratic Socialists of America, Equal Rights Amendment Action operatives in this and other such senseless black on black killings? They will not show up, it is none of their business. It is these kinds of killings that deserve advocating for justice not for suspected criminals. Behind any crime people should ask why it happened not what happened. Scripture says, "He who justifies the wicked and he who condemns the righteous are both alike an abomination to God." [317]

Where were the BLM when Nipsey Hussle, a self-made millionaire got killed by another black man? Nipsey delivered himself from gang life, helped himself and was helping his community by employing the unemployable due to criminal records. Where are the BLM and their masters who claim to care for black people? They will not show up in such cases because they do not fit in their narrative.

When TVCNN operatives stop such militant resistance ideology then, we can work together to build the USA. There is a saying in Hayets' culture that says *Asha z-te-khe-lo le-bam nay ne-qh-lo*— meaning, "What a fool planted, a wise cannot uproot." Four years into Trump Presidency, our division grows bigger because of the divisiveness of TVCNN's propaganda.

Hillary Clinton also has her share in the violence as well for not following American tradition. That is, she did not encourage her voters to work with the winner. She could be the only presidential finalist who has not yet conceded, holding her voter's hostage. On her book 'What Happened,' she blames everybody for her loss, except herself.

As we prepare for the 2020 election, Michael Moore's prediction proved wrong. Trump is not only still the President; he is preparing to win a reelection according to Moore's new prediction.[318]

Socialist parties do not have to do as much competition as in capitalist economy. Since there is no such great reward for the working class, people tend to be less productive. That is why such countries are not as productive as the capitalist economy countries. People cannot and do not want to bring the best results. When one comes with an alternative option to the failing system, that is when they rise to oppose.

DEFUND

Democratic politicians—and some Republicans—hastened to appease the protesters. The Mayors of Los Angeles and New York pledged to cut their cities police budgets. The Minneapolis City Council said it intended to disband the police department.[319] With the existing police presence we have numerous crimes. Without police presence what kind of utopia would we see? It is too sad to see democratically elected leaders being led by lawless mob.

As it is their habit, for the very thing that Democrats built, they are coming back to tear it down saying defund. The Biden bill increased funds, increased prisons, and increased police personnel. The very thing that they voted for to fund, they are coming now against it. Rep. Elham Omar says, "Disband the police." Take a note that the word disband refers to break up or cause an organized group to stop from functioning. Remember, in Somalia where she comes from, since the defunded police and army cannot defend itself, the country is still helped by the African Union. Scripture tell us to beware: "Under three things the earth trembles, under four it cannot bear up: a servant who becomes king, a godless fool who gets plenty to eat, a contemptible woman who gets married, and a servant who displaces her mistress.[320]

Hayet has been under such leadership, of a high school dropout. The worst kind of leadership.

This applies to all the undeserving business, Democratic and Republican leaders who do not have a basic knowledge of our government system and who jump from nowhere to somewhere. They appear to be experts while they are shallow and expose themselves.

The writer of proverbs warns all of us, "Too much talk leads to sin. Be sensible and keep your mouth shut,"[321] on issues that you are not an expert. This warning includes President Trump for saying words that have nothing to do with the situation at hand.

AOC is also one such people. She was fumbling if Democrats work hard, they should and could take the "Three Chambers of Congress," she divided those three "Chambers" as the House, the Senate, and the Presidency. She still left out the Judicial Branch (or "chamber" in her own words). She never corrected the word "chamber" to "branch."[322]

Representative Ilhan Omar, a supporter of the defund the police has a say. She was addressing Muslims regarding the terrorist attack Christchurch, New Zealand. She said what is known as CARE was founded after 9/11 when some people did something. CARE was founded in 1994.

Eventually, the Minneapolis City Council unanimously approved a radical proposal to change the city charter that would allow the police department to be dismantled.[323] Imagine, coming from a country where there is no democracy and rule of law that has not been able to defend itself for thirty years, asking other donors and African Union armies to help defend the nation, being to the one to propose defunding the police.

Mayor Jacob Frey doesn't support abolishing the department, a stance that got him booed off the streets by activists who demonstrated outside his house following Floyd's death and demanded to know where he stood.[324] Some of the Portland protesters harassed and poured paint on senior citizens with BLM signs on their hands for telling them not to damage a building.

President Obama on balancing police and crime once said: "Yes, we need more cops on the streets. Yes, we need fewer guns in the hands of people who shouldn't have them."[325]

As it is said, by its own 'axe haft,' there are some rich black accomplices and house slaves of the white people who hurt the Black People the most. Both, the black and white liberals live protected by security guard all their life in areas safe from where protesters. To the People of Color that protest defund the police, Hayet would love to say think again. To the politicians who are proponents of defund the police; first the Mayors and the Governors defund the rat-infested metropolitan cities that you represent by cleaning them. Second, show the people that you lead and do not need a police force and maybe their proposition could have some considerations.

Additionally, when such leaders call to defund the police, it should include defunding theirs and their spouse's security guards. One should be part of the solution, not part of the problem.

Chapter Sixteen

"In the West, we have reasonably functional, reasonably free, remarkably productive, stable hierarchies that are open to considerations of the dispossessed that hierarchies generate, create. Our societies are freer and functioning more effectively than any societies anywhere else in the world, any societies ever have.

—DR. JORDAN PETERSON

FOR IMMIGRANTS FOCUS ON WHAT THE USA DID *FOR* US INSTEAD OF WHAT USA DID *TO* US

There is a gospel song by Johnson Oatman that says "Count your blessings name them one by one and it will surprise you what the Lord has done. Many immigrants to the USA come from countries where there have been rampant persecutions, imprisonment, exploitation, and much worse killings of the citizens. In their home countries, there have been no presidential elections since the independence. No one ever voted or there has never been a fair presidential election. Although they call themselves presidents, they lead their countries as Kingdoms.

Some unelected or election rigging non-royal, longest ruling national leaders where immigrants come from have served as many as 50 years.

The USA and of course other Western countries gave immigrants a second chance to life, liberty, and the pursuit of happiness. Immigrant citizen are also eligible to vote chances they never had or still don't have in their home countries. America and Western countries have educated our children; giving scholarships that our countries could not, compared to the white folks are given. that our countries could not. America gives immigrants opens door for growth that they did not get in their home countries led by jealous leaders.

Most of the immigrants never had a car or a house in their birth countries, the USA has given them unlimited access to wealth and ownership of automobiles, businesses, and houses worth millions of dollars, which could not be obtained in their birth countries. In fact, most of the leaders of the countries from which immigrants to the USA come from have been accused by the United Nations of leading totalitarian governments responsible for systematic human rights violations that may amount to crimes against humanity, including unjust imprisonments to tens of thousands of people.[326]

The very agitators and house slave masters that are behind inciting civil disobedience want to take the USA to the kind of situation that got the immigrants out of their birth countries. Focus on what the USA did *for* you individually or collectively not on what the USA did *to* us.

The USA treats immigrants, people of color, and all human beings with respect and dignity than our birth nations combined. Everyone has the right to challenge the police force or even the government unlike where we come from, where we cannot challenge the oppressive leaders who are ruthless and brutal.

In Hayet's culture, if one pays evil for the very people who cared and respected them people say *z-be-la-eka-yo y-h-ne-qh-ka* meaning "May what you ate choke you."

An Ivey League student, who is a child of an immigrant hated the racist part of America so much. One summer he went to the birth country of his parents. He saw and compared what it means to live in the USA is. Upon his return, for the first time, "Thank God for the USA," he declared.

An African American contractor also lived and worked in the Middle East for years. He saw how lethal racism in the Middle East for people of color is. He told to Hayet, "I must go home, (the USA), I cannot handle the racism in this country," and he did.

If you hate America, regardless of what color of skin you have, travel around the world. If not right away, at least after the honeymoon is over, you will return and say, "Thank God for the USA."

In a related story, Hayet would like to remind readers of Noah's account. He sent out a raven and a dove one at a time. He first sent out a raven, and it kept flying back and forth until the water had dried up from the earth. (Do you have to do, or should you do the same? Hayet wouldn't.) Then Noah sent out a dove to see if the water had receded from the surface of the ground. But the dove could find nowhere to perch because there was water over all the surface of the earth; so, it returned to Noah in the ark. (Good job, dove). He reached out his hand and took the dove and brought it back to himself in the ark. [327]

As an American citizen, or any person of worth, if you do not feel comfortable where you are, you do not have to keep on flying back and forth in vain, come home, America will accept you! Remember how President Jimmy Carter pardoned thousands draft dodgers. Come home; God will accept you. One thing to reconcile though, "Let the wicked forsake their ways and the unrighteous their thoughts. Let them turn to the LORD, and he will have mercy on them, and to our God, for he will freely pardon."[328]

America does not have to be perfect to be good. Perfection is found only in God. After all, if our own people cannot have mercy on their own people, shouldn't we be grateful for getting mercy from others? There are a lot of imperfections in the USA as are in other countries. There is no better country and continent Hayet would rather stand in fair trial than in the USA. The best way to solve problems is by dialogue, not through threats and intimidations or causing, BLM (Burn, Loot, and Mayhem).

FOCUS ON WHAT HAS BEEN DONE *FOR* US NOT ON WHAT HAS BEEN DONE *TO* US

There are countless negatives issues to look at in any given situation even in a loving family. One should be able to look at the positive encounters. Focusing on 500 years old past negative experiences will not help or bring about any progress for the future. Thinking on the past keeps one stuck in a miry clay, unable to move forward.

There was a teenager who was hated by his brothers for his dreams. At one instance they saw him in the distance, coming to know how they were doing and to bring them some food. Before he reached them, they plotted to kill him. They said to each other "let's kill him and throw him into one of these cisterns and say that a ferocious animal devoured him., we will see what will happen to his dreams."

So, when he came to his brothers, they stripped him of his robe—the ornate robe he was wearing— and they took him and threw him into a cistern. By God's providence, he survived the onslaught, and his brothers sold him for twenty shekels of silver to Ishmaelites traders, who took him to Egypt. Potiphar, an Egyptian who was one of Pharaoh's officials, a Captain of the guard, bought him from the Ishmaelites traders.

The brothers made a pact and told their father that a ferocious animal devoured him. The father wept and mourned for his son while his brothers rejoiced for doing away with the dreamer. The brothers did bad *to* hurt him, but God gave favor *for* him in the eyes of his master and gave him success in everything he did.

At Potiphar's house his master's wife made several attempts to seduce and take him to bed with her. However, out of respect for God and his master he refused. Upon learning he was not likely to go to bed with her, she accused him of attempted rape and had him unfairly incarcerated. His master trusted his wife and did bad *to* him, but God gave favor *for* him in the eyes of the prison warden and he was appointed oversee all other prisoners. One ought to focus on what has been done *for* him not what has been done *to* him regardless of how hard the severity of the persecution is. The best thing one should do while waiting for justice is to humble themselves under God's mighty hand, that he may lift and honor them in due time.

At last God vindicated the victim by enabling him to interpret Pharaoh's dreams, which his magicians and wisemen could not. He got expedited with exaltation and became the second-in-command in Egypt. He was honored by earning Pharaoh's signet ring, without his word no one would lift a hand or foot in all Egypt.

The very people who did bad *to* the man eventually came to Egypt seeking to buy food and were under the care and mercies of their former victim. The former victim did not focus on what his brothers did *to* him, instead, on what God had done *for* him. As he revealed himself to them, he said, "I am your brother Joseph, the one you sold into Egypt! And now, do not be distressed and do not be angry with yourselves for selling me here, because it was to save lives that God sent me ahead of you, to preserve for you a remnant on earth and to save your lives by a great deliverance."

In a related manner, just as Joseph was taken to a foreign land against his will, God brought our African ancestors to the USA. It is a reason which could transcend beyond our comprehension if people take note of what God did for us; that is to help ourselves by working hard to earn and be of a significant help to our people the way Joseph did; but not wait on government donations.

Joseph did not count on what had been done *to* him, instead what God has done *for* him and he assures them saying, 'It was not you who sent me here, but God. God has made me lord of all Egypt and father to Pharaoh, lord of his entire household and ruler of all the country. Now hurry back bring my father, you shall live in the region of Goshen and be near me. You, your children and grandchildren, your flocks, and herds, and all you have. I will provide for you there, because five years of famine are still to come. Otherwise you and your household and all who belong to you will become destitute.'

Evil doers never have peace. Once Joseph was discovered to be alive, his brothers discussed among themselves, "What if Joseph holds a grudge against us and pays us back for all the wrongs, we did *to* him?" So they made up a story and sent word to Joseph, saying, "Your father left these instructions before he died: "This is what you are to say to Joseph: I ask you to forgive your brothers the sins and the wrongs they did *to* you."

Still Joseph did not focus on what they did *to* him, but on what God had done *for* him. He reassured and spoke kindly to them," Don't be afraid. You intended to bring harm *to* me, but God intended it *for* good to accomplish what is now being done, the saving of many lives. So then, do not be afraid. I will provide for you and your children." Details of the story about Joseph are written in Genesis chapters 37 to 52. Now please read the main reason behind Joseph's story and the American unrest of 2020.

By God's Divine Providence, here we are a great multitude that no one can count, to be specific, about 350 million people in the USA, from every nation, tribe, people, and language. The concept "Divine Providence" no matter whether one is a person of faith or not refer to the fact, "that God is the Creator of heaven and earth, and that all that occurs in the Universe takes place under His sovereign guidance and control. According to believers, God governs creation as a loving father, working all things for good."[329]

God is flawlessly good: in all situations. He works for the best, intending the best possible outcomes. Given these suppositions, our initial expectations would be that all of creation, animate and inanimate, is ordained to perfect good: that as creator God pitches his efforts, which none can resist, toward accomplishing the greatest good imaginable, and hence that the world in which we find ourselves is.[330]

The World that we live in, the USA to be specific in our context may contain much good, but it is also a place of suffering, destruction, and death. Life is brief and afflicted with sorrows of every kind—as often as not with no discernible purpose at all, much less a good one. And it ends for each of us in personal destruction—in death, which trumps all worldly hopes, and conceals impenetrably any experience that may lie far off. Nor are these mere human hardships. Every living being dies, all that is beautiful perishes, everything nature builds is destroyed. On one scientific account of the end of things not an atom will escape the cauldron of the Universe's final collapse. And that is not all, in human affairs there is the additional evil of sin: the willful wrongdoing of which we all are at times victims and at other times perpetrators.[331]

"If the good God is in control, why does he not control the pain and suffering that goes on in the world?" Dr. Ravi Zacharias was asked regarding of how evil around us is perpetrated by other people.

He replied, "If you take away responsibility, you actually take away the possibility of any court of law dealing with any act in any nature if it is always someone else's fault. You must have evil explained and that it is not only outside because it is in the inside first. It did not come on the inside from outside. All that is within you is evil and the list of all evils that God gives to us comes from the heart of man that it really defines.[332]

The heart is deceitful above all things and beyond cure. The heart of a person on this context does not refer to the organ, but instead, a way of thinking in relation other people.

Dr. Ravi was asked why God did not stop the trigger when a person killed another man. His reply was that for all that we do the ultimate deciding factor either to do or not to do is love. We are not machines, we have freewill. There is freedom to choose what we want to do or not. If you are asking for God to always stop the trigger, why not God stop everything else next time you hold a cup of boiling water he makes it frozen water instead. Next time you are about to cross the street you are going to be hit he pulls your leg back. Why don't you wait until you stand before God face to face and you will find out there were reasons why he did not stop that trigger so that you will see the heinousness of evil and see the majesty of love and good managing to navigate yourself but as the pilgrim's progress to come to that.[333]

Chapter Seventeen

"Jill and I send our thoughts to President Trump and First Lady Melania Trump for a swift recovery."

— JOE BIDEN

JOE BIDEN'S DAMAGE TO THE MINORITIES

With every person, there is a good and a bad side. Joe Biden may be good and friendly as a person, but there are some issues with his policies. To show how Democrats are tough on crimes, Biden proposed what is known as the Biden Crime Bill of 1993 and Bill Clinton signed it into law.

Biden spoke of how since 1976: "Every minor crime bill has had the name of the Democratic Senator from the State of Delaware, Joe Biden, on that bill, and has had majority votes of the Democratic members of the United States Senate on the bill."[334]

Biden brags about his crime bill that he helped draft, which included 53 offenses worthy of the death penalty. While boasting about his achievement he states, "Weak as it can be, you know?" he added in a sarcastic response to critics who said the bill was too soft. "We do everything but hang people for jaywalking in this Bill."[335]

THE GLORY OF
GOD IS EACH OF
US FULLY ALIVE!

Biden's crime bill has been hurting black and brown Americans, who are disproportionately incarcerated even for first time minor offences. He tells how President Clinton knows the basic way to take back the streets is by more cops, more prisons[336] for which now he opposes.

The Biden crime law imposed tougher prison sentences at the federal level and encouraged states to do the same even for minor crimes. It provided funds for states to build 125,000 new state prison cells, more prisons, to hire 100,000 more cops, and backed grant programs that encouraged police officers to carry out more drug-related arrests — an escalation of the war on drugs."[337] Come to June and July 2020, they call to eliminate or reduce the police force that they created and advocated for.

It is because of such severe crime laws the same year Alice Johnson was taken off the streets in 1993 she was sentenced to life imprisonment without parole. Ms. Johnson's imprisonment happened the year Biden's crime bill became a law, where she spent twenty-one years of her life. She was a desperate woman, first-time offender, a single mother of five kids who was struggling to make ends meet, caught up on quick moneymaking drug-dealing involvement. It is not the saintly Democrats or President Obama who claim to love and care for the black people that commuted her sentence. It is the Man tainted as a bad racist person and a threat for blacks that pardoned the nobody.

President Obama could have commuted Ms. Johnson's sentence, instead he served the interests of his masters by commuting Chelsea Manning transgender person. Manning was sentenced to 35 years in prison for leaking thousands of military and State Department information to WikiLeaks but was released after seven years only.

Look at the comparison, Alice Johnson, economic offender sentenced— to life imprisonment without parole; Manning a political offender 35 years prison sentence. Obama could have released another offender with a less harsh crime, Kristian Saucier, a sailor jailed for taking submarine pictures, who instead was pardoned by Trump.

On his crime bill law speech, the unsympathetic Biden would not ask or care to learn about what made the offenders do 'the crimes,' or how to help them overcome their shortcomings. Even in the face of Republicans asking to deal with the root cause of the crime problem. For Biden, it is 'Not, not.' Criminals must be taken off the street. He further clarifies his lack of concern for offenders saying: I don't care why someone is a "mal" factor in society. I don't care why someone is anti-social. I don't care why they become a sociopath. It doesn't matter whether the offenders were deprived as a youth (one could think that is what the Democrats stand for), they had no background that would enable them to become socialized into the fabric of society. It doesn't matter whether the offenders are the victims of society. They must be taken off the streets.[338]

Just as Margaret Sanger considered certain people feebleminded, Biden refers to the same people as dangerous, children born out of wedlock, immoral, and prostitutes from giving birth to children so that the same character may not continue. The Supreme Court in 1927 passed a law that would allow medical practitioners to do compulsory, forced or even clandestine sterilization in prisons that directly affected about 70,000 Americans.

Although minorities have equal rights as the majorities, it would not apply to a Carrie Buck and her sister who were born to their mother, Emma Buck whose husband abandoned her early in their marriage. People were concerned that if Buck and her sister were let to procreate their generation could be a burden to the society. When the government intrudes on human freedom and forces or mandates people to accept service (including Obamacare health insurance) that becomes a threat to a free society. Legislating, mandating, forcing, and controlling citizens to have or not to one option or the other is expected from Islamic, Socialist, and Communist Marxist country not from the USA.

Although Biden superficially appears to love and care for black people, he fundamentally agrees with Margaret Sanger. Sanger says 'feeble-minded, human weeds should not have children or should be sterilized, should be kept in plantations all their life. Biden also advocates that certain people should be taken out of the street because if they are let to live, they could be a problem to the society.

The very problem created by the government is the underlying condition that caused the problems the inner cities now are facing. Who are Biden's target groups? Here is the list:

Biden urged,

Unless we do something about that cadre of young people - tens of thousands of them - born out of wedlock, without parents, without supervision, without any structure, without any conscience developing because they literally have not had an opportunity. We should focus on them now. If we do not, they will, or a portion of them will, become the predators fifteen years from now. It does not mean, because we created them, that we somehow forgive them or do not take them out of society to protect my family and yours from them. They are beyond the pale, many of those people, beyond the pale, and it is a sad commentary on society. We have no choice but to take them out of society, and the truth is we do not very well know how to rehabilitate them at that point. That's the sad truth.[339]

The Democratic Party and all its affiliates are anti-family, anti-country, anti-God and against faith groups, specifically Christianity. Over the years, people have seen that if one does not say white Republicans are bad and blacks are the victims of racism, they have no room on the liberal Democratic representative anchors.

Democrats' leaders try to be politically correct and avoid even saying Merry Christmas. Obama was the lead for getting rid of prayers and any Christian theme from the White House. Although they try to hide that fact, here and there, they do disclose information. In a couple of instances, Biden would never mention the word God or Creator like it is a pothole that should be avoided. Be it on his tweet or speech, he avoids God or Creator. During one of his speeches he intentionally avoided God or Creator while quoting the declaration of independence. He stated that, "We hold these truths to be self-evident, that all men are created by the ... you know the thing." For Biden, God or Creator is 'the thing.' In contrast, Trump proudly speaks for families, country, and God.

It is not a strange for Biden not to mention God. The broader Democratic leadership is anti-God, anti-family, anti-country, anti-military, and anti-unborn children.

A God sent great American hero, JFK, wanted to reverse the curses of the Democratic Party. However, his life was cut short. May God bless his soul! It is not a strange to see the Democratic Partly specially the junior members choosing to be Trojan hubris. There is no more civility, formal politeness, respect for a person or senior citizens as seen by the Portland protesters, or courtesy in behavior or speech. No more politeness whereby one could bring up an idea for a discussion either to refute or accept. Now what leads America is, threats, fear, shaming, and intimidations.

Ivanka Trump on her RNC 2020 speech stated "We want a culture where differences of opinion and debate are encouraged, not canceled, where law enforcement is respected, where our country's rich diversity is celebrated, and where people of all backgrounds, races, genders and creeds have the chance to achieve their God-given potential. This is the future my father is working to build every day."[340]

BIDEN AND RACISM

The author is a racist, the readers are racists, people of every nation are racists, Biden is racist, Trump is racist, and so is everybody else. (Please allow Hayet to say, there is only one person who is not a racist. That is Annie Hellstrom of Stockholm, Sweden). However, the degree of racism varies from person to person.

Sometimes it is a shame to see the racism that kicks immigrants from their home countries imported to the USA or other Western countries create havoc on people's lives. It is commonly perceived that Trump is the most racist elected president. For media personality Corkin, who covered Trump for a decade, he is not. He is the most generous celebrity.[341] However, the opposite is true of the Democratic career politician of about five decades, Biden.

Perhaps one could say, the so-called racist Trump appears to talk the talk of racism, but Biden walked the walk of racism. Which of them would you rather have?

Congress failed to renew funding the HBCUs However, the one who cares, President Donald Trump signed a bipartisan bill that will permanently provide more than $250 million a year to the nation's historically black colleges and universities, along with dozens of other institutions that serve large shares of minority students. In signing the bill, Trump said historically black schools have "never had better champions in the White House. When I took office, I promised to fight for HBCUs, and my administration continues to deliver," Trump said. The White House and Congress came together and reached a historic agreement,"[342] Good job!

Trump wanted to give an opportunity to students from failing schools to go to school of their choice. He is proponent of the move for saying "A child's zip code in America should never determine their future, and that's what was happening," while Biden was and is opponent of such initiative. Not only was Biden the opponent, he encouraged other Senators to support segregation in schools. The difference between Trump and Biden is, Trump says, a child should be given unlimited access to education; while Biden says, children should be schooled in their zip code, that house the failing schools.

During the election debates run for the 2020 Democratic presidential primaries, Biden's black and white contestants attacked him for his position on anti-bussing. Anti-busing is a legislation opposing students from failing neighborhood schools going to attend in successful schools. When Senator Kamala Harris challenged Biden about his anti-busing policy, her spokesman said, "She spoke wasn't just speaking for herself. She was speaking on behalf of countless black and brown children who were seeking access to better education through school integration."[343]

In 1971, the U.S. Supreme Court ruled in favor of busing to end racial segregation because African American children were still attending segregated schools.[344]

The Supreme Court ruling in favor of bussing was amended and ended because of Senator Biden's move. Senator Harris blamed him for that ruling that personally affected her. The anti-busing crusader, Biden's opposition to court-ordered busing which he would not apologize for is one of the most well-documented views of his career.[345] In the 1968, 1972, and 1976 presidential elections, candidates opposed to busing were elected and reelected each time, and Congress voted repeatedly to end court-mandated busing.[346]

The Holy Scripture teach us, "Watch out for false prophets. They come to you in sheep's clothing, but inwardly they are ferocious wolves. By their fruit you will recognize them. Do people pick grapes from thornbushes, or figs from thistles? Likewise, every good tree bears good fruit, but a bad tree bears bad fruit. A good tree cannot bear bad fruit, and a bad tree cannot bear good fruit."[347]

It is not what one says that matters; it is how one walks that matters. Opposition to busing was purely motivated by racism. Examining and questioning whether Biden might be a racist, he said that he asked the black people on his staff whether he harbored racism in him that's deep-seated that he is not aware off.[348]

Sure enough, he was a racist. Two thousand years ago, a wise teacher told his students:" A good man brings good things out of the good stored up in his heart, and an evil man brings evil things out of the evil stored up in his heart. For the mouth speaks what the heart is full of."[349] It is not what one says, but what one does that matters most.

Biden's white constituents formed an angry anti-busing lobby. They shouted Biden down during one of their meetings, demanding to know what the Senator was going to do to prevent their children from being reassigned to schools that had been majority black. White voters in the state, on whom his re-election in 1978 depended, overwhelmingly opposed busing. Consequently, he chose votes over principles and got reelected, unseating Edward Brooke. Brooke was the only African American Republican Senator then, concerned with the choice of education for blacks, who had never bowed to the anti-busing uproar from white voters, he lost the seat he had held since 1967.[350]

Disapproving of Biden's segregation advocacy, Senator Brooke speaks comparing Biden's intent and its long-term effect as follows: "Biden called busing 'a bankrupt concept' and argued, 'The educational system does not have as its primary purpose the integration of society." His amendment barred the use of federal funds 'to assign teachers or students by race.' Edward Brooke lamented that the Biden amendment was 'the greatest symbolic defeat for civil rights' in years. "It's just a matter of time before we wipe out the civil rights progress of the last decade".[351] In spite of Biden's segregation advocacy in spite of their unpopularity, the schemes that bused children from racially homogenous neighborhoods to racially heterogeneous schools were largely successful.[352]

This is where CNN's Van Jones 'White-lash' should be applied. At a time when African Americans favor integration and show no preference for segregation, Biden was in favor of segregation.

In September 1975, Biden supported an anti-busing amendment to a federal bill. It was proposed by Sen. Jesse Helms of North Carolina, a segregationist until at least the 1960s and regarded by most to be a racist. Delighted by Biden's shift, Helms welcomed him "to the ranks of the enlightened" (the segregationists).[353]

Biden also worked for about three decades and supported an anti-busing amendment by Robert Byrd, a Senator from West Virginia and a Democrat who had a racist past as a recruiter for the Ku Klux Klan.[354]

Senator Byrd was tasked with recruiting 150 people to the Klan. When he involved enough people to start a klavern, a unanimous vote among the recruits named him "Exalted Cyclops" of their group, which is the highest-ranking position in a chapter. Biden photographed with and eulogized Senator Byrd, the second longest serving U.S. Congressman after John Dingell. For being a member of the KKK he regretted later in life.[355] Imagine the backlash should Trump be accused of such allegiance?

Tom Atkins, a Boston NAACP leader, said in March 1975 that opposing busing was racist: "An anti-busing amendment is an anti-desegregation amendment, and an anti-desegregation amendment is an anti-black amendment."[356]

The electorate in South Carolina who do not know the real enemy of the black people resurrected Biden's dying election bid by conspiring against Senator Bernie Sanders in cooperation with the Democrat establishment. This is the second time Democrats' leadership conspired to derail Sanders' favorable bid, the first time being done by Secretary Clinton. Honestly speaking, what Trump promises, he most likely delivers. Whereas, with Biden's Trojan hubris and influence from Democratic Socialist operatives, what promises one would hear from him, gets hijacked by the extremist leftists (led by Obama) and may not be what one would get.

Hip-Hop artist Diddy, who appears to have over 100 times near or with Trump[357] threatens Biden: If You Don't Show You're Going to Improve the Lives of Black People:

> The Black vote is not going to be for free. We're going to have to see some promises. We're going to have to understand what kind of deal we're getting. What are we getting in return for our vote? Because nothing has changed in America for Black America. For us to vote for Biden, we can't be taken for granted like we always are because we're supposed to be Democrats or because people are afraid of Trump. It's whoever that's going to take care of our community. Our vote is not for free. And I will hold the vote hostage if I have to."[358]

The choice is clear, between Biden, a man who is responsible for anti-bussing, imprisonment of thousands of people of color; and Trump, a person who just started politics and is encouraging all to achieve the American Dream.

Chapter Eighteen

"You need to have subcomponents of human existence. You need family, friends, career, educational goal, plans for outside of work, attention to your mental and physical health. If you do not have any of those things, then what you have got left is misery and suffering. That is a bad deal for you."

— DR. JORDAN PETERSON

YOU DETERMINE YOUR WORTH

God has fearfully and wonderfully made human beings in his own image and in his own likeness, for his own glory. All things considered, God knows how humans are worth dying for and

he demonstrated it. Scripture affirms God's love for humanity and says, "Since you are precious and honored in my sight, and because I love you, I will give people in exchange for you, nations in exchange for your life."[359]

It was not with perishables such as silver or gold that humans were redeemed from the empty way of life handed down to them from their ancestors, but with the precious blood of Christ, a lamb without blemish or defect. Thus, since human beings are redeemed and bought at a price, they are not their own, they belong to the one who bought them. Therefore, humans ought to honor God with their bodies. Exchanging, trading, or shortchanging life for anything else cannot be acceptable.

To have clear understanding of the world's worth, it is important to look at the meaning of worth first. Worth refers to "The value equivalent to that of someone or something under consideration; the level at which someone or something deserves to be valued or rated."[360]

Let us use a market analogy. Before merchandise leaves the production plant for the market, the people that produced it know how much merchant should sell it. The merchant always knows the value of the item being sold, and usually gives equivalent value as to how much the item is worth and should be sold. The customer or the consumer on the other side as well knows the worth of the item and how much they would be willing to pay for it. The consumer will not mind if the merchant sells the item half price or even less than that. However, the merchant, or the owner would not be willing to sell the item for less than its worth.

To Hitler, a Jew may mean nothing, but to Jesus every human being matters and is worth dying for. For Jesus, Black Lives Matter, White Lives Matter, Hispanic Lives Matter, Asian Lives Matter, Every Life Matters.

There was a situation where Hayet was traveling on a truck transporting about 100 to 200 goats. One wandered off the truck. Waiting even for one minute in the open country was a threat for Hayet.

"This is a dangerous place, so please let us leave it alone and keep on rolling. I will pay the full price of it," he begged the owners.

"Haven't you read a story of a good shepherd who owned a hundred sheep, and one of them wandered away, would he not leave the ninety-nine on the hills and go to look for the one that wandered off? And when he found it, truly I tell you, he got happy about that one sheep than about the ninety-nine that did not wander off. And when he found it, he joyfully puts it on his shoulders and went home. Then he called his friends and neighbors together and said, 'Rejoice with me; I have found my lost sheep.'"

"I know the story. That is why I am willing to pay the full price for it."

"It is not the market value money that I care about. It is the worth of the life of the goat. If I accept money of its worth and leave it here, to be eaten alive by the wild animals, I will regret all the days of my life for not trying to save it. Sorry, I have no time to talk let me go and catch it before other carnivores do it," he yelled as his voice faded carried on the wind.

For the owner it is not about the money, it is the worth of the goat that cannot be exchanged for money. The further the goat runs away the faster the owner goes after it. After hours of chasing, he manages to get it and bring it back to the herd carrying it on his shoulders.

People may put a price tag on you which you are not worth based on your religion, gender, or skin color. However, in general, every person decides their worth.

In 1963, President Kennedy signed an Equal Pay Act. The Act made it illegal to pay different salaries to males and females working in the same field for the same or similar work. Although the law protects equal pay for all people, there is still much to speak about, fight for, work for, vote for, legislate for, in realizing the practical applicability of the law.

Currently, Black Women in the United States who work full time year-round are typically paid just 62 cents for every dollar paid to White, Non-Hispanic men. For women overall, the wage gap stands at 82 cents for every dollar paid to men. Which is about $23,653 difference per year and $946,120 over a 40-year career.[361] One of the focus areas for Sister-to-Sister International has been to encourage Black Girls to pursue science, technology, engineering, and medicine (STEM) careers, which have the least wage disparities.[362]

In today's market a person's worth is decided by ones' skills, talent, or by ones' education. A person gets paid based on their worth. According to Forbes 2020 of the Top 10 out of 10 Highest-Paid Athletes and Media Personalities in the World happened to be either a mixed race or a minority. These are: Kaylie Jenner (Media) $590 million, Kanye West (Media): $170 million, Roger Federer (Tennis): $106.3 million, Cristiano Ronaldo (Soccer): $105 million, Lionel Messi (Soccer): $104 million, Tyler Perry (Media): $97 million, Neymar (soccer): $95.5 million, Howard Stern (Media): $90 million, LeBron James (Basketball): $88.2 million, Dwayne Johnson (Media): $87.5 million[363]

When employers hire, they figure out how much the job is worth to pay and how much the employer would get in return for hiring that person. The employee has the right either to accept or reject the price tag for that job.

Isaac, an industrial engineer worked for a company for years. However, the company like many others; was shut down due to Obama environmental regulation or high tax. Isaac sold his house and had to move to a state with more employment opportunities. Due to the shutting of the plant, people lost their livelihood; they had no job to take care of themselves and their families. Consequently, family's economies went to shambles. It is at the time the people that lost their jobs got intersected with the Trump, the candidate, who promised to open all the shutdown plants and bring jobs back to the USA.

Trump won the election and fulfilled his promise, giving incentives to multiple companies as well as reopening their manufacturing plants in the USA and reopened their manufacturing plants.

Former employers contacted all employees, including Isaac; to return because the company was open for business. For a former employer to bring back former employees, they should be of notable worth, having good work ethics and productivity. That is how Isaac works. There is no way an employer would bring back a worthless employee.

"Isaac, we want you to come back, we are now open. Your pay will be the same as it was before we shut down," called the Manager. Since the company was buying Isaac's education and experience, they started with the pay rate they used before they shut for business. Had Isaac accepted the rate, it would have been a win for the company.

"I cannot come, I am already settled here" he replied.

The company highly values Isaac's worth and education and his experience are highly sought after. The employer who is race blind Manager asked, "What can we do to make you come?"

Isaac, an African immigrant could have used the race card to submit to the company's offer. Instead, he knew his worth, "If you really want me to come, I want the following items to be met," giving a list of his terms and conditions, which were far higher than what the company offered. Yet since he was irreplaceable, they agreed to honor his worth, accepted his terms and conditions, and he accepted the offer and moved back. What is your worth?

Chapter Nineteen

"When I stand before God at the end of my life, I would hope that I would not have a single bit of talent left, and could say, 'I used everything You gave me.'"

— CHADWICK BOSEMAN

VICTIMHOOD MENTALITY

The worst thing one can do to is to trick another person into believing they are something they are not. To apply it to the current American climate, blacks and minorities believe they are oppressed, victims of systemic racism, while legally they are not.

Prof. Jordan Peterson says that Marxism considers that Capitalism can only prosper on the exploitation of the working class.[364] Everyone who has more than you have obtained their wealth by stealing it from you. Everyone who has more than me received it in a manner that is corrupt; that justifies not only my envy but my action to level the field so to speak and to look virtuously doing it. The worst emotions are resentment, deceit, and arrogance.[365]

Justifying the looting and the burning during the George Floyd's protests, people said that struggle for freedom does not have a single way of achieving the goal; there are many ways to it. In response to the crimes and looting in New York, Rep. AOC says, "The looting has to do with the facts people are not paying their rent and are scared to pay their rent. So, they go out and they need to feed their children and they do not have money. People are being put in a position where they feel they need to shoplift some bread to eat or go hungry that night.[366]

Rep. AOC refuses to acknowledge the truth; it is not the bread houses that were targets for looting. In New York, it is the Luxury Retailers' shelves emptied at dozens of stores from Soho to Midtown such as Bloomingdale's, Chanel, Rolex, Diesel, Gucci, Game Stop, Walgreens, Dolce & Gabbana, among others. To us this is a disgrace to hear such lame excuse instead of condemning the acts. Scriptures tell the believers, "Anyone who has been stealing must no longer steal, but must work, doing something useful with their own hands, that they may have something to share with those in need.[367]

In Ontario, Canada right now, the law society has made it mandatory for lawyers to produce a statement of principle that the government supplied a template for, they tell you what the statement of principle should be. They are basically: equity, diversity, and inclusivity statements. If you don't write out your statement of principle declaring your agreement with these principles simultaneously and essentially you are a racist and you don't get your license.[368]

In Canada, a bill known as "An Act to amend the Canadian Human Rights Act and the Criminal Code (Bill C-16, 2016), is a law passed by the Parliament of Canada. The law adds gender expression and gender identity as protected grounds to the Canadian Human Rights Act, and to the provisions of the Criminal Code dealing with hate propaganda, incitement to genocide, and aggravating factors in sentencing.

The bill was introduced by Justin Trudeau's Liberal government on 17th May 2016. It was passed in the House of Commons by 248–40 votes and in the Senate by 67–11 votes with three abstentions. The bill became law upon receiving Royal Assent on 19 June 2017, coming into force at once.[369] Bill C-16, 2016 in simple terms refers to avoiding the pronoun he and she. If one does not know whether a person identifies as a male or female, one should address them as 'they or them.'

The Ethiopian university students and a few others who have nothing to lose in the community believed the income inequality and oppression people have is due to the few rich owning the resources to make themselves richer. The Communists kept on drumming on the heads of the public about the victimhood mentality and the people believed it. By the help of the Communist regime, they targeted, selectively handpicked, and imprisoned the few productive rich business owners just for being rich, no other wrongdoings or crimes.

The rich were not allowed to have a legal representation, and hence died in prison. Thus, the productive businesses lost their leadership and did not produce what they were intended to do. The businesses ceased to be productive shut their doors. The productive force or employees had no means of supporting their families and were exposed to poverty. The government came in as a sole provider for the public. Due to cutting the productive rich (farmers) from the field in addition to the existing hunger, several Ethiopians died.

The Ethiopian Communist regime followed that of the Russian principles in exterminating the few resource owners, the productive rich, and indiscriminately exterminating human beings in general. There is a common saying that 'Revolution swallows its own children' *Abyot ljochwan twtalech.*

The goal of Marxism is to eliminate one class and replace it by another workable for all. Yet eliminating one and replacing it with another is not good for a healthy community and nation. There should be consistent competition to outdo the other; and doing so produces better quality or services. Competition is part of the game in the capitalist economy.

In the same premise, Prof. Jordan expounds on how victimhood mentality discourse leads to genocide. The discontented operatives make their living by creating a victimhood mentality of one side of the community and instigating irreconcilable hate, conflict, and war on the other. They propagate their agenda telling the so-called victims, "You have been oppressed in a variety of ways. These are the people who did it. They are not going to stop doing it. This time we are going to stop them before they get us." That is the enhancement of victimization.[370]

The USSR cadres made the community, the resentful in the minority, the kind of guys that hang out in the burrows most of the time and who are uncontentious and fail at everything and blame everyone for everything that has failed in their lives. The Russian intellectuals made them believe that this happened to them.

They said,

It is unfair that you have been victimized. Now it is your opportunity to go out and get revenge. Some of the sensible people tried to defend justice (of the rich) surround the farmsteads of the successful people. It did not take long that the defenders were overpowered by the angry and aggressive mob that stripped down into rubble the homes, farmhouses, and businesses of the rich.[371]

The white liberals, the Democratic Marxist operatives, and their Trojan hubris made black people believe they have been and are still being oppressed, brutally killed by white police officers and that they must fight back. Politics and white liberals will not solve the black people's problems.[372] About 1,500 businesses were destroyed by riot in Minnesota over the death of George Floyd. Governor Tim Waltz who did not put any effort to stop the looting, burning, and destruction of businesses declared a major disaster for the state. He requested $500 million from FEMA to repair, rebuild, clear debris, and reimburse expenses.

During his hyper-political eulogy for Congressman John Lewis, President Obama spoke about how the federal government was sending agents to use tear gas and batons against peaceful demonstrators. Yet he failed to acknowledge that those peaceful demonstrators destroyed 1,500 businesses: worth $500 million. However, Gov. Waltz's request was rejected, that the impact to public infrastructure was within the capabilities of the local and state governments to recover.[373] In 2015, under the Obama administration as well, FEMA denied aid to the state of Maryland after rioting in Baltimore over the death of Freddie Gray, a Black man who died in police custody. Maryland appealed the decision and was again rejected.[374]

The Russian operatives handpicked the rich and send them on a train to Siberia with no food and no place to live. They died of hunger, typhoid, and others froze to death. Since the productive rich were exterminated, taken out by the system, there was no food produced. The effects of cutting the productive resulted in the death of six million Ukrainians. People were starving to the point of cannibalism. That is how the idea of victimization and perpetration can go out of hand extraordinarily rapidly.[375]

What needs to be acknowledged is that some historic ugliness and dark history such as slavery happened. There is no way to undo the past. What one can do instead is to learn from the past and avoid repeating the same mistakes and fix the future. The ugly part of our history cannot be neutralized by another modern ugly history. One cannot solve past injustices by a modern injustice. Injustice does not and cannot neutralize injustice.

Dr. Martin Luther King has clearly stated "Injustice anywhere is a threat to justice everywhere. We are caught in an inescapable network of mutuality, tied in a single garment of destiny. Whatever affects one directly, affects all indirectly." Darkness cannot cast away darkness. Only light can. Blood for blood vengeance should have no room in our country. A person calling for retaliation for past mistakes should be held accountable in the USA court of law. In the USA, there is equal rights for all. Should there be a problem, the law accommodates mutual discussion-not violence-to solve the existing issue.

Chapter Twenty

"I predict future happiness for Americans, if they can prevent the government from wasting the labors of the people under the pretense of taking care of them."

— PRESIDENT THOMAS JEFFERSON

A GOVERNMENT WITHIN A GOVERNMENT

The main reason as to why Hayet chose to write this book is after he saw the insanity of protesters barricading and controlling certain part of Seattle. He said, "Enough is Enough."

There should be only one government in a country. What makes America and most of the developed countries unique is the presence of checks and balances. A leader cannot abuse certain powers. Unlike the Communist, Socialist, Marxist, Islamic and other countries where most immigrants come from, leaders can do whatever they want and there is no one who can challenge them.

As Hayet takes a walk by the swimming pool in his neighborhood he comes across his neighbor Corey, "Hi, Hayet," Corey calls out. "Have you seen or heard the ordinance and demands by BLM on business owners in Louisville?"

"No! Who did you say is demanding? Is it the City Council or the State's delegated person for that responsibility?"

"No, it is the Black Lives Matter Movement."

"A government within a government? What are their demands and why?"

She speaks fast like a shooter shooting a whole magazine at once. "Slow down please, you are too fast."

"Okay, here we go slowly. Like 23% of staff are 'Black or Indigenous Persons of Color' (BIPOC)."

"This is not a Communist rationing. As a person involved in business, company should hire based on ability and talent that the individual brings to the business not on diversity demands. Look at most of our inner cities leadership are BIPOC, you know those places are the worst to bring up a child."

"What else?"

"23% of inventory should be from BIPOC retailers?"

"How would I know which inventory is from BIPOC retailers?"

"I don't know either."

"How could you echo what you do not know?"

"I am just telling you what is going on in the street."

"By the way, I went to three BIPOC car service."

"How did it go?" shops.

"Horrible!"

"Why?"

"At the first business I was so happy to see minority owning business and hoping to recommend them to other friends and relatives. However, three of them were so discriminating, disrespectful, and not business minded. Are they going to blame the white people for not doing well?"

"Tell me about that."

After the service, the first man said, "My card reader is not working please go to Quick Trip, withdraw money from the ATM and pay me cash. I did it and so hated that business. I do not think he would do the same with a white customer. The second and the third are open for business throughout 24 hours. The business owner said that he was going to charge me $40 for the service. I told him that "Walmart charges $15, but to support you, okay" I replied. After the service, during checkout, I gave him a card to pay. The man was so furious demanding cash pay. I managed to get $35 dollar bills and the last five in quarters which I personally received from another customer. For the quarters, "I am not a beggar that you give me coins. This is an insult," He yelled. He refused to accept the quarters even when myself and my wife begged him. He told me to go away and I had to leave.

"Really? Corey interjected.

"I am telling you!"

"Take 160 quarters or an equal value in dimes, nickels or pennies to a white business owner and they would accept it happily. I guarantee you; they would never do the same with a white customer. Try it for yourself. If three of them accept your card payment, I will cover all the cost."

On the third one, after the service he said, "My card reader is not working go to Chevron, get cash and pay me."

"If it is random ATM vendor, they charge money. Can I go to my bank ATM and bring you cash?" I asked believing he would trust me.

"You can either call someone to bring you the money or leave your driver's license with me."

"At that moment I wanted to call 911 but did not want to harm the business of my African brother. Eventually, I went to get money without my ID just to get away from him. Driving without an ID was foolishness, risking myself of getting a ticket."

"Coming back to you. Would you go back to such businesses?"

"No!"

"Would you recommend such businesses to friends and family?"

"Absolutely not! It is about how one serves not about what race one is."

"Thank you! I did what you would do. If a business in a local area has no repeat customers and referrals from customers, it cannot survive. Then such business owners blame the white man for taking their job away. Improve customer service and your business will grow. Moreover, I guarantee you again, they would never treat a white customer the way they did to me."

"What else?"

"Dress code accommodating BIPOC patrons and employees."

"What is new about that, we already have it. I have been to several countries where students as well as employees are required to put on uniforms due to the need for safety. If one does not comply to the safety standards of the company then they should leave or have their own company that does not require any dress code."

"What else?"

"Mandated diversity and inclusion training."

"Business owners know what is working for their businesses and should be free to do what is good for their companies, serving customers. This is not a government bureaucracy or Communist ration vending. This sounds like the Communist reeducation camp."

"What else?"

"Business owners should display left-wing messaging to support 'reparations."

"Business owners should display neither left-wing nor right-wing messages. Only what is good for everybody. Such requirements are from Communist and Marxist countries and I have lived in such places. I never thought I would see such ignorance in the USA."

"All these demands are from jealous people who do not know how to run a successful business."

CAVING INTO DETRACTORS

Until one achieves the goal 100% and keeps on maintaining and sustaining the achievement, they should not let up or give in even an inch to the detractors. When word came to Sanballat, Tobias, Geshem the Arab, and the rest of the enemies that Nehemiah had rebuilt the wall and no gap was left in it—though up to that time he had not set the doors in the gates— Sanballat and Geshem sent him this message: "Come, let us meet together in one of the villages on the plain of Ono."

If doors are not set, Nehemiah's mission is incomplete. A house without a gate is not a safe place. Nehemiah's detractors, after having several failed attempts (as Trump has experienced from his detractors), they produced another conspiracy, for a discussion. The discussion was not in the best interest of the Jews, but a scheme to harm them and derail the work. The same is going on with the unrest in the USA, not for the benefit of the black people but for the benefit of the Democratic feudalists. It is for the interest of the nobles, who are also conspiring to enforce their hidden agenda.

Nehemiah was not intimidated by their threats and schemes. He sent messengers to the detractors with this reply: "I am carrying on a great project and cannot go down. Why should the work stop while I leave it and go down to you? Four times they sent me the same message, and each time I gave them the same answer."

Detractors tirelessly and shamelessly make up senseless and un-corroborating story after story even if it results on exonerating a non-guilty verdict on their target.

Here for the fifth time, the deaf detractor Sanballat sent his aide to Nehemiah with the same message, and in his hand was an unsealed letter that had a made up story written as: "It is reported among the nations—and Geshem says it is true—that you and the Jews are plotting to revolt, and therefore you are building the wall. Moreover, according to these reports you are about to become their king and have even appointed prophets to make this proclamation about you in Jerusalem: 'There is a king in Judah!' Now this report will get back to the king; so, come, let us meet."

The purpose here again was to make the target negotiate over nonnegotiable matters and ultimately get detracted. However, the discerning Nehemiah was aware of their scheme. Although there was no need of negotiating with terrorists, he replied: "Nothing like what you are saying is happening; you are just making it up out of your head."

The detractors were trying to frighten the Jews, thinking, "Their hands will get too weak for the work, and it will not be completed."

In such times, the best solution for the Israelites, as is also for the Americans comes from the Lord, the maker of the heavens and the earth.

The Scriptures order believers to pray for all government officials even to the undeserving. Contrary to mayhem advocacy, Saint Paul calls "I urge, then, first of all, that petitions, prayers, intercession and thanksgiving be made for all people   for kings and all those in authority, that we may live peaceful and quiet lives in all godliness and holiness."[376] Whereas Fifth column detractors who really do not care for the American people appearing in different names, the kind of groups Michael Moore encourages to join advocate have been engaged in destruction, and not to protect and unite the country.

Whether or not one agrees with the political party leader at the time, it is the responsibility of the believers to "seek the peace and prosperity of the city to which I have carried you into exile. Pray to the LORD for it, because if it prospers, you too will prosper" (Jeremiah 29:7). Therefore, sincere prayer is needed for the country and the city one lives in, and for Trump and America.

On July 4th weekend, in Atlanta, there were eleven separate shootings, 31 injuries and five deaths that included an eight-year-old girl, confronted by a group of armed BLM protesters in downtown Atlanta.[377] If the law enforcement does not take control of the city and the street, soon the USA will be like any other lawless countries.

When Nehemiah's enemies saw that they could not slow him down (Trump), they keep on manufacturing another approach each time. Thank God! Trump train no slow and no stop. The worst attack that Nehemiah faced as Trump did, was from the very people that were supposed to be on his side. These were the nobles who were in it for their benefit and not for the truth.

One day Nehemiah went to Shemaiah son of Delilah, the son of Mehetabel's home, who is a prophet. The prophet said to Nehemiah, "Let us meet in the house of God, inside the temple, and let us close the temple doors, because men are coming to kill you—by night."

The main reason the prophet came to Nehemiah was not because he cared for him, but because he sought benefits. It is good that the discerning Nehemiah realized that God had not sent him, but that he had prophesied against him because Tobias and Sanballat had hired him. He had been hired to intimidate him so he would commit a sin by doing this, and then they would give him a bad name to discredit him.

How many people have been hired to discredit Trump? The list is endless. Some credible starting points, others, baseless accusation. What matters is what God says who you are regardless of one's history!

One-time God showed Zechariah, Joshua the high priest standing before the angel of the Lord, and Satan standing at his right side to accuse him. The Lord said to Satan, "The Lord rebuke you, Satan! The Lord, who has chosen Jerusalem, rebukes you! Is not this man a burning stick snatched from the fire?"

Joshua was dressed in filthy clothes as he stood before the angel. The angel said to those who were standing before him, "Take off his filthy clothes."

Then he said to Joshua, "See, I have taken away your sin, and I will put fine garments on you." Then he said, "Put a clean turban on his head." So, they put a clean turban on his head and clothed him, while the angel of the Lord stood by.[378]

When all Nehemiah's (Trump's) enemies heard about the completion of the wall building, (work that career politicians could not achieve in 50 years) the surrounding nations were afraid and lost their self-confidence, because they realized that this work had been done with the help of God.

As usual, the detractors still have other conspiracies. In those days, the nobles of Judah were sending many letters to Tobias and replies from Tobias kept coming to them. Many people in Judah were under oath to him (not to the Jewish State/ not to America), since he was son-in-law to Shekaniah son of Arah, and his son Jehohanan had married the daughter of Meshullam son of Berekiah. Moreover, they kept reporting to him his honorable deeds and then telling him what Nehemiah said. And Tobias sent letters to intimidate him.[379]

It is sad that some priests, prophets, and the nobles (establishment Democrat and Republicans alike) care more for the wellbeing of the Jewish enemies than they do for their own people. They valued mere benefits such as money, friendship, and relationships over their country. The countries, (America, China, Russia, you name each country that should come first), not benefit; because after each leader is gone, the country remains.

The good thing though is that the silent majority was more effective in achieving their goal than the few vocal pundit critics of the leadership. Nehemiah's detractors have had generations to fix the existing problem, and return to God, which they did not. Now the fresh face to the system appears to clean the corruption and mess of the old system, they are jealous of him. They want to do all they can to detract him from getting the credit that should have been theirs.

HONORING THE FAKE

These are the kind of days whereby Paul gave charge to Timothy: "Preach the Word; be prepared in season and out of season; correct, rebuke, and encourage—with great patience and careful instruction. For the time will come when people will not put up with sound doctrine. Instead, to suit their own desires, they will gather around them a considerable number of teachers to say what their itching ears want to hear. They will turn their ears away from the truth and turn aside to myths. But you, keep your head in all situations, endure hardship, do the work of an evangelist, discharge all the duties of your ministry.[380]

Usually, the fake TVCNN pundits are louder and more visible, audible, destructive than silent warriors. No matter how long it may take, how loud TVCNN wailing may be, the truth vindicates the deserving.

In 2 Chronicles 18, there is a story whereby the king of Israel, Ahab and the king of Judah, Jehoshaphat wanted to go to war against Ramoth Gilead. However, before moving on, Jehoshaphat wanted to seek God's counsel whether to go or not. So, king Ahab brought together four hundred of his prophets and asked them, whether they should go to war or not. The prophets answered in unison "Go, for God will give victory into the king's hand". However, the discerning and wise king Jehoshaphat not trusting the prophecy inquired, "IS there no longer a prophet of the Lord here whom we can inquire?" he probed.

"There is still one prophet through whom we can inquire of the Lord, but I hate him because he never prophesies anything good about me, but always bad. He is Micaiah son of Imlah," Ahab replied.

The main issue with king Ahab is he was not interested in the truth but hearing what he wanted to hear and not what he needed to hear. The current aggressive Media, Academics, Big Tech companies, and Lawyers only keep you around if you sing their tone, and when one speaks the truth refusing to be their Trojan horse, they are cut off air.

Examples: New Orleans Saints tight end Benjamin Watson was invited to speak on CNN about his perspective over the wake of 18 years old black, Michael Brown's death who got killed by a white police officer. The anchor expected Watson to sing to her tune, such as 'this racism'. Instead, he sang to his tune pointing out the main problem in America as sin, which is a departure from God. The mention of God is not good news to CNN. It got worse when he stated to bring the subject of healing from racism and prejudice, "we need salvation through Jesus Christ," the interview was cut off.[381] If people do not sing to their tone chances are that they cannot be invited again.

Jehoshaphat suggested that Micaiah be brought. Immediately, Ahab ordered one of his officials to bring the prophet. The messenger who had gone to summon Micaiah said to him, "Look, the other prophets without exception are predicting success for the king. Let your word agree with theirs and speak favorably."

How many people are bamboozled, tricked, recruited, enticed, paid to say what most likely would hurt or trap President Trump?

"As surely as the Lord lives, I can tell him only what my God says," replied Micaiah.

When he arrived, king Ahab asked him, "Micaiah, shall we go to war against Ramoth Gilead, or shall I not?"

Micaiah eventually replied that Ahab should not go, if he goes, he would die.

Upon hearing the disapproval of the other prophet's prophecy, "Didn't I tell you that he never prophesies anything good about me, but only bad?" Ahab yelled furiously, threatening imprisonment, accompanied by one prophet slapping Micaiah in the face.

Consequently, Micaiah was put in prison for speaking against what king Ahab wanted to hear. Eventually, the kings went to war in disguise disregarding Micaiah's prophecy and he died (2 Chronicles 18).

The same is going on in America today to the people who use their unalienable freedom either to keep silent or speak in favor of what is hemorrhaging the USA. When God wants to honor a person, God's omnipotence overrides any injunction or ceases and desists. God blesses a person irrespective of their flaws. God does not call a person because he or she is perfect. God calls people and uses them with their flaws. If people were to be perfect, they would not be looking for a Savior. Accepting people with their flaws the Bible declare, "What shall we say then? Is there injustice on God's part? By no means! For he says to Moses, "I will have mercy on whom I have mercy, and I will have compassion on whom I have compassion."[382]

OPPOSITION WITHIN YOUR FAMILY

Every now and then, an enemy comes out from within. There are so many enemies born within that have become a great threat to the family, to the nation, and to the World.

The Muslim Malcom X's enemies were his own people. He could handle the fight against the white liberals who are the most dangerous for humanity and the white conservatives, but his own people. He was killed by another black Muslim.

Mary Trump, who is Trump's niece, a licensed clinical psychologist published a book. Ms. Trump's tell-all book portrays Trump as a damaged man with lethal flaws who threatens the World's health, economic security, and social fabric. His father Fred caused him terror; Donald suffered deprivations that would scar him for life.[383]

There could be two approaches to Ms. Trump's comments. First, it could be for neutralization or damage control to the Trump's name. Second, this could be spewing a personal beef or fight of one family member against the other in which money is the main reason.

When Fred Trump Sr. died in 1999, Mary and her brother Fred III contested their grandfather's will. Mr. Fred Sr.'s will left the bulk of his estate, in equal shares, to his children. His grandchildren were each left with $200,000. When Mary's father predeceased him, Fred Sr.'s lawyers had recommended amending his will, to leave Mary and her brother, Fred III, larger shares than the grandchildren with living parents. They anticipated Fred Sr.'s will would be challenged if it were not amended by descendants who would argue his intent was that each child would eventually leave a portion of his or her share of the estate to his or her own descendants.

Shortly after Fred Sr.'s death, Mary's sister-in-law gave birth to a son with a rare and debilitating medical condition—one that would require a lifetime of expensive medical care. Fred Sr. had set up a foundation that paid the medical expenses of his family. After Mary and Fred III had filed suit against Donald Trump and two of his siblings, Mary and Fred III were advised that the medical foundation would no longer pay for their medical expenses. The lawsuit was settled in 2001. The final settlement of the dispute over sharing Fred Sr.'s estate did not award Mary and her brother the share their father would have inherited, had he been alive when Fred Sr. died.[384]

The title of the book as it portrays: *Too Much and Never Enough: How My Family Created the World's Most Dangerous Man* appears to care for her perceived damage Trump is inflicting to the USA and the World. Mary may be trying to take revenge because the legal settlement did not give her what she wanted or deserved. The Trump family fight should remain among them; there is no need of bringing it out for the World to justify one against the other. This book is a big deal and big news to the TVCNN, but of no value to the American public. The book could be like previous books, Michael Wolff's *Fire and Fury* or even John Bolton's *The Room Where It Happened*, intended to harm Trump but turned out to be fruitless nuisances.

Speaking the truth, who is perfect? Mary Trump is not perfect herself too like her uncle Donald Trump. Scriptures tell, "God's righteousness is given through faith in Jesus Christ to all who believe. There is no difference between Jew and Gentile, for all have sinned and fall short of the glory of God, and all are justified freely by his grace through the redemption that came by Christ Jesus."[385]

WHEN YOUR CHILDREN BECOME YOUR TIME BOMB

King David experienced enmity in his family. He describes it how sever it was, "Even my close friend, someone I trusted, one who shared my bread, has turned against me." [386] His own son wanted to kill him. Yet, David still was merciful.

In the Bible, Joseph's enemies were his jealous brothers. Jesus' enemies were his own family and countrymen; they were looking some way to get rid of him.[387] David's enemies were, his brothers, King Saul whom he served faithfully, his son Absalom, and his confidant Ahithophel.

In relation to children and their parents the writer of Proverbs tells, "There are those who curse their fathers and do not bless their mothers. Those whose eyes are ever so haughty; whose glances are so disdainful. The eye that mocks a father, that scorns an aged mother, will be pecked out by the ravens of the valley; will be eaten by the vultures.[388]

A time bomb is a bomb whose detonation is triggered by a timer. What makes a time bomb dangerous it that, it is right by your side, under your shade and you do not know that it could be set to detonate in hours, weeks, or months over a period of time. For example, the Grand Hotel bombing in Brighton (1984) which was targeted at British Prime Minister Margaret Thatcher the result of time bomb which had been placed in the hotel nearly a month before it detonated. Thatcher escaped harm, though 5 people perished, and 31 others were injured.[389]

What makes the author to give this subtopic is that, your children becoming your time bomb is that, they live with you, you trust them, you bring them up to represent the very thing that you love and care about. However, it is sad and shocking to see when these same children intentionally and totally turn against their parent's views. It is okay to have independent children, but there is a limitation. A pro-life father was shocked when his teenage daughter spoke of being for pro-choice; that abortion is okay and stating that a woman can do whatever she wants with her body.

The premise, 'a woman can do whatever she wants with her body' is the work of Nicolaitan, one that God detests. The word Nicolaitan comes after Nicolas of Antioch, one of the seven men chosen to serve the church in Jerusalem.

The works or deeds of Nicolaitan reasoned that the human body was evil anyway and only the spirit was good. Christians, therefore, could do whatever they desired with their bodies because they had no importance. The spirit, on the other hand, was the recipient of grace, which meant that grace and forgiveness were theirs no matter what they did. Sexual relations outside marriage were completely acceptable in such a society. They were ready to compromise with the world. They were judged by the author of Revelation to be the most dangerous because the results of their teachings conformed Christianity to the World rather than having Christianity change the World.[390]

The pro-life people speak about the body inside the human body. Parents also bring up their children to believe a marriage should be between a biologically male and a biologically female. They teach that it is okay to get married to whomever you love as long as they are opposite to your gender. Where do you stand? One of King David's son was time bomb for his father.

Absalom at times would get up early and stand by the side of the road leading to the city gate. Whenever anyone came with a complaint to be placed before the king for a decision, Absalom would call out to him, "What town are you from?" He would answer,

"Your servant is from one of the tribes of Israel."

Then Absalom would act prideful and would say to people that came seeking solutions, "Look, your claims are valid and proper, but there is no representative of the king to hear you. If only I were appointed judge in the land! Then everyone who has a complaint or case could come to me and I would see that they receive justice."

Whenever anyone approached Absalom to bow down before him, he would reach out his hand, take hold of them and kiss them. Absalom behaved in this way toward all the Israelites who came to the king asking for justice, and so he stole the hearts of the people of Israel." That was not all. After four years of disloyalty and rebellion to the king, who was loyal to the people and to the family, Absalom eventually declared himself a king at a place called Hebron. This is treason. Scripture disapproves off such behavior, "Do not plot harm against your neighbor, who lives trustfully near you."[391] Ahithophel's defection from the king to join Absalom was a big blow to David, big news to the TVCNN. That is why David had to pray, "LORD, turn Ahithophel's counsel into foolishness."[392]

Although Absalom was out there to harm his father, David was kind enough to say to the men heading to the war, which would kill twenty-four thousand people "Deal gently with the young man Absalom for my sake."

The result of children who rebel against their parents and people that rebel against authority is death. Paul has warned Timothy of the same, "There will be terrible times in the last days. People will be lovers of themselves, lovers of money, boastful, proud, abusive, disobedient to their parents, ungrateful, unholy, without love, unforgiving, slanderous, without self-control, brutal, not lovers of the good, treacherous, rash, conceited, lovers of pleasure rather than lovers of God— having a form of godliness but denying its power. Have nothing to do with such people."[393]

Furthermore Paul states, "They are the kind who worm their way into homes and gain control over gullible women, who are loaded down with sins and are swayed by all kinds of evil desires, always learning but never able to come to a knowledge of the truth. Just as Jannes and Jambres opposed Moses, so also these teachers oppose the truth. They are men of depraved minds, who, as far as the faith is concerned, are rejected. But they will not get far because, as in the case of those men, their folly will be clear to everyone."[394]

As the battle raged, "Absalom rode on a mule. The mule went under the thick boughs of a great terebinth tree, and his head caught in the terebinth; so, he was left hanging between heaven and earth. And the mule which *was* under him went on." Absalom died at that spot.

In a related subject, "Please for the love of God do not vote for my dad': Republican's daughter Stephanie Regan who is an advocate systemic racism tweets, white privilege exists and Black Lives Matter. She voiced opposition against her father Robert Regan who was running for election. Mr. Regan who describes himself as a conservative blames the education system for perverting the clear conscience of the country and, family-loving children when they head to college. He stated "When they go off to college, quite frankly they get involved with these Marxist, Socialist universities, and they start getting indoctrinated with things that are completely opposite from where and what you raised them. The only place where Mr. Regan really sees systemic racism would be the abortion clinic because they target the African American community.[395]

The then 14 years old 10th grader, daughter asked her dad referring to 2016 election, "Who are you going to vote for?"

"I don't think I will vote, but if I vote it will be for Trump."

"If you ever get to vote for Trump, I will never get to talk to you. Hillary won in our school voting; she should win the presidential election too," she asserted.

This is how our young generation today in the World are dangerous. Grandparents have been threatened and told that they would never be able to see their grandchildren for voting for Republican Party. This is the liberal's Socialist and Marxist America. They bring their aggressive political view to the class, to work, and to home. This cannot and should not be tolerated. In the true America, you can vote whoever you want to vote for, and at the dinner table you eat together as if you have the same political view.

There is so much incompatible political dissension and division in American families of the young generation than any other time in history. Students whose school fees are paid either by the government or by their parents are indoctrinated to hate America and all that the USA stands for. The very kids expect to inherit from their parent's but would not love what their parents love. It is understandable that American children should have their own opinions. However, it is wrong to consider themselves as national experts while they have no experience. They speak as if they are all-knowing. They disrespect and lambast their parents openly. This is a dishonorable act and cut one's life short. This is contrary to what the Scriptures command "Honor your father and mother so that you may live long in the land the LORD your God is giving you."

There are several instances where things will not go well for dishonorable children. There is a curse, or a blessing associated with obeying or disobeying one's parents. There is a man called Samson in the Biblical stories. His parents told him not to marry a woman out of his culture. He was adamant, chose to go his way, and he did. He lost the first woman he wished; he kept on making the same mistake. Eventually, he got entrapped by the snare his parents told him to avoid.

There is another Scriptural example. Isaac commanded Jacob: "Do not marry a Canaanite woman. Go at once to the house of your uncle and take a wife for yourself there, from among the daughters. He also blessed him saying may God Almighty bless you and make you fruitful and increase your numbers until you become a community of peoples. May he give you and your descendants the blessing given to Abraham, so that you may take possession of the land where you now live as a foreigner, the land God gave to Abraham."[396] Jacob honored his father and mother by doing all that they told him to do. As a result, his name still exists.

On the contrary, "Esau then realized how displeasing the Canaanite women were to his father Isaac; so, he went to Ishmael and married Mahalath, the daughter of Ishmael son of Abraham, in addition to the wives he already had."[397] Due to his disobedience, all did not go well with him and his descendants. Scriptures refer to God as the of God Abraham, Isaac, and Jacob. It could and should have been the God Abraham, Isaac, and Esau.

It is so painful for a parent to see children deviate from what they have been trained and are expected to behave. For the most part, defiant behavior is temporary. Sometimes it comes with irreversible scars, heartaches, injuries, or even death. However, a lot of times, there is a scriptures' promise, "Start children off on the way they should go, and even when they are old, they will not turn from it."[398] Until one sees the fulfillment a parent ought to be a parent that is loving and caring even for undeserving sons and daughters.

Chapter Twenty-One

"One of the saddest lessons of history is this: If we've been bamboozled long enough, we tend to reject any evidence of the bamboozle. We're no longer interested in finding out the truth. The bamboozle has captured us. It is simply too painful to acknowledge, even to ourselves, that we've been taken. Once you give a charlatan power over you, you almost never get it back."

— CARL SAGAN, THE DEMON-HAUNTED WORLD: SCIENCE AS A CANDLE IN THE DARK

TRUMP GOOD OR BAD FOR THE USA

This is an important question one should answer honestly. Should one ask, Chris Cuomo, Don Lemon, Michael Moore, or his disciples as well as all other TVCNN, if they have a single good to praise for Trump's goodness. One time, a Ghanaian preacher Dr. Mensa Otabil said, "Criticizers will criticize you even if you cut your hand and give them. Just do all that should and need to be done." As for the author, excluding Trump's character flaws, he is one of the best Presidents who did good to the USA. It is possible that you may not like a person's personality, but personal hatred should not impede one's honest judgement.

It is too sad to see that the Jealous, Angry, Aggressive, Crying Liberal, Democrat, Militants (JAACLDM) and anchors hatred lead the people like a lamb to the slaughter including the academia who in turn use their students as accessories to achieve their anti-America rhetoric.

A president of any nation's priority is to take care of the citizens and the country. Right after the September 11, 2001 terrorist attack, which changed America for good, President George Bush said that his priority was to protect Americans. That is what President Trump's motto has been: "America first." That is what he promised during the campaign and that is what he is doing, and he is unapologetic for it. Trump should not be blamed for putting America first. If Hayet were to add one word to Trump's motto, it would be 'Americans,' to make it "America and Americans first."

The world has seen President Obama tour to apologize for America's past wrong and to forge good relationship with other nations, most of which did not like America and Americans. In his first 100 days (about 3 and a half months) he visited three continents apologizing for America's past mistakes, but skipped America's closest ally, Israel.

We have been used to leaders who put America into debt to feed and defend other nations at the cost of billions and perhaps trillions of dollars every year. However, with President Trump, all those days are behind us. Although when it comes to foreign policy Democrats and Republicans have the same perspective, one is worse than the other. It appears Democrats want to globalize, export democracy, and control the entire World, while Republicans appear to take control more of themselves, within the USA.

As a businessman, Trump appears to lead the nation from a business perspective showing assets, $+ (plus); or from liability $- (minus). Over the past 100 years or so, we have seen American leaders being taken advantage of by other nations and would do nothing to correct it. But not in Trump's America.

Donald Trump, character wise, was the least electable person in the eyes of the electorate, but he came at a time when multiple predecessors failed the American people. The predecessors came to the Presidency and left the Office without fulfilling what they promised to fix. Americans lost faith in their elected leaders. As a result, several electorates discontented.

At such a time as this, there was a need for a reviving leader and Trump showed up and promised to fix all wrongs in America. Of course, for some people wrong and right are subjective, it depends on the perspective of a person from which angle one looks at it. All those who were in distress over the handling of American problems or discontented by their leaders gathered around him, they voted for him and he became the commander in chief of the USA.

To be a great leader in the USA, one should lead from three fronts. The first one is to coordinate government leaders. This includes appointing judges that would uphold family values. Since his election, Trump has appointed more conservative judges than any other president in American history.

Second, coordinate faith leaders. Faith leaders do play a key role to either build or tear down the country. The faith leaders would directly influence each family leader (a father) to nurture the family giving right leadership of providing, protecting, nurturing, and leading the family. A nation is a collection of families. When the family stays strong, so does the nation.

Third, coordinate "We the People." When Nehemiah started his project, a vision birthed within him, then he coordinated the people. Some were for the work others were not. A leader is only one, to achieve common goals, or more of the people, he or she ought to be involved for a sustainable achievement.

TRUMP GOOD OR BAD FOR MINORITIES, BLACKS, and IMMIGRANTS

To say that Trump is good or bad for minorities and blacks; it depends on which angle one considers. The main thing to look at is that if you cannot take care of yourself, nobody cares about you.

Within about a year of his Presidency, he recognized and signed into law a bill for 'Ebenezer Baptist Church and King's burial site; to have all been upgraded from a national historic site to a national historic park.[399] This is a big deal for Trump; three of his predecessors could not do within twenty-four years.

Majority of the people in the Democratic Party, including Joe Biden, believe poverty is tied to the minorities, more so to the People of color. If one is black, the assumption is they are poor and in need of help. While addressing Asian & Latino Coalition group in Des Moines, Iowa he said, "We have this notion that somehow if you're poor, you cannot do it. Poor kids are just as bright and just as talented as white kids."[400]

Hayet works for a company where minors and teenagers are the clients. One Hispanic teen asks, "Who are you going to vote for?"

"We have been told not to talk about politics, I cannot tell you," replied Hayet.

"My grandfather told me that Democrats are good for minorities."

"Why?"

"He told me, if Democrats find a jobless people on the street, they give them food. If Republicans find the same, they give them a job application form."

"So, which one would you rather choose? Getting a job application to find a job or getting food."

"For immediate need, you need food. However, for the long run and future sustainability getting a job is better. Because you will not ask for food again."

"Thank you for realizing the truth. I am afraid to say that we need leaders who would give us jobs not who would give us food."

The Black people and the minorities are among the people that Trump calls the forgotten people. During his inaugural speech he said "The forgotten men and women of our country will be forgotten no longer," he told the crowd as the cold breeze hammers the people that came out to see the inauguration of the 45th President in Washington DC. "And I will fight for you with every breath in my body, and I will never, ever let you down" And he appears to be fulfilling his promises.

Democrat leadership loves intrusion, regulation of production and market, control of everything, including faith-based organizations, big government spending in and out of the country. However, Republican leadership, encouraged people to have responsibility to think for themselves on spending so that there is less government spending and intervention.

people have responsibility to think for themselves on spending, there is less government spending and intervention.

The single largest annual budget for the about 80-plus federal welfare programs amounts roughly to $1.03 trillion (about $3,200 per person in the US).[401] The $1.03 budget includes salaries of the employees. A substantial portion of the distributed budget goes to the workers than to the beneficiaries.

TRUMP'S IMMIGRATION POLICY

In some cases, Trump's immigrant policy is discriminatory and favors rich immigrants. European nations, mainly the French and the British have done that for generations, and it did turn out well. It is not fair and just to deny poor immigrants' permanent legal status, also known as green card, if they are deemed likely to use government's benefit programs such as food stamps and subsidized housing. Wealthier immigrants, who are defined as less likely to require public assistance, will be able to obtain green card.[402]

The concern for such policy is that vast numbers of immigrants may drop out of programs they need because they fear retribution by immigration authorities.[403]

It is true and cannot be denied that there are some immigrants and refugees that take advantage of the generosity of the system. It is wrong. If you do not need government assistance, you should leave it for the people that need the assistance. After all, such undeserving assistance keeps people in poverty.

When given a moment while volunteering among the refugees Hayet tells them to set themselves free from government assistance as early as possible. He tells clients from his experience.

One thing Hayet would like to tell the immigrants, blacks, and other minorities is that God has brought you to this land: work for yourself. God has promised you, "There need be no poor people among you, for in the land the Lord your God is giving you to possess as your inheritance, he will richly bless you, if only you fully obey the Lord your God and are careful to follow all these commands I am giving you today."[404] To be rich, one precondition is to obey God.

Chapter Twenty-Two

"Your pride for your country should not come after your country becomes great; your country becomes great because of your pride in it."

— IDOWU KOYENIKAN

TRUMP THE NEHEMIAH OF OUR GENERATION

According to ancient writings, Nehemiah is known for building the wall of Jerusalem. He was the Jewish cupbearer of King Artaxerxes in Babylonia. While in exile, he loved his country and would ask about the remnants. He met some people who came from Judah and asked them about the remnants at the homeland and about Jerusalem. He was informed that the wall of Jerusalem was broken down, and its gates had been burned with fire.

It is obvious that Nehemiah may not have been the only person who learned about the sad news of the remnants and about Jerusalem. Although other leaders also knew about the existing (America's/Jerusalem's) problem, none dared to fix it due to political correctness. At a time as such, God raised up a man who is so concerned about his country. He began to pray, and God stared creating the necessary connections.

A meaningful and lasting change starts within a person not from outside help. Nehemiah birthed a vision to build the wall out of his own initiative. Spoon-feeding an adult to be an adult would never help either side. For the 2020 election, we have two main leaders. It appears that as he was in 2016, Trump with all his "character inadequacies", has his own initiative to run for the Presidency and win. Whereas Biden does not appear have his own initiative, energy, enthusiasm that he would have to offer to the American people. He always appears fragile. He speaks of a consensus in his family; the most important people in his life and his grandchildren shove him to run for Presidency for the third time.[405]

> A meaningful and lasting change starts within a person not from outside help.

Unlike Biden, Bernie Sanders, who got cheated by the Democrat establishments for the second time, had his own initiative to be one. God forbid should Biden get elected, the very people who shoved him to run for Presidency, the far left, the antifa, BLM that Trojan horse the Democratic Party will run our country, which would be a disaster.

As per the author's experience, the far left, Democratic Socialist of America (DSA), Black Lives Matter, are temporarily working together Trojan horsing the Democratic Party. There is a proverb that says, "the enemy of my enemy is my friend." Once they defeat their common enemy, the Republican Party, a fierce fight will insinuate between the Democratic Party and all the other factions as one team. At last, the Democratic Party will be defeated, then America becomes a Socialist country, persecution will come, Americans have nowhere to go from the last land where freedom stands. *Enough is ENOUGH!*

NANCY PELOSI

Nancy Patricia Pelosi (D) is an American politician serving as a Congresswoman from California and is the two-time Speaker of the United States House of Representatives. She is the only woman in U.S. history to serve as a Speaker, and is the highest-ranking female elected official in United States history.[406] Hayet had great respect for her, a person who knows the book (governance in the USA). However, when she succumbed to the powers of darkness that fuel hate in the USA, by their lame impeachment trial, she lost the respect. Instead of a leader, she became a follower.

She is one of the close friends of Joe Biden. These very people direct what Biden should say and should not what Biden should do or should not. They come guise inside Biden as Greeks used Trojan horse to enter the independent city of Troy and won the war. They introduce him and say what has never been done or said in the USA history for the run of presidential office.

For example, Congresswoman Nancy Pelosi, Speaker of the United States' House of Representatives, is the only person to shred a President's speech in the history of the USA. She appears to have a standing ovation from House Democrats.

It is a formality for a current President to hand the document to the Speaker of the House to be archived as part of our history. A Speaker of the House may have disagreements with the addressing President's, address shredding the document is a dishonorable act. It is an unprecedented behavior of a person who cannot control her emotions. The document is not a personal junk mail with no accountability for it to be discarded. It belongs to the American people. This is the first time for a person to despise the office and bring a personal hatred to the State of the Union address. It is possible to disagree with policy, a person, or a President. However, the disagreement should not affect how one performs the duty of Speakership of the House of Representatives or any other office.

Out of the 223 annual State of the Union messages, she robbed Americans a legal document and she would not apologize for what she did.

The first person to shred a legal document is proposing for the first time in the USA history a presumptive nominee to skip a presidential debate in a series that have already been reduced to three due to Covid-19. Why? She reasons that Trump disrespected the office and has engaged in "skullduggery" referring to the debate handling during the 2016 election,[407] and how he could repeat the same. What greater disrespect of an Office is there than ripping a legal document that belongs to "We the People?"

Skullduggery is the dishonorable proceedings, dishonest, trickery, underhanded, or unscrupulous behavior[408] of a person.

For the scheduled debates Pelosi is using to skip the Biden-Trump debate, in 2016, Veteran Democratic operative Donna Brazile finally admitted that she used her former position as a CNN commentator to relay questions ahead of debates to Hillary Clinton during the Democratic primary.[409] Is that not a skullduggery what the Democrats are known for during the past four years? They did skullduggery to Trump on 2016 election what they accuse him that he could do for the 2020 elections. They were in such multiple activities and were caught.

During a debate, candidates hit and are hit by ideas. The voters then decide the best based on what the candidate promises to offer. If Biden cannot survive a debate with just a single person, how is he going to lead this great nation when criticized by the internal and external adversaries of the USA? Trump has proved himself that he can survive the skullduggery of the Democrats and Republicans single handedly.

Pelosi could have been one of the people that shoved Biden to run for the office. How long will he be covered and hidden by his handlers that shove him in? Biden is not a Trojan horse; he should come out and speak for himself. If he knows that he cannot win due to medical or other limitations it is better to hand over the torch to somebody else capable to win.

SUCCESSFUL ACHIEVEMENT

Some of the characteristics of Trojan horses are, they have ears, but cannot hear they have eyes, but they cannot see; they have noses but cannot smell for themselves. They cannot have successful achievement of their own. It is the handler's duty to determine and decide where and how to deal with them. Trojan horses have no say of their own. It is the handlers that do the talking, pushing, driving, the shoving and you name it.

Earlier, Robert Gates said that Biden has been wrong on nearly every major foreign policy and national security issue over the past four decades. If Biden was wrong when he was energetic, what is going to change now? Hayet has no problem with Biden as a person, but the failed policy that he embodies is part of the reason that got Trump elected.

If God gives a vision, He gives a way to fulfill it. If people give a vision, they must find a way to make it work. God makes a way where there seems to be no way. God bringing Trump to the Presidency is a testimony of His miraculous work and love for America. Nehemiah was nobody, just a cupbearer, with perhaps no architectural experience. When a nobody makes a divine connection with God's purpose, then they become a somebody. When a man's way pleases God, He causes their enemies to make peace with them.[410] God gives favor for others to whoever is willing to achieve his purpose.

For there is no favoritism, no respect of persons with God. Sometimes he uses a person people did not expect to achieve his goal. At least in two instances, God calls a heathen King, "my servant." With my great power and outstretched arm, I made the earth and its people and the animals that are on it, and I give it to anyone I please (Clinton or Trump on 2016, Biden or Trump on 2020). Now I will give all your countries into the hands of my servant Nebuchadnezzar king of Babylon; I will make even the wild animals subject to him.[411]

Nehemiah had not been sad in the king's presence before, and the king asked him, "Why does your face look so sad when you are not ill? This can be nothing but sadness of heart."

Nehemiah was afraid to give the right answer and he replied, "May the king live forever! Why should my face not look sad when the city where my ancestors are buried lies in ruins, and its gates have been destroyed by fire?"

The king said to him, "What is it you want?"

"If it pleases the king and if your servant has found favor in his sight, let him send me to the city in Judah where my ancestors are buried so I can rebuild it."

"How long will your journey take, and when will you get back?" Nehemiah set a time and was given provisions to enable him.

Focusing on the sentence "What is it you want?" Hayet would like to elaborate a couple of points on how cooperation could bring great result.

Shortly after Trump became the winner of the 2016 election, the Obama transition team reached out to a real man, Steve Harvey to help Trump reach out to the African American communities in the inner cities. Hayet highly commends the transition team for their wish for Trump's success. Steve has been friends and had several encounters with President Obama. He could have said no because Trump is not his kind of person. After all Steve told Trump that he did not vote for him and he told people on his show not to vote for Trump. That showed real enmity.

For his willingness to work with the Trump team, Steve experiences some brutality and name calling, such as Uncle Tom, sell out, coon, shoeshine, and many other names. Steve went to Trump Tower and had some common interest conversation with Trump.

Amid conversation, Steve stated, "What can I do for you," just as what Nehemiah was asked "What is it you want?" asked Trump.

King Ahasuerus also asked, "What is it, Queen Esther? What is your request? Even up to half the kingdom, it will be given you. She used the silver lining and she got what she wanted, saving her people from death.

"There is nothing I really want you to do for me. I want to do something for you."

"You want to help me?" winner Trump asked.

"Yes," Steve replies. "You appointed Dr. Ben Carson to head the HUD, I would like to help him. I do not think he has the celebrity notoriety to get to the inner cities. I can help him with the urban situations. I want to do something to help him."

"So, what do you want to do?"

"I have a mentoring program, which is restricted because I can only help about a thousand boys, one time a year in each city. I want to create vision centers around the country. I can take these schools that you are closing in the inner cities using HUD funds, refurbish these school buildings and turn them into vision centers where boys and girls can come, learn life-skills and parents can come, learn financial, and literacy skills to provide a better life for themselves. Eventually I would like to build vision homes around the Vision Center to help support the community so that we have wonderful communities. I want people who are less fortunate to have a better way of life."

"I like that. Let me get Ben Carson right now," Trump said emphatically. Within two minutes he had Dr. Ben Carson on the phone. Steve and Dr. Carson began talking. Steve introduced the concept of vision homes.

"It is a done deal," Dr. Carson affirmed.

The man Trump is for work. If one is willing to work, Trump is behind that person. Remember how the North Korean peace deal came through Dennis Rodman. No other President Trusted that such peaceful deal would come through unlikely person. If you are for work, Trump is behind you.

When Steve and Trump went to do the briefing to the media waiting outside, Trump, being unpredictable, spoke different than what they spoke upstairs which humiliated Steve. Anyway, Steve held his ground because he had a purpose to achieve to help the less fortunate.[412]

Steve's perseverance reminds Hayet of how Saint Paul refused to be bound by cultural expectations to benefit others. Explaining his experience Paul says, "To the Jews I became like a Jew, to win the Jews. To those under the law I became like one under the law (though I am not under the law), to win those under the law. To those not having the law I became like one not having the law (though I am not free from God's law but am under Christ's law), to win those not having the law. To the weak I became weak, to win the weak. I have become all things to all people so that by all possible means I might save some."[413]

Steve used a one-time chance, a silver lining, and several poor Americans are benefiting because of his vision even in June 2020, because of his courage and his choice to humble himself. Steve needed nothing from Trump and vice versa. However, when they spoke their visions, something good for the community was born. Steve could have said, "I hate Trump," and refuse to work together. He did not vote for Trump and told people not to vote for him. He took the American Spirit with him. The American Spirit is that people fight until elections, after elections the winner and the loser work together for the betterment of America. Learning from Steve's achievement can help someone forget the difference and focus on the good of the majority.

FORCING PEOPLE TO HATE WHAT YOU HATE

The election of President Trump has created more hate groups than any other time. Who is to blame? Trump? Of course not. It is the American enemies, foxes coming in sheep clothing

Before the inauguration of Trump, people like far-left group, never thought that the 45th President would make it to that point. That is the time when Moore declared war on Trump. All the rioting, killing, destruction of property is a joy for the Trojan handlers. That is why out of the nearly 100 DNC 2020 speakers, not even a single person addressed the riots, lootings, and destruction in our cities. By doing so, they did not want to offend their Trojan handlers. They thought the lawlessness was going to hurt Trump; it did not go as they hoped. Now, they are going after damage control. One the other side, most of the RNC speakers addressed the need for law and order.

One thing to note is that Trump is not a perfect person. The problem for the creation of all the hate groups is the Trojan horse handlers and the dangerous hubris coming undercover.

Whatever the USA is now facing under Trump has been there for generations. American leaders are so blinded in the name of being nice to other countries while wasting our money for no reward. Trump promised to change the bad deals that Americans have been accustomed to such as allowing other nations take advantage of their country including defending the rich Arab countries by our money, and NATO members not paying their fair share. No more under Trump's Presidency.

Other Trojan masters lost their income because of the disruption created by Trump. They are afraid that while draining the swamp the Man will expose them.

Trump's former friends now turned his enemies. The political establishment that hate Trump are being exposed; they keep on fueling hate. They force, entice, and trick others to hate what they hate. They do not have a clear reason. Here is one example.

The Goya Foods CEO, Robert Unanue is facing a backlash for his desire to work with Trump. In the Democrat plantation, there is no individual freedom of choice on who to support and who not to. The rich and the black should automatically disown Trump. As per Biden, if you are black, you have no other choice but to vote for him. Otherwise it would be treason.

Voicing his right of how the CEO worked with Obama and should do the same with Trumps he stated, "You're allowed to talk good or talk praise to one President but you're not — when I was called to be part of this commission to aid in economic and educational prosperity and you make a positive comment, all of a sudden that's not acceptable," Unanue said. "If you are called by the President of the United States, you're going to say, 'No I am sorry, I am busy, no thank you?' I didn't say that to the Obamas, and I didn't say that to President Trump."[414]

Democrats are like a jealous spouse or a dictator. They do not want their spouse to speak to other people.

For the past decades, it has been a tradition for champions of all sporting events to receive an invitation to the White House. Instead of doing so, Warriors spent a day with local children at an African American history museum.[415] Hayet understands that every child has a worth and a value. Yet there are better approaches to reaching out to millions instead of few people.

It was unfortunate that the Warriors, Cavaliers, and part of Patriots including Tom Brady refused to do the tradition of visiting the White House in order not to offend a part of their fans who hate Trump and probably also, they did not agree with his ideas. Remember, Steve Harvey did not agree with Trump, but he accepted the invitation and multiple people are still benefiting because of his decision. The teams appear to have an un-American, partisan issue. They are unaware that if their visit offends one side, not visiting also offends the other side. Sports teams and musicians should know that they are not property of a President, but fun entertainment for 'We the People' and 'We the World.' For accepting the tradition, their fun and the matter would have been understandable.

One may disagree with the person Trump, or any other president, but one should differentiate from disagreeing with the office of the president. Sports Champions are nobody for Trump the person and Trump the President. People do not get invited to the White House because they know the President. It is if the President knows you that you get invited to the White House, for which the Champions traditionally qualify for that.

The Champions should have humbled themselves to help others. Some of them may have probably visited with the previous Presidents, but the outcome of each visit is different. Steve Harvey visited the White House and had several encounters with President Obama. But no other visit resulted in as much good as did the visit to Trump Tower. Nobody has a legitimate reason to not accept Trump's invitation as Steve did, because he said words against Trump.

Trump was mature, forgiving, to Steve. Steve refers him "congenial." The teams that refused to visit the White House missed a silver lining. They could have used that door to tell him what they would love to achieve to help or reach out to multitudes the way Steve did. Kanye and Kardashian West's visit to the White House secured the Presidential pardon of Alice Johnson. Hayet hopes that no other sports team would repeat what the Champions did during Trump's term.

Life is not about living just for yourself. It is about serving others. To serve others, there are times when one would be offensive and times when one would be defensive; there are times one would do the undoable and go to places they ought not. There are more challenges to do in the offensive than the defensive, and it is only the team that goes on the offensive wins. That is what Steve Harvey did.

Coming back to Nehemiah, when Sanballat the Horonite and Tobias the Ammonite official heard about this, they were very much disturbed that someone (Trump) had come to promote the welfare of the Israelites (Americans).

After inspecting the wall, he told his people of the gracious hand of his God had been on him and how God gave him favor before the eyes of the king, "You see the trouble we are in: Jerusalem lies in ruins, and its gates have been burned with fire. Come, let us rebuild the wall of Jerusalem, and we will no longer be in disgrace."

"Let us start rebuilding," the people agreed in one accord and began. This excellent work continued expeditiously for the people worked with all their heart.

When Sanballat, Tobias and Geshem the Arab, the people of Ashdod heard that the repairs to Jerusalem's wall had gone ahead and that the gaps were being closed, they were very angry, and greatly incensed, mocked and ridiculed Nehemiah and his team Trump and his team, as what Moore would call Trump Thump out.

The insinuating mockery included, "What are those feeble Jews doing? Will they restore their wall? Will they finish in a day? Can they bring the stones back to life from those heaps of rubble—burned as they are? What they are building—even a fox climbing up on it would break down!"

Detractors could come from within, from outside and in different forms. For Job of the Bible his main detractor was his wife. It is easy to identify and fight the enemy from outside, but hard to fight and defend oneself from the enemy within.

It is the custom of any party; the previous party leaders would support any presumptive nominee. All 2016 presidential candidates signed a pledge to eventually support the party nominee. However, Bush Sr. and Bush Jr., Jeb Bush, Carly Fiorina, Lindsey Graham, Colin Powell, Condoleezza Rice, John Kasich, Mitt Romney (who voted to convict Trump), John McCain, Justin Amash, and Joe Heck did not honor the party tradition of support after Trump became the Republican presidential nominee.[416]

The very people who did not vote for Trump in 2016 have resurfaced for the 2020 election as well, General James Matis, part of the veterans' group joined the opposition list. The opposition of prominent Republicans who promised to vote for Biden has grown to over 100. It is big news for TVCNN, but not for the silent Americans who matter most. If God is for us, who can be against us?

No worries! They are Nehushtan protecting their legacy and doing "scratch my back" and "I will scratch yours." They do not like Trump because he is overturning their work and for those who were not elected are jealous of Trump's achievements.

Nehushtan was the bronze snake that Moses made and up to the time of King Hezekiah the Israelites were burning incense to it. Hezekiah said Enough is Enough.

King David also experienced a defection of his greatest confidant and counselor, Ahithophel. Not only did he defect, but Ahithophel also aligned himself with people that hated David. It was a big blow to David, big news to the TVCNN.

Nehemiah's detractors plotted together to come and fight against Jerusalem and stir up trouble against the project. It sounds the same with all of Trump's detractors coming together against him in the form of the groups Michael Moore encourages people to join. There are also others who call themselves "Evangelicals against Trump." The nobles, TVCNN, and detractors in general, keep on searching for people and cases that would threaten (Nehemiah's/Trump's) leadership. Even matters not newsworthy is a big deal for them.

The Jews who lived near their enemies came and told Nehemiah ten times over, "Wherever you turn, they will attack us. Because they have already said "Before they know it or see us, we will be right there among them and will kill them and put an end to the work." The purpose is to discourage the dedicated people and stall the project.

These are the days where individual American freedom is vanishing because of threats from vigilantes, forcing people on the streets to kneel and apologize, for the wrongs they did not commit. People are getting intimidated in their homes; their businesses are being looted, destroyed, and burned.

To protect people and property from further destructions, Nehemiah therefore stationed (as Trump did to troops) some of the people behind the lowest points of the wall at the exposed places, posting them by families, with their swords, spears, and bows. He reminded the Jews, "Don't be afraid of them. Remember the Lord, who is great and awesome, will fight for your families, your sons and your daughters, your wives, and your homes."

When the Jews' enemies heard that they were aware of their plot and that God had frustrated it, Nehemiah and the builders returned to the wall, each to their own work. This is the time; America is at a crossroad by the people who are behind the agendas that hate the values America was founded upon. Thus, from that day one, half of Nehemiah's team did the work, while the other half was equipped with spears, shields, bows, and armor. The officers posted themselves behind all the people of Judah who were building the wall. Those who carried materials did their work with one hand and held a weapon in the other, and each of the builders wore their swords at their sides as they worked. The more one caved in, the more one would be demanded to keep silent. This is the time to fight back for America, for yourself, for your family, wisely.

WAYS TO FIGHT BACK

In every battle, one should fight to win, not to survive. There are seven ways to fight back:

1st. Economically: one must be stable. If not, one would be forced to wait on government handouts.

2nd. Legally: one must know what is lawful and what is not. The law is the final arbiter. One would be considered guilty by the law and face all the consequences of it; another would be set free by the law.

3rd. Vote: One who does not vote ought not to complain. A person who voted yet the vote is not in their favor, should accept the outcome.

4th. Defend the country: During naturalization oath, a person makes the following declaration which ought to be sincere: "I hereby declare, on oath, that I absolutely and entirely renounce and abjure all allegiance and fidelity to any foreign prince, potentate, state, or sovereignty, of whom or which I have heretofore been a subject or citizen; that I will support and defend the Constitution and laws of the United States of America against all enemies, foreign and domestic."

5th. Arm yourself: In these days of defund, disband, and dismantle the police, 911 call may not be so efficient. One ought to defend themselves against law breaking invaders. Nehemiah's team armed themselves with one hand while working with the other hand.

6th. Equip your house and yourself with a video camera or phone that is capable of recording, as proof should you need it as evidence for your case.

7th. Finally, pray: Saint Paul instructs the believers, "For our struggle is not against flesh and blood, but against the rulers, against the authorities, against the powers of this mysterious world and against the spiritual forces of evil in the heavenly realms.[417]

On one of his major fights David told his enemy, "You come against me with a sword and a spear and a javelin, but I come against you in the name of the LORD Almighty, the God of the armies of Israel, whom you have defied."[418]

OUR STRUGGLE IS NOT AGAINST FLESH AND BLOOD

There are so many proofs that our struggle is not against flesh and blood. The first proof is that common sense is intentionally ignored. Common sense means a sound and prudent judgment based on a simple belief of the situation or facts.[419] That does not require sophisticated intellectual thinking. Commonsense could easily identify black from white; darkness from light; rainy seasons from dry seasons.

For the Trojan hubris whom the Scriptures refer to as "They claim to be wise, they became fool" who intentionally ignore going against common sense, a fetus in the womb is not a person. Again, after birth, live birth abortion, unwanted baby, or a survivor of abortion is not a person. According to the CDC categorization, "The legal definition of live birth includes any sign of life, e.g., breath, heartbeat, pulsation of the umbilical cord, or definite movement of voluntary muscles."[420]

In the age of live birth abortion, children who come out of the uterus, given intentional murder death certificate with a code P96.4 recorded were between less than ten minutes to one day or more. Infant deaths for a 12-year period between 2003 — and 2014 assigned to code ICD-10 code P96.4 – Termination of pregnancy, affecting fetus and newborn were reviewed. During this period there were 315,392 infant deaths and 49,126,572 live births. The purpose of CDC's analysis is to provide some other information about infant deaths with this cause of death code. This category includes both spontaneous terminations of pregnancy and induced terminations of pregnancy. Analysis of the text as reported by the cause-of-death certifier show that of 588 deaths with mention of P96.4.[421] This is the same murderous spirit that legally killed thousands of children shortly after Jesus was born and is still prevalent in the Western societies. This murder is prevalent in Canada as well where 491 babies born alive during botched abortion were left to die in their immediate aftermath.[422]

For the people who intentionally refuse to acknowledge common sense, a male can be a female and a female can be a male should they so choose.

Nehemiah's team continued the work with half of the men holding spears, from the first light of dawn till the stars came out. He further instructed his people to "Have every man and his helper stay inside Jerusalem at night, so they can serve as guards by night and as workers by day." Neither he, his brothers, his men nor the guards with him took off their clothes; each had (armed, concealed) their weapon, even when they went for water.

At the same time, there was economic disaster and outcry; people were mortgaging their fields, vineyards, and homes, to get grains to survive the famine. Others were subjecting their children to slavery to Jews and others. He accused and rebuked the people who were exploiting or taking advantage of the economic calamity. He told them, "You are charging your own people interest!" It is at a time as such that Trump called Feds to lower interest below zero amid the Covid-19 fallout.

Nehemiah called together a large meeting to deal with nobles and said: "As far as possible, we have bought back our fellow Jews who were sold to the Gentiles. Now you are selling your own people, only for them to be sold back to us!" The nobles are the establishment people, who care to protect their own interests only.

He continues, "What you are doing is not right. Shouldn't you walk in the fear of our God to avoid the reproach of our Gentile enemies? Nehemiah's brothers and his men were also lending the people money and grain. (This sounds similar as to what Trump allowed - lending to business owners and banks to save America's economy). Nehemiah challenged the nobles, so let us stop charging interest! Give them back their fields at once, vineyards, olive groves and houses, and the interest you are charging them—one percent of the money, grain, new wine and olive oil."

The nobles accepted Nehemiah's challenge, "We will give it back," they said. "And we will not demand anything more from them. We will do as you say."

Just as Trump is in favor of faith groups, so was Nehemiah. Democrat leadership, specifically with Obama, who knows the Biblical principles better than Trump does, was engaged in discrediting the faith contribution, taking prayers and God out of the White House, our schools, and the court systems. Trump has been doing the opposite, bringing God back to the White House.

Trump has been involving faith groups prayers in his administration. People say Trump is fake, using the Church. The choice we have here is between those who try to discredit and persecute faith groups and the so-called faking people that give credit to the Church. Which one would you rather have?

A few years back Pastor Jentezen Franklin preached about a woman praying for food. A mocker of the society who heard the prayer went and bought all the food that he believed was necessary for a family and dropped them by her doorstep. The woman thanked God for the provision. Sometime later, the mocker told the woman, "Are you going to say God gave you the food and thank him? You should thank me."

"Praise God," the woman replied. "I prayed for food and God used the devil as a courier to bring me what I asked for." The opposition says that Trump may be fake, or the devil. Sometimes God uses the devil to do his will. There was a time when God used Nebuchadnezzar the king of Babylon to achieve his goal. Paul also speaks of how people that rejected the faith have suffered. He handed two men over to Satan to be taught not to blaspheme.

Nehemiah as well, summoned the priests and made the nobles and officials take an oath to do what they had promised. He also shook out the folds of his robe and said, "In this way may God shake out of the house and possessions of anyone who does not keep this promise. So, may such a person be shaken out and emptied!" At this the whole assembly said, "Amen," and praised the Lord. And the people did as they had promised.

Chapter Twenty-Three

"A government big enough to give you everything you want is a government big enough to take from you everything you have."

— PRESIDENT GERALD R. FORD

LET MY PEOPLE GO

God instructed Moses to tell Pharaoh "let my people go." My people refer to the Israelites. From where, where to go to? They have been slaves in Egypt and God wanted to deliver them let

them go to their homeland after about four hundred years. Their plight in Egypt was not accidental. God had informed their ancestor Abraham about it. The fulfillment started from Joseph whose jealous brothers wanted to get rid of and sold him to Egyptian slave traders. This reminds one how Black Africans were sold into forced slavery to white folks. Just as Joseph was sold into slavery by his own brothers, it is Africans that sold their fellow Africans for financial gain. The main culprit for selling Joseph were his own brothers, so were the culprit for the African slaves their own brothers.

Eventually, they multiplied so greatly that they became extremely powerful and filled the land. Outnumbering and becoming stronger than the Egyptians, became a threat for them. Consequently, the Egyptians devised a plan to keep them from growing even more. Thus, the Egyptians said, if we do not control their number, and if war breaks out, they will join our enemies and fight against us. Then they will escape from the country. So, the Egyptians made the Israelites their slaves.

They appointed brutal slave drivers over them, hoping to wear them down with crushing labor. But the more they were oppressed, the more they multiplied and spread; so, the Egyptians came to dread the Israelites and worked them ruthlessly. They made their lives bitter with harsh labor in brick and mortar and with all kinds of work in the fields; in all their harsh labor the Egyptians worked them ruthlessly.

Still the ruthless overwork did not slow the Israelites from increasing in numbers. Therefore, Pharaoh told the Egyptians midwives "When you are helping the Hebrew women during childbirth on the delivery stool, if you see that the baby is a boy, kill him; but if it is a girl, let her live." How come the killing of born alive male Israelites in Egypt is called a murder, while the born alive American, Canadian, and other Western countries children is not?

The midwives feared God and did not do what the king of Egypt had told them to do. They had brains compared to the merciless, murderous, brainless, bloodless Presidents, Governors, Prime Ministers who are enablers of the born alive abortion murderers. For not killing infants, God was kind to the midwives and gave them families of their own, the Israelites increased and became even more numerous.

Just as what Pharaoh did, there was a woman engaged in an intentional genocide and extermination of the black race, called Margaret Sanger. In about the time she was born, "When Mississippi rejoined the Union in 1870, former slaves made up more than half of that state's population."[423] She believed "A free race cannot be born of slave mothers."[424] On the outside she appeared good on her recruitment of black facilitators, but behind the scene on the inside, she was scripted saying "We do not want word to go out that we want to exterminate the Negro population."[425] That was systemic racism, treating one favorably over others.

As it is said a tree is cut by its own 'axe haft' Sanger wanted to use black doctors and nurses to achieve her goal. To prove her point she said,

> the colored Negroes have profound respect for black ministers and professionals. They can get closer to their own members and lay their cards on the table, which means their ignorance, superstitions, and doubts. They do not do this with the white people and if we can train the Negro doctor at the Clinic, he can go among them with enthusiasm and with knowledge, which, I believe, will have far-reaching results among the colored people. His work in my opinion should be entirely with the Negro profession and the nurses, hospital, social workers, as well as the County's white doctors. His success will depend upon his personality and his training by us.[426]

Sanger also wanted to recruit a male minister (preacher) with an engaging personality who could straighten out that idea if it ever occurred to any of their more rebellious members, "should be trained, perhaps by the Federation as to our ideals and the goal that we hope to reach."[427]

It was sad to hear Dr. King fit that description of a male black minister Sanger wanted to recruit. He received awards from Planned Parenthood Foundation. On the acceptance letter read by Mrs. King, he referenced on how striking kinship between their movement and Margaret Sanger's early efforts were. Although it is unlikely Dr. King would agree with the woman who wanted to exterminate the very people he wanted to liberate, if there is any wrongdoing it is a betrayal. Perhaps he was deceived.

AGREEING TO DISAGREE

In most American elections when the winner gets named the one who did not win concedes, and all Americans stand behind the winner. However, in Michael Moore's World about Trump, it is not so. When it comes to Biblical perspective (when seen on the outside), Trump is unpopular of all-American presidential candidates. The very moral weapons that tripped and cut short the political campaigns of previous contestants would not work on him, "No weapon forged against you shall prosper."

Trump numerous sexual misconduct allegations including the controversial Access Hollywood tape. In American history, nobody has been tainted with barrages of real or fake TVCNN accusation as Trump did. There is something that is sustaining the morally weakest of all presidential candidates, respectively a president.

Sometimes it is obvious and difficult to defend Trump who could kick friends and enemies alike. The Trump axe is like a double-edged sword, merciless to everybody, sometimes it could help or hurt himself too. Referring to the handover of his business responsibility to his children, he stated that, after I complete my term, I will see how my children handled my business. If they did an excellent job, great. If not, I will fire them.

Perhaps no American president has hired and fired as President Trump. At the beginning, Hayet did not like the constant hiring and firing, but later he realized that it is justifiable. The reason is that the corrupt state, federal, and FBI employees were treating their jobs as means of partisan politics instead of serving for the good of the USA, entrapping the incoming Trump team in one way or the other. One goes out to defend the truth even if it hurts or else it will eventually hurt nationally.

Now and then people do see some politicians during a debate, instead of attacking the issues that the other competitor stands for, they go after their family, the wife, the children, or parents. That should be out of bounds. If your issue is with the candidate, deal with him or her do not talk about the wife, husband, children, or even their parents. In America, it is not acceptable to inflict harm on other family members who have done no wrong and be a scapegoat.

One, specifically the Democrats ought to differentiate or distinguish between Trump the person and Trump the President. On the same level, one ought to distinguish between Secretary Clinton the person from Secretary Clinton the Presidential candidate. Trump as well as Clinton the person refers to the character, weaknesses, and strengths of personhood. Trump or Clinton the Presidential candidate refers to what the person does and says to be an elected official. If one has hatred, enmity, or issue with Trump the person as the morally unfit President they should deal with it separately. The same applies to people who do not like Secretary Clinton.

Referring to being against and hating Trump the person, and their loss, Chuck Schumer, Clinton's former New York colleague in the Senate stated that, "So what did we do wrong? People did not know what we stood for, just that we were against Trump. And still believe that."[428] What Senator Schumer is pointing out is that they did not have promising ideas to present to the American voters. They were against Trump the person. He still believes that after Clinton's loss to Trump. Yet having clear understanding of Democrat's hate for Trump the person, Senator Schumer lead Senate and Congress Democrats repeatedly with one after the other baseless accusations that culminated up to the lame, unsuccessful Impeachment Trial. The more the lying of the Democrats get exposed the more people hate them. That is why Hayet decided to write this project saying enough is enough.

Chastising Secretary Clinton and her voters as well as the TVCNN Senator Schumer said that, "When you lose to somebody who has 40 percent popularity, you don't blame other things — Comey, Russia — you blame yourself."[429]

Having said so, the only way we could bring solution to the hurting USA and the world at large is acknowledge our wrongdoing and return to God. Let us have a discerning Spirit and see what is good and bad personally and nationally, and say no, to where no is due.

It appears there are external forces that try to influence and change the USA's history to be like any other nation. America's uniqueness is based on the USA's distinctiveness. God made America and the first World countries prosperous because of adopting Christian principles as a manual. When they abandon what made them prosperous in the name of human freedom purported by people who do not love God, they become like the ungodly nations. Thus, Christianity as it did for 2,000 years will survive without the first World nations. However, the first World nations cannot survive without Christianity that made them prosperous. Thus, let the population of first, second and third world nations return to God so that it may be well with them.

God bless you!

291

Although we cannot promise to reply for every e-mail, the author would love to hear from the readers as to what has been said good, what has been said bad. Please email to:

EmpoweringMessage@gmail.com

The author's photograph was taken by Portrait Innovations.

THE END

ENDNOTES

[1] Wikipedia, William Lloyd Garrison
https://en.wikipedia.org/wiki/William_Lloyd_Garrison#:~:text=Lloy
d%20Garrison%2C%20was%20a%20prominent,by%20Constitutional
%20amendment%20in%201865. Accessed 06/26/2020

[2] Graham, Billy, "My Heart Aches for America'
https://billygraham.org/story/billy-graham-my-heart-aches-for-
america/
[3] Ibid
[4] The Bible, (Habakkuk 2:1).
[5] Ibid, (Habakkuk 1:5-7).
[6] Ibid, (Matthew 11:21)

[12] Kenneth Baker (ed.), *The New International Version Study Bible*,
Grand Rapids, MI: Zondervan Publishing House, 1995. (Psalms
139:13-18).
[13] Baby's development in the womb
https://www.mydr.com.au/babies-pregnancy/baby-s-development-in-
the-
womb#:~:text=By%2024%20weeks%20your%20baby's,thin%20with
%20little%20underlying%20fat. Accessed 09/11/2020

[14] The Bible (Jeremiah 15:16)
[15] The Bible, (Colossians 1:16)
[16] New York Post, Joe Biden claims there are 'at least 3'

genders during Iowa campaign stop, blows up at college student
https://nypost.com/2019/08/10/joe-biden-claims-there-are-at-least-3-
genders-during-iowa-campaign-stop-blows-up-at-college-student/
Accessed 08/23/2020

[17] The Bible, (Genesis 5:2)
[18] Abrams Mere, 64 Terms That Describe Gender Identity and
Expression https://www.healthline.com/health/different-genders
Accessed 08/23/2020
[19] The Bible (Genesis 1:28).

[20] The Bible (Luke 1:26-38)
[21] The Bible (Luke 1:39-56)
[22] Foust Michael, Christian Headlines, Megachurch Pastor:
Abortion 'Is Consistent with' Christianity and 'I Will Fight' to Keep it
Legal https://www.christianheadlines.com/contributors/michael-
foust/megachurch-pastor-abortion-is-consistent-with-christianity-and-
i-will-fight-to-keep-it-legal.html 08/24/2020
[23] The Bible (Revelation 2:2).
[24] The Bible (Galatians 1:6-9).
[25] The Bible (Jude 4)
[26] Foust Michael, Christian Headlines, Megachurch Pastor:
Abortion 'Is Consistent with' Christianity and 'I Will Fight' to Keep it
Legal https://www.christianheadlines.com/contributors/michael-
foust/megachurch-pastor-abortion-is-consistent-with-christianity-and-
i-will-fight-to-keep-it-legal.html 08/24/2020

[27] The Bible (1 Samuel 2:30)
[28] Torchbearers for Christ, Them that honor me, I will honor
http://www.torchbearers-for-
christ.org/templates/System/details.asp?id=28827&PID=397540#:~:t
ext=God%20is%20saying%20to%20us%20that%20if%20any,some%2
0person%20in%20recognition%20of%20a%20worthy%20act.
08/20/2020

[29] Wikipedia, Just Do It,
https://en.wikipedia.org/wiki/Just_Do_It Accessed 08/09/2020
[30] The Bible (Philippians 3:12-14).

[31] YouTube Meet Curtis "Wall Street" Carroll: A Finance Prophet Currently Serving Life https://www.youtube.com/watch?v=vv3AxJNsuyM Accessed 07/04/2020

[32] The Bible (1 Kings 18-19)

[33] Ibid, (1 Corinthians 10:26)

[34] Ibid, (Matthew 6:25-34)

[35] Ibid, (1 Samuel 13:19-20)

[36] Chinese Scientist Says Covid-19 Came From Government Lab In Wuhan: Report https://www.ndtv.com/world-news/chinese-virologist-li-meng-yan-claims-coronavirus-was-made-in-wuhan-lab-report-2295323 Accessed 09/15/2020

[37] World Health Organization, WHO Coronavirus Disease (COVID-19) Dashboard https://covid19.who.int/?gclid=EAIaIQobChMI2u-t1fn86gIVM_3jBx1wlQ0GEAAYASAAEgKuMPD_BwE%2009/13/2020 Accessed 09/13/2020

[38] The Bible, (Matthew 2:18)

[39] Ibid, (Mark 4:9)

[40] Ibid, (Revelation 1:7)

[41] Ibid, (Galatians 5:15)

[42] Ibid, (Ephesians 5:15-16)

[43] Ibid, (Isaiah 55:6-9)

[44] Ibid, (1 Timothy 4:1-2)

[45] Ibid, (Proverbs 1:24-27)

[46] Fox News, Todd Starnes: Middle school students taught Trump is 'an idiot' – Anti-Trump hatred infects schools https://www.foxnews.com/opinion/todd-starnes-test-depicts-trump-as-an-idiot-one-more-example-of-schools-as-indoctrination-centers 09/23/2020

[47] The Bible, (Proverbs 17:5)

[48] Ibid, (Deuteronomy 24:16)

[49] Ibid, (Matthew 24:38-39)

[50] Ibid, (Jonah 3:5-10)

[51] The Washington Post, Joe Biden's CNN Town Hall An Accusational Whopper https://www.washingtonpost.com/politics/2020/09/17/joe-bidens-

cnn-town-hall-an-occasional-whopper/ Accessed, 09/18/2020

[52] The Bible (Psalms 119:9)

[53] Ibid, (2 Timothy 3:1-5-1-5; Romans13:1-10)

[54] Ibid, (Matthew 23:1-4)

[55] Wikipedia, Trojan Horse,
https://en.wikipedia.org/wiki/Trojan_Horse Accessed, 08/02/2020

[56] Google Dictionary, Trojan Horse
https://www.google.com/search?q=what+is+Trojan+horse+meaning
&oq=&aqs=chrome.0.69i59l8.234989j0j7&sourceid=chrome&ie=UTF
-8 Accessed, 08/02/2020

[57] Merriam Webster Dictionary, Trojan Horse
https://www.merriam-webster.com/dictionary/Trojan%20horse
Accessed, 08/02/2020

[58] Investopedia, Hubris,
https://www.investopedia.com/terms/h/hubris.asp Accessed,
08/02/2020

[59] Encyclopedia Britannica, Hibris,
https://www.britannica.com/topic/hubris Accessed, 08/02/2020

[60] Wikipedia, the free Encyclopedia, Hubris,
https://en.wikipedia.org/wiki/Hubris Accessed, 08/02/2020

[61] The Bible, (1 Samuel 2:3)

[62] News Week, Obama Tweets Rainbow White House Image
and Wishes Happy Pride Month After Supreme Court Delivers Victory
for LGBTQ Rights, https://www.newsweek.com/barack-obama-
lgbtq-supreme-court-civil-rights-act-1511077 Accessed, 07/06/2020.

[63] NBC News, Trump admin tells U.S. embassies they can't fly
pride flag on flagpoles https://www.nbcnews.com/politics/national-
security/trump-admin-tells-u-s-embassies-they-can-t-fly-n1015236
Accessed, 07/10/2020

[64] Wikipedia, the free Encyclopedia, Hubris,
https://en.wikipedia.org/wiki/Hubris Accessed, 08/02/2020

[65] The Bible (Isaiah 14:12-15)

[66] Ibid (Isaiah 32:8)

[67] Ibid, (Acts 16:16-24)

[68] Ibid, (Psalms 34:19-20)

[69] What Christians Want to Know, Who Was Legion in The Bible https://www.whatchristianswanttoknow.com/who-was-legion-in-the-bible/ Accessed, 07/16/2020

[70] The Bible (Mark 5:1-17)

[71] Ibid, (Matthew 13:15)

[72] The Washington Times, Federal judge blocks Seattle's ban on crowd-control tools as police brace for weekend protests https://www.washingtontimes.com/news/2020/jul/25/federal-judge-blocks-seattles-ban-crowd-control-to/ Accessed, 07/25/2020

[73] The Bible (Matthew 15:14)

[74] Share America, Federal government: More than the White House and Congress https://share.america.gov/what-does-federal-government-do/ Accessed, 08/15/2020

[75] The Bible (2 Kings 7:3-20)

[76] Helsel Phil, Obama: 'I Continue to Believe Trump Will Not Be President', https://www.nbcnews.com/politics/2016-election/obama-i-continue-believe-trump-will-not-be-president-n519751 Accessed, 08/15/2020

[77] Town Hall, Trump Does The Unthinkable https://townhall.com/columnists/lizcrokin/2016/07/10/trump-does-the-unthinkable-n2190160 Accessed, 07/25/2020

[78] Ibid

[79] The Bible, (Proverbs 16:7)

[80] Google Search, Vulturing https://www.google.com/search?q=vulturing+meaning&rlz=1C1CH BF_enUS813US813&oq=vulturing&aqs=chrome.0.69i59l2j69i57j0l5.1 1198j0j7&sourceid=chrome&ie=UTF-8 Accessed, 07/25/2020

[81] The Bible, (Deuteronomy 28:7).

[82] Ibid, (Deuteronomy 28:25)

[83] Google Search, Vulturing https://www.google.com/search?q=vulturing+meaning&rlz=1C1CH BF_enUS813US813&oq=vulturing&aqs=chrome.0.69i59l2j69i57j0l5.1 1198j0j7&sourceid=chrome&ie=UTF-8 Accessed, 07/25/2020

[84] The Bible, (Job 22:21-25).

[85] Davis Susan and Wolf Richard, USA Today, U.S. Senate goes 'nuclear,' changes filibuster rules https://www.usatoday.com/story/news/politics/2013/11/21/harry-

reid-nuclear-senate/3662445/ 08/25/2020

[86] Ibid

[87] Chung Andrew, Democrats prepare bill limiting U.S. Supreme Court justice terms to 18 years https://www.reuters.com/article/us-usa-court-termlimits/democrats-prepare-bill-limiting-u-s-supreme-court-justice-terms-to-18-years-idUSKCN26F3L3

[88] The Bible, (Deuteronomy 28:67).

[89] The WhiteHouse.Gov, Unclassified https://www.whitehouse.gov/wp-content/uploads/2019/09/Unclassified09.2019.pdf Accessed, 08/25/2020

[90] C-SPAN, Biden Tells Story of Getting the Ukraine Prosecutor Fired https://www.c-span.org/video/?c4820105/user-clip-biden-tells-story-ukraine-prosecutor-fired Accessed, 08/25/2020

[91] SHRM, Trump Approves Paid Parental Leave for Federal Workers https://www.shrm.org/resourcesandtools/legal-and-compliance/employment-law/pages/trump-approves-paid-parental-leave-for-federal-workers.aspx Accessed, 08/30/2020

[92] The Atlantic, Robert Gates Thinks Joe Biden Hasn't Stopped Being Wrong for 40 Years https://www.theatlantic.com/politics/archive/2014/01/robert-gates-thinks-joe-biden-hasnt-stopped-being-wrong-40-years/356785/ Accessed, 08/29/2020

[93] Boston Globe, In 2006. Democrats were saying 'build the fence!' https://www.bostonglobe.com/news/politics/2017/01/26/when-wall-was-fence-and-democrats-embraced/QE7ieCBXjXVxO63pLMTe9O/story.html Accessed, 08/15/2020

[94] Nowrasteh Alex, Deportation Rates in Historical Perspective, https://www.cato.org/blog/deportation-rates-historical-perspective?queryID=dd9b273670332e800d182fbf4524f7c8 Accessed, 08/15/2020

[95] The Hill, Deportations lower under Trump administration than Obama: reporthttps://thehill.com/latino/470900-deportations-lower-under-trump-than-obama-report Accessed, 08/15/2020

[96] Nowrasteh Alex, Deportation Rates in Historical Perspective, https://www.cato.org/blog/deportation-rates-historical-perspective?queryID=dd9b273670332e800d182fbf4524f7c8 Accessed, 08/15/2020

[97] Wikipedia, Deferred Action for Childhood Arrivals https://en.wikipedia.org/wiki/Deferred_Action_for_Childhood_Arrivals#:~:text=Deferred%20Action%20for%20Childhood%20Arrivals%20(DACA)%20is%20a%20United%20States,for%20a%20work%20permit%20in Accessed, 08/25/2020

[98] AP News, AP FACT CHECK: Michelle Obama and the kids in 'cages' https://apnews.com/2663c84832a13cdd7a8233becfc7a5f3 Accessed, 08/24/2020

[99] US News, AP FACT CHECK: Michelle Obama and the Kids in 'Cages' https://www.usnews.com/news/politics/articles/2020-08-18/ap-fact-check-michelle-obama-and-the-kids-in-cages Accessed, 08/18/2020.

[100] The Bible, (Matthew 7:3-5)

[101] Ibid, (Matthew 23:4)

[102] Ibid, (Proverbs 7:21-23)

[103] Ibid, (Job 18:8-10)

[104] The Bible, (Jeremiah 29:11)

[105] Lyrics Freak, Bob Marley – Could You Be Loved Lyrics https://www.lyricsfreak.com/b/bob+marley/could+you+be+loved_20021754.html Accessed, 08/08/2020

[106] The White House President Barack Obama, FACT SHEET: Obama Administration's Record and the LGBT Community https://obamawhitehouse.archives.gov/the-press-office/2016/06/09/fact-sheet-obama-administrations-record-and-lgbt-community Accessed, 08/15/2020

[107] Wikipedia, Patriot Act https://en.wikipedia.org/wiki/Patriot_Act Accessed, 08/15/2020

[108] Wikipedia, Barack Obama on Mass Surveillance https://en.wikipedia.org/wiki/Barack_Obama_on_mass_surveillance Accessed, 08/15/2020

[109] Obama Speeches, Floor Statement – PATRIOT Act Reauthorization – Complete Text http://obamaspeeches.com/053-Floor-Statement-S2271-PATRIOT-Act-Reauthorization-Obama-

Speech.htm Accessed, 08/15/2020

[110] Wikipedia, Barack Obama on Mass Surveillance https://en.wikipedia.org/wiki/Barack_Obama_on_mass_surveillance Accessed, 08/15/2020

[111] The Washington Post, What's the evidence for 'spying' on Trump's campaign? Here's your guide. https://www.washingtonpost.com/politics/2019/05/06/whats-evidence-spying-trumps-campaign-heres-your-guide/ Accessed, 08/15/2020

[112] Google Dictionary, Antidote https://www.google.com/search?q=antidote&rlz=1C1ZKTG_enUS7 77US777&oq=antidote&aqs=chrome..69i57j0l4j46j0j46.7319j1j9&sour ceid=chrome&ie=UTF-8 Accessed, 09/30/2020

[113] News Yahoo, Cuomo Announces $2.3 Billion Revenue Shortfall: 'God Forbid If the Rich Leave' https://news.yahoo.com/cuomo-announces-2-3-billion-230018445.html Accessed, 09/10/2020

[114] De Lea Brittany, Fox Business, New York's wealthy taxpayers may not return, Cuomo fears https://www.foxbusiness.com/lifestyle/new-yorks-wealthy-taxpayers-return-cuomo Accessed, 09/10/2020

[115] The Seattle Times, Howard Schultz, former Starbucks CEO, is preparing to run for president as an independent https://www.seattletimes.com/seattle-news/politics/howard-schultz-former-starbucks-ceo-is-preparing-to-run-for-president-as-an-independent/ Accessed, 07/15/2020.

[116] Ibid

[117] Ibid

[118] Our Documents.Gov Transcript of President John F. Kennedy's Inaugural Address (1961) https://www.ourdocuments.gov/doc.php?flash=false&doc=91&page=transcript Accessed, 07/15/2020

[119] Ibid

[120] Ballotpedia News, Trump has appointed second-most federal judges through June 1 of a president's fourth year Newshttps://news.ballotpedia.org/2020/06/03/trump-has-appointed-

second-most-federal-judges-through-june-1-of-a-presidents-fourth-year/ Accessed, 08/23/2020

[121] CBS News, Pence knocks Chief Justice John Roberts as a "disappointment to conservatives" https://www.cbsnews.com/news/mike-pence-chief-justice-john-roberts-disappointment-conservatives/ Accessed, 08/07/2020

[122] FiveThirtyEight, John Roberts Has Cast A Pivotal Liberal Vote Only 5 Times https://fivethirtyeight.com/features/john-roberts-has-cast-a-pivotal-liberal-vote-only-5-times/ Accessed, 07/04/2020

[123] Town Hall, READ: Justice Gorsuch Torches Roberts and the Liberal Wing of SCOTUS in Nevada Church Case...In One Paragraph https://townhall.com/tipsheet/mattvespa/2020/07/25/roberts-has-abandoned-his-oath-bushs-chief-justice-sides-with-liberals-again-n2573111 Accessed, 07/25/2020

[124] Ibid

[125] The Christian Science Monitor, Why Gorsuch upheld civil rights for LGBTQ Americans https://www.csmonitor.com/USA/Justice/2020/0616/Why-Gorsuch-upheld-civil-rights-for-LGBTQ-Americans Access, 07/04/2020

[126] Wikipedia, List of people granted executive clemency by Donald Trump https://en.wikipedia.org/wiki/List_of_people_granted_executive_clemency_by_Donald_Trump Accessed, 07/13/2020

[127] Wasson Erika, MSN News, Pelosi Plans Bill to Limit Pardons in Wake of Stone Commutation https://www.msn.com/en-us/news/politics/pelosi-plans-bill-to-limit-pardons-in-wake-of-stone-commutation/ar-BB16Cke4?li=BBnb7Kz Accessed, 07/11/2020

[128] Livingston Mercey, These are the major brands donating to the Black Lives Matter movement C Net, https://www.cnet.com/how-to/companies-donating-black-lives-matter/ Accessed, 07/02/2020

[129] Abusaid Shaddi, The Atlanta Journal-Constitution, Atlanta-based activist faces federal fraud charges over BLM funds https://www.ajc.com/news/atlanta-based-activist-faces-federal-fraud-charges-over-blm-funds/CQUVQKJYWBF3BLB3TVIW3OG5AY/ Accessed, 10/02/2020

[130] NPR, A Company That Profits Off Of The Black Lives

Matter Movement https://www.npr.org/2020/06/16/878852994/a-company-that-profits-off-of-the-black-lives-matter-movement Accessed, 07/02/2020

[131] YouTube, Robert Ray Barnes Black Lives Matter Foundation Causes Fundraising Confusion with BLM https://www.youtube.com/watch?v=VIKDcei7Bms Accessed, 08/15/2020

[132] New York Times, Black Lives Matter co-founder describes herself as 'trained Marxist' https://nypost.com/2020/06/25/blm-co-founder-describes-herself-as-trained-marxist/ Accessed, 08/24/20

[133] Ibid

[134] Wikipedia, John F. MacArthur, https://en.wikipedia.org/wiki/John_F._MacArthur Accessed, 08/18/2020

[135] Garza Alicia, Lesbian Who Tech, Meet the Lesbians Who Tech & Allies Speakers https://lesbianswhotech.org/speakers/alicia-garza/ Accessed, 07/28/2020

[136] Ibid

[137] YouTube, John MacArthur: Black Lives Matter https://www.youtube.com/watch?v=WKXAykFtehY Accessed, 07/10/2020

[138] Brainy Quote, Pope John Paul II https://www.brainyquote.com/quotes/pope_john_paul_ii_138667 Accessed 09/26/2020

[139] Complex, Lil Wayne on George Floyd's Death: 'If We Want to Place the Blame on Anybody, It Should Be Ourselves' https://www.complex.com/music/2020/05/lil-wayne-on-george-floyd-death-if-we-blame-anybody-ourselves Accessed, 07/02/2020

[140] Hotchkiss Sam, Reconnect, Rayshard Brooks: In his own words https://reconnect.io/rayshard-brooks-in-his-own-words/ Accessed, 07/28/2020

[141] Grace Jamie, Live About It, https://www.google.com/search?q=jamie+grace+live+about+it+lyrics&rlz=1C1ZKTG_enUS777US777&oq=jamy+grace+live+a&aqs=chrome.2.69i57j46j0.13967j0j4&sourceid=chrome&ie=UTF-8 Accessed 09/30/2020

[142] FBI News, FBI Releases 2019 Statistics on Law Enforcement Officers Killed in the Line of Duty https://www.fbi.gov/news/pressrel/press-releases/fbi-releases-2019-statistics-on-law-enforcement-officers-killed-in-the-line-of-duty Accessed, 06/28/2020

[143] The Bible, (Genesis 4:4-16)

[144] Knox Patric, REVELING IN DEATH Portland BLM activist shockingly says 'I'm not sad a f***ing fascist died' as US flag is burned The U.S. Sun, https://www.the-sun.com/news/1392659/blm-portland-killing-fascist-us-flag-burned/ Accessed 10/02/2020

[145] The Bible, (Matthew 5:44).

[146] Owens Candace, YouTube, Candace Owens Closing Remarks BLEXIT https://www.youtube.com/results?search_query=candace+owens+blexit+speech Accessed, 10/03/2020

[147] Ibid, (Matthew 7:2)

[148] Ibid, (Proverbs 28:1)

[149] Mastrangelo Dominick 'He's promoting racism': Jason Whitlock says Lebron James is 'a bigot' https://www.washingtonexaminer.com/news/hes-promoting-racism-jason-whitlock-says-lebron-james-is-a-bigot Accessed, 08/30/2020

[150] The Bible, (Ecclesiastes 9:4).

[151] Ibid, (Matthew 5:25-26)

[152] Ibid, (Philemon 11-18).

[153] The Moguldom Nation, Steve Harvey TV Show Cancelled After Preaching Rich People Don't Get Sleep, But Host Keeps Positive Attitude https://moguldom.com/202270/steve-harvey-tv-show-cancelled-after-preaching-rich-people-dont-get-sleep-keeps-positive-attitude/?utm_source=taboola&utm_medium=cpc&utm_campaign=202270#tblciGiBLhXMpoEptMlqss1VgL9zDRR9e2n9kf29-VTNeV8R7oSCnvEI Accessed, 07/14/2020

[154] Ibid

[155] FBI: UCR, 2018 Crime in the United States, https://ucr.fbi.gov/crime-in-the-u.s/2018/crime-in-the-u.s.-2018/tables/expanded-homicide-data-table-6.xls Accessed, 08/21/2020.

[156] The Race, What's the Homicide Capital of America? Murder

Rates in U.S. Cities, Ranked.,
https://www.thetrace.org/2018/04/highest-murder-rates-us-cities-list/
Accessed, 08/21/2020

[157] Star Tribune, A timeline of events leading to George Floyd's death as outlined in charging documents
https://www.startribune.com/a-timeline-of-events-leading-to-george-floyd-s-death-as-outlined-in-charging-documents/570999132/
Accessed, 07/02/2020

[158] Complex, Lil Wayne on George Floyd's Death: 'If We Want to Place the Blame on Anybody, It Should Be Ourselves'
https://www.complex.com/music/2020/05/lil-wayne-on-george-floyd-death-if-we-blame-anybody-ourselves Accessed, 07/02/2020

[159] Ali Ayaan Hirsi, America Doesn't Need a New Revolution
https://www.wsj.com/articles/america-doesnt-need-a-new-revolution-11593201840 Accessed, 07/20/2020

[160] The Bible, (Luke 22:31-32).

[161] Ali Ayaan Hirsi, America Doesn't Need a New Revolution
https://www.wsj.com/articles/america-doesnt-need-a-new-revolution-11593201840 Accessed, 07/20/2020

[162] McLellan David, Marxism
https://www.britannica.com/topic/Marxism Accessed, 07/10/2020

[163] Hawaii.Edu, UNDERSTANDING CONFLICT AND WAR: VOL. 3: CONFLICT IN PERSPECTIVE
https://www.hawaii.edu/powerkills/CIP.CHAP5.HTM Accessed, 07/13/2020

[164] Merriam Webster Dictionary, Feminism
https://www.merriam-webster.com/dictionary/feminism Accessed, 07/20/2020

[165] Stanford Encyclopedia of Philosophy, What is Feminism?
https://plato.stanford.edu/entries/feminist-philosophy/#WhatFemi Accessed, 08/06/2020

[166] Connelly Patricia, On Marxism and Feminismhttps://www.tandfonline.com/doi/abs/10.1080/19187033.1983.11675655?src=recsys Accessed, 07/13/2020

[167] Bryson Valerie, Taylor and Francis Online, Marxism and feminism: can the 'unhappy marriage' be saved?https://www.tandfonline.com/doi/full/10.1080/135693103200

0167454?src=recsys Accessed, 07/13/2020

[168] Ibid

[169] Wikipedia, Red Terror
https://en.wikipedia.org/wiki/Red_Terror Accessed, 06/20/2020

[170] YouTube, I'm a Christian and a Marxist Jordan B Peterson
https://www.youtube.com/watch?v=fvmn1wLglak Accessed,
07/19/2020

[171] Wikipedia, Xinjiang re-education camp
https://en.wikipedia.org/wiki/Xinjiang_re-
education_camps#:~:text=As%20of%202018%2C%20it%20was,inter
nment%20camps%20which%20are%20located Accessed, 07/19/2020

[172] Business Insider, China is harvesting thousands of human organs
from its Uighur Muslim minority, UN human-rights body hears
https://www.businessinsider.com/china-harvesting-organs-of-uighur-
muslims-china-tribunal-tells-un-2019-9 07/19/2020 Accessed,
07/20/2020

[173] Friedman George, Marxism, Violence, and Tyranny
https://www.cambridge.org/core/journals/social-philosophy-and-
policy/article/marxism-violence-and-
tyrann/49A90091235920E10803784BEE89718E Accessed,
07/13/2020

[174] Hudson Institute, 100 Years of Communism—and 100
Million Dead https://www.hudson.org/research/13994-100-years-of-
communism-and-100-million-dead Accessed, 07/28/2020

[175] Research Gate, Marxism in Theory, Violence in Practice
https://www.researchgate.net/publication/333642800_Marxism_in_T
heory_Violence_in_Practice Accessed, 07/13/2020

[176] The Hill, Maxine Waters: 'I don't respect this president'
https://thehill.com/homenews/house/329856-maxine-waters-i-dont-
respect-this-president Accessed, 07/14/2020

[177] Wermund Benjamin, Houston Chronicle, Houston
Democrat spars with Trump over impeachment quote
https://www.houstonchronicle.com/politics/texas/article/Houston-
Democrat-spars-with-Trump-over-14434996.php Accessed,
10/03/2020

[178] Gray Bryson, Trump is Your President,
https://www.google.com/search?q=bryson+gray+trump+is+your+pr
esident+lyrics&rlz=1C1ZKTG_enUS777US777&oq=bry&aqs=chrom

e.0.69i59l3j69i57j69i59j69i60l3.17126j0j4&sourceid=chrome&ie=UTF-8 Accessed, 10/03/2020

[179] Wikipedia, Hubris https://en.wikipedia.org/wiki/Hubris Accessed, 08/02/2020

[180] YouTube, Rep. Waters on Trump administration: 'Tell them they're not welcome' https://www.youtube.com/watch?v=tJCDe7vdFfw Accessed, 06/26/2020

[181] The Bible, (Matthew 7:2).

[182] MPR News, Council advances plan to dismantle Minneapolis Police Dept https://www.mprnews.org/story/2020/06/26/minneapolis-council-puts-plan-to-dismantle-police-in-motion Access, 06/26/2020

[183] The Amazon blog, Amazon donates $10 million to organizations supporting justice and equity https://blog.aboutamazon.com/policy/amazon-donates-10-million-to-organizations-supporting-justice-and-equity Accessed, 07/22/2020

[184] Washington Examiner, Six Trump donors Joaquin Castro tried to shame also gave to him and brother Julián https://www.washingtonexaminer.com/news/six-trump-donors-joaquin-castro-tried-to-shame-also-gave-to-him-and-brother-julian Accessed, 06/26/020

[185] YouTube, Whoopi lambasts Debra Messing's call to shame Trump donors https://youtu.be/VwRzMpr5zWM Accessed, 07/10/2020

[186] Ali, Ayaan Hirsi, Washington Street Journal, America Doesn't Need a New Revolution https://www.wsj.com/articles/america-doesnt-need-a-new-revolution-11593201840 Accessed, 07/20/2020

[187] YouTube, Margaret Sanger, Planned Parenthood's Racist Founder https://www.youtube.com/watch?v=kEja-1emRic Accessed, 06/06/2020

[188] Wikipedia, Margaret Sanger https://en.wikipedia.org/wiki/Margaret_Sanger Accessed, 07/16/2020

[189] The Time, What Margaret Sanger Really Said About

Eugenics and Race Accessed, 06/25/2020

[190] AP Publications, Margaret Sanger Labeled 'Racist' https://ajph.aphapublications.org/doi/pdf/10.2105/AJPH.71.1.91 Accessed, 07/12/2020

[191] Encyclopedia of World Biography, Margaret Sanger Biography https://www.notablebiographies.com/Ro-Sc/Sanger-Margaret.html Accessed, 07/17/2020

[192] Ibid

[193] YouTube, Hillary Clinton honors Margaret Sanger https://www.youtube.com/watch?v=dBFEyN0sAqQ Accessed, 06/16/2020

[194] Rolling Stone, The Violence That Shaped Our Nation https://www.rollingstone.com/culture/culture-features/tulsa-race-massacre-juneteenth-american-violence-1017511/ Accessed, 06/21/2020

[195] Ibid

[196] US Senator for Texas, Ted Cruz, Conservative Members of Congress Demand Immediate Removal of Margaret Sanger Bust from Display https://www.cruz.senate.gov/?p=press_release&id=2476 Accessed, 06/16/2020."

[197] Ibid

[198] Genetics Generation Education is Our Motivation, Introduction to Eugenics https://knowgenetics.org/history-of-eugenics/ Accessed, 07/12/2020

[199] Ibid

[200] US Senator for Texas, Ted Cruz, Conservative Members of Congress Demand Immediate Removal of Margaret Sanger Bust from Display https://www.cruz.senate.gov/?p=press_release&id=2476 Accessed, 06/16/2020.

[201] YouTube, 21 Quotes by Margaret Sanger https://www.youtube.com/watch?v=20mxoigI0cc Accessed, 06/16/2020

[202] Cultural Legacy Restoring Life and Liberty, Abortion for profit, https://www.culturallegacy.org/abortion-profit Accessed, 07/10/2020

[203] Kagan Julia, The Meaning to Tx Exempt
https://www.investopedia.com/terms/t/tax_exempt.asp#:~:text=Tax
%2Dexempt%20refers%20to%20income,shown%20for%20informatio
nal%20purposes%20only. Accessed, 07/11/2020

[204] Ibid

[205] Cultural Legacy Restoring Life and Liberty, Abortion for
profit, https://www.culturallegacy.org/abortion-profit Accessed,
07/10/2020

[206] Wooding, Dan and Peter, Identity Network, He was the
product of a rape and later nearly shot his father and then took his
surnamehttps://www.identitynetwork.net/apps/articles/default.asp?ar
ticleid=44622&columnid= Accessed, 07/11//2020

[207] Planned Parenthood of Western Pennsylvania
https://www.plannedparenthood.org/planned-parenthood-western-
pennsylvania/patients/fees-services# Accessed, 07/11/2020

[208] The Center for Medical Progress, Planned Parenthood
Testimony On Selling Baby Parts Unsealed, New Videos Released
http://www.centerformedicalprogress.org/2020/05/planned-
parenthood-testimony-on-selling-baby-parts-unsealed-new-videos-
released/ Accessed, 07/11/2020

[209] Ibid

[210] Mail Online, Shocking new Planned Parenthood sting video
shows graphic footage of doctors haggling over the price of dissected
fetal tissue https://www.dailymail.co.uk/news/article-3177372/Latest-
Planned-Parenthood-video-features-undercover-footage-doctors-
dissecting-aborted-fetal-tissue-discussing-pricing-parts.html Accessed,
08/29/2020

[211] Vox, The controversy around Virginia's new abortion bill,
explained https://www.vox.com/2019/2/1/18205428/virginia-
abortion-bill-kathy-tran-ralph-northam Accessed, 06/27/2020

[212] CNN, https://www.cnn.com/2019/04/29/politics/fact-
check-trump-abortion/index.html Accessed, 07/14/2020

[213] Reilly Briana, The Cap Times, Governor Tony Evers vetoes
four abortion bills, including 'born alive' legislation
https://madison.com/ct/news/local/govt-and-politics/evers-vetoes-
four-abortion-bills-including-born-alive-legislation/article_5256a045-

3489-5cff-b775-be9dd2fd67a9.html Accessed, 07/04/2020

[214] The News and Observer, Fact check: 'Born alive' scenario is focus of NC abortion debate. How often does that happen? https://www.newsobserver.com/news/politics-government/article230992798.html Accessed, 07/04/2020

[215] The New York Times, Our Supreme Court Correspondent on This Week's Abortion Ruling https://www.nytimes.com/2020/07/03/insider/our-supreme-court-correspondent-on-this-weeks-abortion-ruling.html Accessed, 07/04/2020

[216] Wikipedia, Michael Moore https://en.wikipedia.org/wiki/Michael_Moore Accessed, 06/10/2020

[217] Business Insider, Michael Moore makes a new Trump prediction: He may quit 'before he even takes office' https://www.businessinsider.com/michael-moore-trump-prediction-quit-the-presidency-2016-12 Accessed, 06/10/2020

[218] Ibid

[219] Michael Moore, DO THESE 10 THINGS, AND TRUMP WILL BE TOAST https://michaelmoore.com/10PointPlan/ Accessed, 06/10/2020

[220] Law Enforcement Today, Michael Moore wishes unrest plays out like movie where 'heroes swoop in and kill the murderous cops' https://www.lawenforcementtoday.com/michael-moore-wants-to-see-heroes-swoop-in-and-kill-the-murderous-cops/ Accessed, 08/28/2020

[221] The Washington Post, Kamala Harris Tweeted Support for a bail fund, but the money didn't just assist protestors https://www.washingtonpost.com/politics/2020/09/03/kamala-harris-tweeted-support-bail-fund-money-didnt-just-assist-protestors/ Accessed, 08/30/2020

[222] ACLU https://www.aclu.org/ Accessed, 06/10/2020

[223] Ibid

[224] Ibid

[225] George Justin, What's Really in the First Step Act? https://www.themarshallproject.org/2018/11/16/what-s-really-in-the-first-step-act Accessed, 08/29/2020

[226] Thought Co., Communism Vs Socialism
https://www.thoughtco.com/difference-between-communism-and-socialism-195448#:~:text=The%20main%20difference%20is%20that,by%20a%20democratically%2Delected%20government. Accessed, 08/20/2020

[227] The Bible, (2 Chronicles 15:2).
[228] Resource Workable, News Anchor responsibilities include
https://resources.workable.com/news-anchor-job-description#:~:text=As%20a%20news%20anchor%2C%20you,informative%2Cinteresting%20and%20unbiased%20way Accessed, 06/11/2020
[229] YouTube, Minister Louis Farrakhan - Obama's Legacy must be destroyed by Donald Trump
https://www.youtube.com/watch?v=AHPAwLRkrqI Accessed 06/11/2020
[230] The Guardian, Barack Obama tells African states to abandon anti-gay discrimination, https://www.theguardian.com/us-news/2015/jul/25/barack-obama-african-states-abandon-anti-gay-discrimination Accessed, 06/25/2020
[231] YouTube, Ravi Zacharias on the Christian View of Homosexuality #Apologetics
https://www.youtube.com/watch?v=nPYRXop7aPA Accessed, 06/25/2020

[232] The Bible, (Isaiah 55:8-9).
[233] Wikipedia, United States Electoral College,
https://en.wikipedia.org/wiki/United_States_Electoral_College Accessed, 08/17/2020
[234] Reflections by Roseylinn, Electoral Voted Presidentshttps://roseylinn.wordpress.com/2016/11/10/electoral-voted-presidents/ Accessed, 08/17/2020
[235] Wikipedia, 2016 United States presidential election https://en.wikipedia.org/wiki/2016_United_States_presidential_election Accessed, 07/18/2020
[236] White J. Adam, The Washington Examiner, Obama Admin: Religious Organizations Could Lose Tax-Exempt Status If Supreme Court Creates Constitutional Right to Same-Sex Marriage

https://www.washingtonexaminer.com/weekly-standard/obama-admin-religious-organizations-could-lose-tax-exempt-status-if-supreme-court-creates-constitutional-right-to-same-sex-marriage Accessed, 07/29/2020

[237] Good Reads Quotes, Martin Luther https://www.goodreads.com/quotes/757798-you-cannot-keep-birds-from-flying-over-your-head-but#:~:text=%E2%80%9CYou%20cannot%20keep%20birds%20from%20flying%20over%20your%20head,a%20nest%20in%20your%20hair%E2%80%9D Accessed, 06/08/2020

[238] YouTube, Ben Carson Defends His Endorsement of Donald Trump - The View https://www.youtube.com/watch?v=W3XqRhfLpg8 Accessed, 07/05/2020

[239] Zunes, Stephen, Institute for Policy Studies, U.S. Policy Toward Jerusalem: Clinton's Shift To The Right https://ips-dc.org/us_policy_toward_jerusalem_clintons_shift_to_the_right/ Accessed, 06/14/2020

[240] NPR, Donald Trump's Been Saying The Same Thing For 30 Years https://www.npr.org/2017/01/20/510680463/donald-trumps-been-saying-the-same-thing-for-30-years Accessed, 06/14/2020

[241] Google Dictionary, Opportunist https://www.google.com/search?q=opprtunist&oq=opprtunist&aqs=chrome..69i57j0l7.17853j1j9&sourceid=chrome&ie=UTF-8 Accessed, 07/04/2020

[242] NBC News, O'Rourke says churches against gay marriage should lose tax benefits, draws backlash https://www.nbcnews.com/politics/2020-election/o-rourke-says-churches-against-gay-marriage-should-lose-tax-n1065186 Accessed, 06/20/2020

[243] White J. Adam, Washington Examiner, Obama Admin: Religious Organizations Could Lose Tax-Exempt Status If Supreme Court Creates Constitutional Right to Same-Sex Marriage https://www.washingtonexaminer.com/weekly-standard/obama-admin-religious-organizations-could-lose-tax-exempt-status-if-supreme-court-creates-constitutional-right-to-same-sex-marriage Accessed,

06/27/2020

[244] The Bible, (Jude 7).

[245] The Bible, (Genesis 19:1-25)

[246] The Bible, (Jude 5-6).

[247] Fox New, Washington Post columnist warns of need to 'burn down the Republican Party' to wipe out Trump supporters https://www.foxnews.com/media/trump-republican-party-2020-burn-down Accessed, 06/28/2020

[248] Ibid

[249] The Bible, (Jeremiah 15:19).

[250] Wikipedia, Executive Order 13672 https://en.wikipedia.org/wiki/Executive_Order_13672#:~:text=Exec utive%20Order%2013672%2C%20signed%20by,and%20employment %20to%20additional%20classes Accessed, 06/20/2020.

[251] The Bible, (James 4:17)

[252] Huppke Rex, Chicago Tribune, 2017: PROOF that liberal protesters are paid https://www.chicagotribune.com/columns/rex-huppke/ct-paid-protesters-huppke-20170227-story.html Accessed,

[253] USCCB What is Systemic Racism? http://www.usccb.org/issues-and-action/human-life-and-dignity/racism/upload/racism-and-systemic-racism.pdf Accessed, 07/04/2020

[254] NBC News Joe Biden didn't just compromise with segregationists. He fought for their cause in schools, experts say. https://www.nbcnews.com/news/nbcblk/joe-biden-didn-t-just-compromise-segregationists-he-fought-their-n1021626 Accessed, 07/20/2020

[255] History, Emancipation Proclamation https://www.history.com/topics/american-civil-war/emancipation-proclamation Accessed, 07/03/2020

[256] Wikipedia, Jim Crow Law, https://en.wikipedia.org/wiki/Jim_Crow_laws#:~:text=Jim%20Crow %20laws%20and%20Jim,U.S.%20military%20was%20already%20segre gated Accessed, 07/03/2020

[257] Google Dictionary, Compartmentalize https://www.google.com/search?q=compartmentalized&oq=compart ment&aqs=chrome.5.69i57j0l7.10089j0j7&sourceid=chrome&ie=UTF

-8 Accessed, 07/03/2020

[258] Wikipedia, Compartmentalization (Psychology) https://en.wikipedia.org/wiki/Compartmentalization_(psychology) Accessed, 07/03/2020

[259] BBC News, Kanye West suggests African-American slavery was 'a choice' https://www.bbc.com/news/world-us-canada-43970903 Accessed, 07/03/2020

[260] BBC.Com, The World's Strongest Animal Can Lift Staggering Weight http://www.bbc.com/earth/story/20161121-the-worlds-strongest-animal-can-lift-staggering-weights Accessed, 07/03/2020

[261] The Bible, (Titus 1:15)

[262] Wikipedia, Fascism https://en.wikipedia.org/wiki/Fascism Accessed, 06/27/2020

[263] Ibid

[264] Ibid

[265] Ibid

[266] Vox, I asked 5 fascism experts whether Donald Trump is a fascist. Here's what they said. https://www.vox.com/policy-and-politics/2015/12/10/9886152/donald-trump-fascism Accessed, 06/27/2020

[267] Ibid

[268] Moore Mark, BLM leader: If change doesn't happen, then 'we will burn down this system' https://nypost.com/2020/06/25/blm-leader-if-change-doesnt-happen-we-will-burn-down-this-system/ Accessed, 07/04/2020

[269] Vox, I asked 5 fascism experts whether Donald Trump is a fascist. Here's what they said. https://www.vox.com/policy-and-politics/2015/12/10/9886152/donald-trump-fascism Accessed, 08/27/20

[270] Ibid

[271] Ibid

[272] Lexico Dictionary, Populist https://www.lexico.com/en/definition/populist Accessed, 06/27/2020

[273] Constitutional Right Foundation, Race and Voting

https://www.crf-usa.org/brown-v-board-50th-anniversary/race-and-voting.html Accessed, 06/27/2020.

[274] Snoopes, Elijah Cummings Said Democrats Gave Black People the Right to Vote? https://www.snopes.com/fact-check/elijah-cummings-said-democrats-gave-black-people-the-right-to-vote/ Accessed, 06/27/2020

[275] The Washington Post, Gov. Ralph Northam admits he was in 1984 yearbook photo showing figures in blackface, KKK hood https://www.washingtonpost.com/local/virginia-politics/va-gov-northams-medical-school-yearbook-page-shows-men-in-blackface-kkk-robe/2019/02/01/517a43ee-265f-11e9-90cd-dedb0c92dc17_story.html Accessed, 06/27/2020

[276] Wikipedia, Presidency of Ulysses S. Grant https://en.wikipedia.org/wiki/Presidency_of_Ulysses_S._Grant Accessed, 07/03/2020

[277] Good Reads, Malcom X Quotes https://www.goodreads.com/quotes/8869214-the-white-liberal-is-the-worst-enemy-to-america-and Accessed, 08/29/2020

[278] Musto Julia Fox News, https://www.foxnews.com/media/alveda-king-john-lewis-funeral-obama Accessed, 08/08/2020

[279] Google Dictionary, Cry Wolf https://www.google.com/search?q=crying+wolf+meaning&oq=cryin g+wol&aqs=chrome.5.0j46j69i57j46j0l4.7753j0j7&sourceid=chrome&i e=UTF-8 Accessed, 08/08/2020

[280] Glenn Radio, The Blaze, African Christian University Dean: 'Black people in America are the FREEST and MOST PROSPEROUS black people in the world' https://www.theblaze.com/glenn-radio/the-truth-about-black-americans-and-oppression?rebelltitem=1#rebelltitem1 Accessed, 07/01/2020

[281] The Bible, (Job 42:2)

[282] Glenn Radio, The Blaze, African Christian University Dean: 'Black people in America are the FREEST and MOST PROSPEROUS black people in the world' https://www.theblaze.com/glenn-radio/the-truth-about-black-americans-and-oppression?rebelltitem=1#rebelltitem1 Accessed, 07/01/2020

[283] Ibid

[284] Ali, Ayaan Hirsi, The Wal Street Journal America Doesn't

Need a New Revolution https://www.wsj.com/articles/america-doesnt-need-a-new-revolution-11593201840 Accessed, 07/20/2020

[285] Ibid

[286] Ibid

[287] Glenn Radio, The Blaze, African Christian University Dean: 'Black people in America are the FREEST and MOST PROSPEROUS black people in the world' https://www.theblaze.com/glenn-radio/the-truth-about-black-americans-and-oppression?rebelltitem=1#rebelltitem1 Accessed, 07/01/2020

[288] The Times News, Blacks' biggest enemy is a white liberal https://www.thetimesnews.com/opinion/20190104/editorial-blacks-biggest-enemy-is-white-liberal Accessed, 07/25/2020

[289] The New York Times, Obama's Father's Day Remarks https://www.nytimes.com/2008/06/15/us/politics/15text-obama.html Accessed, 07/02/2020

[290] YouTube, Black Americans Failed by Good Intentions: An Interview with Jason Riley https://www.youtube.com/watch?v=zorEMP8GxBA&feature=youtu.be Accessed, 07/10/2020

[291] Concha Joe, the Hill, Van Jones: A 'white, liberal Hillary Clinton supporter' can pose a greater threat to black Americans than the KKK https://thehill.com/homenews/media/500158-van-jones-a-white-liberal-hillary-clinton-supporter-can-pose-a-greater-threat Accessed, 10/03/2020

[292] The Times News, Blacks' biggest enemy is a white liberal https://www.thetimesnews.com/opinion/20190104/editorial-blacks-biggest-enemy-is-white-liberal Accessed, 07/25/2020

[293] Ibid

[294] The Bible, (2 Kings 6:24-27).

[295] Ali Ayaan Hirsi, The Washington Journal https://www.wsj.com/articles/america-doesnt-need-a-new-revolution-11593201840 Accessed, 07/20/2020

[296] YouTube, Don Lemon – Black People! Cleanup your act! https://www.youtube.com/watch?v=EsGdCBk_18 Accessed, 07/09/2020

[297] Ibid

[298] The Times News, Blacks' biggest enemy is a white liberal https://www.thetimesnews.com/opinion/20190104/editorial-blacks-biggest-enemy-is-white-liberal Accessed, 07/25/2020

[299] Good Reads, Malcom X Quotes https://www.goodreads.com/quotes/8869214-the-white-liberal-is-the-worst-enemy-to-america-and Accessed, 08/29/2020

[300] Ibid

[301] Ibid

[302] Montgomery County Department of Police, Three Suspects Charged for Vandalism to Walt Whitman High Schoolhttps://www.mymcpnews.com/2020/06/16/three-suspects-charged-for-vandalism-to-walt-whitman-high-school/ Accessed, 06/16/2020

[303] Vincent Milly, Mail online, Frederick Douglas Statue Hacked, https://www.dailymail.co.uk/news/article-8494083/Statue-abolitionist-Frederick-Douglass-hacked-base-damaged-repair.html Accessed 09/30/2020

[304] Wikipedia, Christian Abolitionism https://en.wikipedia.org/wiki/Christian_abolitionism Accessed, 06/29/2020

[305] Lawrence Andrea, Milwaukee Journal Sentinel, Hans Christian Heg was an abolitionist who died trying to end slavery. What to know about the man whose statue was toppled in Madison https://www.jsonline.com/story/news/local/wisconsin/2020/06/24/hans-christian-hegs-abolitionist-statue-toppled-madison-what-know/3248692001/ Accessed, 06/29/2020

[306] Bradford Betz, Fox News, Shaun King: Statues of Jesus Christ are 'form of white supremacy,' should be torn down https://www.foxnews.com/media/shaun-king-jesus-christ-statues-white-supremacy Accessed, 06/23/2020

[307] Manzoni Mike and Salahi Lara, 10 Boston, Virgin Mary Statue Set on Fire Outside Boston Church, Authorities Say https://www.nbcboston.com/news/local/virgin-mary-statue-set-on-fire-outside-boston-church/2158037/#:~:text=Boston%20police%20are%20investigating%20after,they%20found%20the%20burned%20statue. Accessed, 07/14/2020

[308] Albany Update, Federal Court Says Cuomo Wrong to Limit

Worship Services https://www.albanyupdate.com/federal-court-says-cuomo-is-wrong-to-limit-worship-services/ Accessed, 06/28/2020

[309] New York Post, BLM leader: If change doesn't happen, then 'we will burn down this system' https://nypost.com/2020/06/25/blm-leader-if-change-doesnt-happen-we-will-burn-down-this-system/ Accessed, 07/04/2020

[310] France Lisa Respers, CNN, Madonna: 'Blowing up White House' taken out of context https://www.cnn.com/2017/01/23/entertainment/madonna-white-house/index.html Accessed, 09/29/2020

[311] The Bible, (Matthew 7:15-23).

[312] Ibid (Mark 2:16-17)

[313] The Washington Times, Black Lives Matter cashes in with $100 million from liberal foundations https://www.washingtontimes.com/news/2016/aug/16/black-lives-matter-cashes-100-million-liberal-foun/ Accessed, 07/01/2020

[314] The Times News, Blacks' biggest enemy is a white liberal https://www.thetimesnews.com/opinion/20190104/editorial-blacks-biggest-enemy-is-white-liberal Accessed, 07/25/2020

[315] ABC News, Woman arraigned in killing of security guard over virus mask https://abcnews.go.com/US/wireStory/woman-arraigned-killing-security-guard-virus-mask-70516361 Accessed, 07/01/2020

[316] Maxouris Christina, A security guard was shot after telling a customer to wear a face mask, officials say. His widow calls the killing 'senseless and stupid' https://www.cnn.com/2020/05/06/us/security-guard-shot-mask-wife/index.html Accessed, 07/01/2020

[317] The Bible, (Proverbs 17:15).

[318] Nededog Jethro, Business Insider, Michael Moore makes a new Trump prediction: He may quit 'before he even takes office' https://www.businessinsider.com/michael-moore-trump-prediction-quit-the-presidency-2016-12 Accessed, 06/09/2020

[319] Ali Ayaan Hirsi, The Washington Journal https://www.wsj.com/articles/america-doesnt-need-a-new-revolution-

11593201840 Accessed, 07/20/2020

[320] The Bible, (Proverbs 30:21-23).

[321] The Bible, (Proverbs 10:19)

[322] AMAC, Ocasio-Cortez Calls for Democrats to Take Over "All Three [?] Chambers of Government" in 2020 https://amac.us/ocasio-cortez-calls-for-democrats-to-take-over-all-three-chambers-of-government-in-2020/ Accessed, 07/20/2020

[323] MPR News, Council advances plan to dismantle Minneapolis Police Department https://www.mprnews.org/story/2020/06/26/minneapolis-council-puts-plan-to-dismantle-police-in-motion Accessed, 06/26/2020

[324] Ibid

[325] The New York Times, Obama's Father's Day Remarks, https://www.nytimes.com/2008/06/15/us/politics/15text-obama.html Accessed, 07/02/2020

[326] Wikipedia, Isaias Afwerki, https://en.wikipedia.org/wiki/Isaias_Afwerki Accessed, 07/01/2020

[327] The Bible, (Genesis 8:6-12)

[328] Ibid, (Isaiah 55:7)

[329] Stanford Encyclopedia of Philosophy, Divine Providence, https://plato.stanford.edu/entries/providence-divine/ Accessed, 06/30/2020

[330] Ibid

[331] Ibid

[332] YouTube, Why doesn't God stop evil" Ravi Zacharias https://www.youtube.com/results?search_query=ravi+on+evil+and+good Accessed, 06/30/2020

[333] Ibid

[334] Daily Kos, Biden's Crime Bill Speech from 1993: full transcript https://www.dailykos.com/stories/2020/6/19/1954559/-Biden-s-Crime-Bill-Speech-from-1993-full-transcript Accessed, 06/24/2020

[335] CTPOST, Biden's criminal justice plan differs sharply from '94 law https://www.ctpost.com/news/article/Biden-announces-criminal-justice-policy-sharply-14115722.php Accessed, 07/10/2020

[336] Daily Kos, Biden's Crime Bill Speech from 1993: full transcript https://www.dailykos.com/stories/2020/6/19/1954559/-

Biden-s-Crime-Bill-Speech-from-1993-full-transcript Accessed, 06/24/2020

[337] Vox, Lopez German, The controversial 1994 crime law that Joe Biden helped write, explained https://www.vox.com/policy-and-politics/2019/6/20/18677998/joe-biden-1994-crime-bill-law-mass-incarceration Accessed, 06/21/2020

[338] Daily Kos, Biden's Crime Bill Speech from 1993: full transcript https://www.dailykos.com/stories/2020/6/19/1954559/-Biden-s-Crime-Bill-Speech-from-1993-full-transcript Accessed, 06/24/2020

[339] Ibid

[340] Ivanka Trump on her RNC 2020 speech

[341] Corkin Liz, Town Hall, Trump Does The Unthinkable https://townhall.com/columnists/lizcrokin/2016/07/10/trump-does-the-unthinkable-n2190160 Accessed, 07/25/2020

[342] Binkley Collin, AP News, Trump signs bill restoring funding for black colleges, https://apnews.com/c4834e48841d97c5a93312b1bf75302a Accessed, 06/29/2020

[343] The Washington Post, Joe Biden Called Bussing a Liberal Train Wreck Now His Stance On School Integration is an Issue https://www.washingtonpost.com/politics/joe-biden-called-busing-a-liberal-train-wreck-now-his-stance-on-school-integration-is-an-issue/2019/06/28/557705dc-99b3-11e9-830a-21b9b36b64ad_story.html Accessed, 06/29/2020

[344] Wikipedia, Desegregation Bussing Criticism https://en.wikipedia.org/wiki/Desegregation_busing#:~:text=In%20the%201968%2C%201972%2C%20and,entailed%20far%20more%20distant%20busing. Accessed, 06/29/2020

[345] The Washington Post, Joe Biden Called Bussing a Liberal Train Wreck Now His Stance On School Integration is an Issue https://www.washingtonpost.com/politics/joe-biden-called-busing-a-liberal-train-wreck-now-his-stance-on-school-integration-is-an-issue/2019/06/28/557705dc-99b3-11e9-830a-21b9b36b64ad_story.html Accessed, 06/29/2020

[346] Lockhart P.R. Joe Biden's record on school desegregation busing, explained https://www.vox.com/policy-and-politics/2019/6/28/18965923/joe-biden-school-desegregation-busing-democratic-primary 06/29/2020

[347] The Bible, (Matthew 7:15-18)

[348] Goodman Alana, Washington Examiner Joe Biden embraced segregation in 1975, claiming it was a matter of 'black pride' https://www.washingtonexaminer.com/politics/joe-biden-embraced-segregation-in-1975-claiming-it-was-a-matter-of-black-pride Accessed, 06/29/2020

[349] The Bible, (Luke 6:45)

[350] Goodman Alana, Washington Examiner Joe Biden embraced segregation in 1975, claiming it was a matter of 'black pride' https://www.washingtonexaminer.com/politics/joe-biden-embraced-segregation-in-1975-claiming-it-was-a-matter-of-black-pride Accessed, 06/29/2020

[351] LSE US Center, How Senator Joe Biden got it wrong on busing in the 1970s https://blogs.lse.ac.uk/usappblog/2019/05/16/how-senator-joe-biden-got-it-wrong-on-busing-in-the-1970s/ Accessed, 08/08/2020

[352] Ibid

[353] Goodman Alana, Washington Examiner Joe Biden embraced segregation in 1975, claiming it was a matter of 'black pride' https://www.washingtonexaminer.com/politics/joe-biden-embraced-segregation-in-1975-claiming-it-was-a-matter-of-black-pride Accessed, 06/29/2020

[354] Ibid

[355] Dallas County News, Fact check: Photo shows Biden with Byrd, who once had ties to KKK but wasn't a grand wizard https://www.adelnews.com/zz/news/20200615/fact-check-photo-shows-biden-with-byrd-who-once-had-ties-to-kkk-but-wasnt-grand-wizard Accessed, 06/29/2020

[356] Goodman Alana, Washington Examiner Joe Biden embraced segregation in 1975, claiming it was a matter of 'black pride' https://www.washingtonexaminer.com/politics/joe-biden-embraced-segregation-in-1975-claiming-it-was-a-matter-of-black-pride Accessed, 06/29/2020

[357] Gitty Images, https://www.gettyimages.com/photos/diddy-trump?family=editorial&phrase=diddy%20trump&sort=mostpopular Accessed, 07/30/2020

[358] Brown Ann, The Mogul Nation, Diddy Threatens Biden: If You Don't Show You're Going To Improve The Lives of Black

People, I'll Hold The Vote Hostage
https://moguldom.com/275441/diddy-threatens-biden-if-you-dont-show-youre-going-to-improve-the-lives-of-black-people-ill-hold-the-vote-hostage/ Accessed, 07/14/2020

[359] The Bible, (Isaiah 43:4)

[360] Google Dictionary, Worth, https://www.google.com/search?q=worth+meaning&rlz=1C1CHBF_enUS813US813&oq=worth+mean&aqs=chrome.0.0j69i57j0l6.6774j1j7&sourceid=chrome&ie=UTF-8 Accessed, 06/17/2020

[361] Ramaswamy Swapna Venugopal, MSN, Black Women's Equal Pay Day highlights how Black women lose nearly $1M over their careers https://www.msn.com/en-us/news/us/black-women-s-equal-pay-day-highlights-how-black-women-lose-nearly-1m-over-their-careers/ar-BB17SAdx?ocid=msedgntp Accessed, 08/13/2020

[362] Ibid

[363] Forbes, THE WORLD'S HIGHEST-PAID CELEBRITIES https://www.forbes.com/celebrities/ Accessed, 07/23/2020

[364] Trueman C N, History Learning Site, Marxist Concepts https://www.historylearningsite.co.uk/sociology/theories-in-sociology/marxist-concepts/ Accessed, 07/12/2020

[365] YouTube, Jordan Peterson: Why is Marxism so Attractive? https://www.youtube.com/watch?v=MkWS1Q069pU Accessed, 7/12/2020

[366] YouTube, AOC Goes On DERANGED Rant Defending the Looters In NYC https://www.youtube.com/watch?v=AzlRVUJLOwo Accessed, 07/29/2020

[367] The Bible, (Ephesians 4:28).

[368] YouTube, Jordan Peterson: Why is Marxism so Attractive? https://www.youtube.com/watch?v=MkWS1Q069pU Accessed, 7/12/2020

[369] Wikipedia, An Act to amend the Canadian Human Rights Act and the Criminal Code, https://en.wikipedia.org/wiki/An_Act_to_amend_the_Canadian_Human_Rights_Act_and_the_Criminal_Code 07/28/2020   Accessed,

07/28/2020

[370] YouTube, When Victimhood Leads to Genocide - Prof. Jordan Peterson on Dekulakization https://www.youtube.com/watch?v=DeYRK16PIlA Accessed, 07/16/2020

[371] Ibid

[372] The Times News, Editorial: Blacks' biggest enemy is a white liberal https://www.thetimesnews.com/opinion/20190104/editorial-blacks-biggest-enemy-is-white-liberal Accessed, 07/25/2020

[373] Star Tribune, With FEMA aid to rebuild from riots denied Minnesota looks elsewhere https://www.startribune.com/with-fema-aid-to-rebuild-from-riots-denied-minnesota-looks-elsewhere/571731112/ Accessed, 07/16/2020.

[374] Ibid

[375] YouTube, When Victimhood Leads to Genocide - Prof. Jordan Peterson on Dekulakization https://www.youtube.com/watch?v=DeYRK16PIlA Accessed, 07/16/2020

[376] The Bible, (1 Timothy 2:1-2)

[377] 11 Alive, There were 11 shootings in Atlanta during the July 4th weekend. Out of the 31 victims, 5 of them died. https://www.11alive.com/article/news/crime/july-fourth-shooting-statistics-atlanta-police/85-da8960d3-ed66-4ecf-b9f0-9b1885bf7531 Accessed, 07/07/2020

[378] The Bible, (Zechariah 3:1-5)

[379] Ibid, (Nehemiah 6).

[380] Ibid, (2 Timothy 4:2-5).

[381] YouTube, NFL Star Benjamin Watson Mic Cut Off On CNN When He Mentions Jesus Christ https://www.youtube.com/watch?v=36VXifuEeq8 Accessed, 06/26/2020

[382] The Bible, (Romans 9:13-15).

[383] Stelter Brian, CNN Business, The explosive tell-all book by Trump's niece is coming out two weeks earlier than expected https://www.cnn.com/2020/07/06/media/mary-trump-book-release-

date/index.html 07/07/2020

[384] Wikipedia, Mary L. Trump, https://en.wikipedia.org/wiki/Mary_L._Trump Accessed, 07/24/2020

[385] The Bible, (Romans 3:22-25).
[386] Ibid, (Psalms 41:9)

[387] Ibid, (Luke 22:2).
[388] Ibid, (Proverbs 30:11,13, 17).

[389] Wikipedia, Time Bomb, https://en.wikipedia.org/wiki/Time_bomb Accessed, 08/16/2020

[390] Encyclopedia of the Bible, Nicolaitans https://www.biblegateway.com/resources/encyclopedia-of-the-bible/Nicolaitans Accessed, 09/10/2020
[391] The Bible, (Proverbs 3:29).
[392] Ibid, (2 Samuel 15:31).
[393] Ibid, (2 Timothy 3:1-5).
[394] Ibid, (2 Timothy 3:6-9).

[395] The Guardian, 'Please for the love of God do not vote for my dad': Republican's daughter voices opposition https://www.theguardian.com/us-news/2020/jun/26/please-do-not-vote-for-my-dad-republican-daughter-robert-reagan-michigan Accessed, 06/26/2020
[396] The Bible, (Genesis 28:1-4).
[397] Ibid, (Genesis 28:8-9).
[398] Ibid, (Proverbs 22:6).
[399] Defender Network, Martin Luther King Jr. birthplace designated a national historic park https://defendernetwork.com/news/national/trump-designates-martin-luther-king-jr-birthplace-national-historic-park/ Accessed, 07/07/2020
[400] The Guardian, Biden criticized after saying: 'Poor kids are as bright as white kids' https://www.theguardian.com/us-

news/2019/aug/09/joe-biden-poor-kids-white-gaffe-iowa

[401] Sessions Jeff, United States Senate Budget Committee
https://www.budget.senate.gov/imo/media/doc/CRS%20Report%20
-
%20Welfare%20Spending%20The%20Largest%20Item%20In%20The
%20Federal%20Budget.pdf Accessed, 07/24/2020

[402] Shear Michael D and Sullivan Eileen The New York Times,
Trump Policy Favors Wealthier Immigrants for Green Cards
https://www.nytimes.com/2019/08/12/us/politics/trump-
immigration-policy.html Accessed, 08/30/2020

[403] Ibid

[404] The Bible, (Deuteronomy 15:4-5).

[405] Martin Jonathan, The New York Times, Biden's Family Is
Urging Him to Run in 2020
https://www.nytimes.com/2019/02/26/us/politics/biden-2020-
family.html Accessed, 07/03/2020

[406] Wikipedia, Nancy Pelosi
https://en.wikipedia.org/wiki/Nancy_Pelosi 08/30/2020

[407] RT Question More 'Skullduggery': Pelosi says Biden should
NOT 'dignify' Trump with a debate as president 'disrespects' office
https://www.rt.com/usa/499241-pelosi-debates-trump-biden/
08/27/2020

[408] Merriam Webster Dictionary, Skullduggery
https://www.merriam-webster.com/dictionary/skulduggery Accessed,
08/27/2020

[409] Scarry Eddie, Washington Examiner, Donna Brazile finally
admits she shared debate questions with Clinton campaign
https://www.washingtonexaminer.com/donna-brazile-finally-admits-
she-shared-debate-questions-with-clinton-campaign 08/27/2020

[410] The Bible, (Proverbs 16:17).

[411] Ibid, (Jeremiah 27:5-6).

[412] YouTube, Steve Harvey on the Donald Trump Visit
https://www.youtube.com/watch?v=BGbo9EXWGcI Accessed,
07/03/2020

[413] The Bible, (1 Corinthians 9:20-22).

[414] Dunmore Royce, News One, Goya CEO Cites 'Obamas' To Defend Praising Trump https://newsone.com/3974266/goya-ceo-cites-obamas-defend-praising-trump/ Accessed, 07/13/2020

[415] Cato Tim and Medworth Whitney SB Nation, Why the Warriors didn't visit the White House https://www.sbnation.com/2018/2/27/17058176/warriors-white-house-washington-dc-children-museum-local-kiddos-good-job-yall Accessed, 07/05/2020

[416] Wikipedia, List of Republicans who opposed the 2016 Donald Trump presidential campaign https://en.wikipedia.org/wiki/List_of_Republicans_who_opposed_the_2016_Donald_Trump_presidential_campaign#Former_U.S._presidents Accessed, 07/05/2020

[417] The Bible, (Ephesians 6:12).

[418] Ibid, (1 Samuel 17:45).

[419] Google Dictionary, Commonsense https://www.google.com/search?q=commonsense+definition&oq=commonsense+&aqs=chrome.3.69i57j0l7.8489j0j7&sourceid=chrome&ie=UTF-8 07/24/2020

[420] CDC, Mortality Records with Mention of Termination of Pregnancy https://www.cdc.gov/nchs/health_policy/mortality-records-mentioning-termination-of-pregnancy.htm Accessed, 07/24/2020

[421] Ibid

[422] Sullivan Nora, Charlotte Lozier Institute, Born Alive, Left to Die https://lozierinstitute.org/born-alive-left-to-die/ 07/24/2020

[423] Constitutional Rights Foundation, Race and Voting, https://www.crf-usa.org/brown-v-board-50th-anniversary/race-and-voting.html Accessed, 06/27/2020.

[424] Wikipedia, Margaret Sangerhttps://en.wikiquote.org/wiki/Margaret_Sanger Accessed, 06/27/2020

[425] Ibid

[426] Ibid

[427] Ibid

[428] The Washington Post, Charles Schumer shot at Hillary Clinton, https://www.washingtonpost.com/news/the-

fix/wp/2017/07/24/charles-schumers-shot-at-hillary-clinton/
Accessed, 06/18/2020
[429] Ibid

Made in the USA
Columbia, SC
05 October 2020